PENGUIN CL

FOUNDER EDITOR (1944-), ...

PRESENT EDITORS:
Betty Radice and Robert Baldick

XENOPHON was an Athenian country gentleman born about 430
B.C. He may have helped to publish Thucydides' *History*, and certainly wrote his own *Hellenica* as a continuation of it. By his own
(probably reliable) account he was a fine officer and outstanding
leader, but his admiration for Sparta and devotion to Socrates,
among other causes, led to his banishment. In exile he wrote history,
biography, memoirs and specialist treatises. He had too much enthusiasm and too little judgement for a historian or a philosopher,
and his moralizing is sometimes prosy, sometimes excessively rhetorical; but the *Memoirs*, at their best, give a most interesting and
entertaining picture of Athenian society at the end of the fifth century B.C.

HUGH TREDENNICK, Professor Emeritus of Classics in the
University of London, was born in 1899 and educated at King
Edward's, Birmingham, and Trinity Hall, Cambridge, where he
got a double First in Classics. He was appointed Professor of
Classics at Royal Holloway College in 1946. He was Dean of the
Faculty of Arts at London University from 1956 to 1960, and joint
editor of the *Classical Review* from 1961 to 1967. His *Last Days of
Socrates* is a Penguin Classic, and he has also edited and translated
works by Aristotle.

XENOPHON

MEMOIRS OF SOCRATES
AND
THE SYMPOSIUM
(*The Dinner Party*)

TRANSLATED
WITH AN INTRODUCTION BY
HUGH TREDENNICK

PENGUIN BOOKS

Penguin Books Ltd, Harmondsworth, Middlesex, England
Penguin Books Inc., 7110 Ambassador Road, Baltimore, Maryland 21207, U.S.A.
Penguin Books Australia Ltd, Ringwood, Victoria, Australia

—

This translation first published 1970

—

Copyright © Hugh Tredennick, 1970

—

Made and printed in Great Britain
by Richard Clay (The Chaucer Press) Ltd,
Bungay, Suffolk
Set in Monotype Bembo

CONTENTS

INTRODUCTION

THOSE who know Socrates only from Plato's dialogues may find Xenophon's *Memorabilia* a little disappointing. Some of the magic has disappeared. Socrates is still a highly impressive character, but it is not so easy to see why he had such a compelling influence upon the minds and hearts of many (including some of the unlikeliest) of his fellow-citizens. In fact, some of the moral discourses which Xenophon puts into his mouth seem trite and tedious. Critics have even maintained that the two portraits of Socrates are so different that one at least must be false, and since Xenophon was clearly the less inventive writer, Plato has been charged with re-creating Socrates in his own image.

There is an element of truth in the charge. It is obvious to most people that in his 'middle' period (whatever he had done before) Plato developed his Socrates into a suitable mouthpiece for the views that he wanted to express. The intellectual stature of Socrates is much greater in *Republic* or even in *Phaedo* than it is in *Charmides* or *Lysis*. But the personality is, upon the whole, much the same. And if we make due allowance for the differences between Plato and Xenophon – many and substantial differences, not least in sheer intellect and literary artistry – the surprising thing is how closely Xenophon's picture corresponds with Plato's in depicting a man *eager for goodness*. This is the essential Socrates: from this formula all the rest can be deduced.

The formula may not appeal much at first sight to believers in an inverted morality or in no morality at all; but it is worth investigating. The Greek words *agathos* and *aretê*, corresponding roughly to the English 'good' and 'goodness', were used to describe any kind of excellence. When applied to persons they denoted originally high rank, then prowess in fighting,

7

then general efficiency; and these implications (especially the last) tended to persist, whether consciously or not, even when the words came in the fifth century to be used specifically of moral character. Now in every branch of life – certainly in all the arts and crafts – efficiency is the result of knowledge, while errors are (for the most part, at any rate) due to ignorance. Hence if you want to be 'good' at anything you must get to know about it; and when you have got your knowledge you will naturally use it. A skilled craftsman does not botch a simple piece of work: no more will a man, seeing clearly what he ought to do, deliberately do something else. This is the Socratic paradox that Virtue is Knowledge.

Of course this is not quite the whole story, as Ovid[1] and St Paul[2] (to name only two) have acutely observed; but there is a great deal of truth in it. The trouble is that when it comes to 'good' conduct many people don't really care, or are positively afraid of appearing priggish; you will hear ten people appeal to artistic integrity (whatever that means) for every one that would venture to suggest moral integrity as a decisive factor. But if you want to be 'good' at the art of living, you will seek what knowledge is relevant to it; and if you care at all for others you will involve them in the search too, especially if you believe that intelligent discussion is the best if not the only way of discovering the truth and passing it on to others. And the search must be systematic and unflinching, even if the result seems likely to be unpalatable. That is the basis of Socrates' intellectual honesty.

What about the will? This question is not treated explicitly by Socrates in either Plato or Xenophon; the real Socrates, we may be sure, had not analysed the psyche into 'parts' at all, as Plato makes him do in *Republic*, 434–41; but it is answered by implication. One cannot live well without health of body

1. *Metamorphoses* vii, 20 f.
2. *Romans* vii, 15 ff.

8

and soul, which can only be secured by strict self-discipline, i.e. by the exercise of will-power. This is made quite clear in *Memorabilia*, ii, 1.

To return to semantics: if *agathos*, the Greek word for 'good', (there are of course others) has more than one meaning, *kalos*, the Greek word for 'beautiful', has quite as many, because it can describe not only aesthetic and moral beauty but anything that appeals to the imagination as admirably effective (cf. our 'beautiful' shot or in-swinger); a fact which helps to justify the association of beauty with function in *Memorabilia*, iii, 8. The two words *kalos* and *agathos* are often used together to describe a man who has the highest physical and moral qualities; originally with a strongly aristocratic flavour (since it is the ruling class that sets the standards), but tending more and more to express the notion of ideal manhood. This combination is a translator's nightmare; fifty years ago 'gentleman' would still have served in most instances (although it lacks a convenient abstract formation), but the word now seems quite *déclassé* and has no obvious substitute. As the connotation naturally varies according to context, a number of different phrases have been tried, but few of them have satisfied the translator. The literal 'beautiful and good' has naturally been excluded as sounding merely sarcastic in contemporary idiom. However, this concept lies at the very heart of Xenophon's *Memoirs*; indeed it represents his own ideal. It is time to consider what kind of man he was.

Xenophon, the son of Gryllus, of the deme Erchia,[3] was born about 430[4] and died about 355 B.C. He must have learned a good deal about soldiering in the later years of the Pelopon-

3. Probably near the modern Spata, about ten miles east of Athens.
4. Possibly three or four years later (Delebecque); but there are difficulties.

nesian War – say 412–404 – probably in the cavalry. He himself has told in his *Anabasis* how in 401 he became involved as a private person in Cyrus' expedition to win the crown of Persia, and how, when Cyrus was killed at Cunaxa and the senior Greek officers were soon afterwards treacherously seized and murdered, he not only restored morale but was elected as one of the new generals, and with the Spartan Chirisophus (the other replacements seem to have been quite overshadowed) took charge of the Greek troops and led them for hundreds of miles through difficult, hostile and unknown country back to civilization at Trapezus (Trebizond) on the Black Sea, and thence westwards along the coast to Chalcedon. This was not the end of their adventures; but Xenophon brought them at last to Pergamum and handed them over to the Spartan general Thibron early in the year 399.

One might have expected Xenophon now to return to Greece. Indeed he says of himself[5] while still at Lampsacus that he was openly making preparations to return home, *because sentence of banishment had not yet been passed upon him at Athens*, but his friends begged him not to leave until he had led the force to its destination and handed it over to Thibron. If this means anything it surely implies that he learnt of his banishment very soon afterwards and changed his plans accordingly. At any rate he seems to have stayed in Asia serving under different commanders, finally under the Spartan king Agesilaus, who was trying to win his country an empire overseas. But in 394 Sparta had to face a powerful confederacy in Greece headed by Thebes, Athens, Corinth and Argos; Agesilaus was recalled to help his country, and took with him the remainder of the Greek mercenaries who had followed Cyrus: among them Xenophon.

5. *Anabasis* vii, 7, 57.

Some authorities seem to assume that Xenophon was exiled for treasonable conduct in fighting for Sparta against Athens and her allies at Coronea. He was certainly present, and apparently expected to fight,[6] although his description[7] of the battle seems more appropriate for a spectator than for a participant. But the important point is that if (as seems probable) he was already an exile, to fight on the Spartan side would have been unpatriotic, perhaps, but not treasonable. He should at least be given the benefit of the doubt.

On his banishment Sparta provided him with an estate at Scillus near Olympia, where he lived for over twenty years combining the pursuits of a country gentleman with the writing of numerous books. In about the year 370 political events compelled him to move, and at about the same time his sentence was repealed; but although his sons returned to Athens and he himself probably paid visits to the city he seems to have lived mainly at Corinth – as a sort of neutral territory? – until his death.

If Xenophon was banished in or shortly after 399, what was the immediate cause? Was he regarded as an associate of Socrates? Was Socrates an enemy of democracy? It is logical to take the last question first.

Nothing that we are told about Socrates suggests that he would have tolerated the oppression or exploitation of one class by another; on the contrary both Plato and Xenophon show him insisting that the primary concern of government is the welfare of the subject. Thus he undoubtedly condemned the selfish and tyrannical policy of the extreme oligarchs. But he was no egalitarian: he continually stressed that orders should be given by 'the man who knows', i.e. that government is a matter for experts; and he derided the practice of making

6. *Anabasis* v, 3, 6.
7. *Hellenica* iv, 3, 15 ff.

public appointments by lot without regard for qualifications. There was another side to this question: lot was a safeguard against bribery, undue influence and intimidation; but it did not make for efficiency. Further, there is evidence that Socrates considered the Demos to be, upon the whole, ignorant and gullible: as no doubt it was. Secondary and higher education were not available for the average citizen; and the sovereign Assembly, when it lacked the guidance of a wise and trusted statesman, was not only easily swayed by appeals to prejudice and emotion; like all undisciplined crowds it was prone in times of crisis to rush wildly from one extreme to the other. It is true that the restored democracy is reputed to have shown commendable forbearance towards the revolutionaries, but the evidence is rather one-sided. After all, it was a democratic court that condemned Socrates to death; and the only justification for such a verdict (if you can call it justification) was political (the charge of heresy[8] was, *pace* Bury and others, merely a pretext): that he was critical of the democracy and that most of his friends and admirers were from the wealthier and more highly educated class. If this is a fair statement (as it is meant to be) it is a heavy indictment.

When Xenophon left Athens in 401 he must have known (even if he was not one of the 'inner circle') what Socrates' views were and how they were regarded by his fellow-countrymen. He himself was obviously proud of his country and of her past achievements, which he often recalls. At the same time, being a man of wealth and education, he would naturally share the outlook of the propertied class, which

8. The Greek word *asebeia* properly denotes lack of (outward) reverence towards men or gods. As the ground of an indictment it implies that the accused has departed, by commission or omission, from the code of religious observance enjoined by the state. In such a context 'heresy' seems a better rendering in English than 'impiety', which suggests rather an attitude of mind such as has not usually been regarded as an indictable offence.

looked more to the Right than to the Left: he might fairly be called an oligarch – but a supporter not of Critias (whose crimes he evidently detested) but of Theramenes, whose moderation and courage he no less clearly admired.[9] All oligarchs were *ipso facto* suspected of Laconism, because Sparta was an oligarchy and was constantly intriguing to set up oligarchies in rival states. As a soldier Xenophon must have admired the professional discipline and efficiency of Spartan troops, and in Asia[10] he served either with or under such capable Spartan commanders as Clearchus, Chirisophus and (above all) his hero Agesilaus. He seems also to have had a curiously high regard not only for the Spartan way of life (which at its best had an alluring air of primitive simplicity and order)[11] but also for the Spartan character, to which he attributed a quite fictitious virtue.[12]

The immediate cause of Xenophon's banishment is unknown. The charge must surely have been Laconism, and there were certainly some grounds for such a charge, but they hardly seem adequate. The date, too, is uncertain, but if it was in or soon after 399 (as seems likely) one wonders whether there was any link with Socrates' execution. Both events must have shocked Xenophon profoundly: that Athens should treat as criminals two[13] men of such absolute integrity was surely a sign of political dementia. No wonder that he accepted the asylum provided by Sparta. But another disillusionment awaited him: Sparta abused her renewed supremacy by treacherous and tyrannical acts, notably by her seizure of

9. Cf. *Hellenica* ii, 3, 15–56.

10. Of course this was after he left Athens, but the experience would have improved his feelings towards Sparta.

11. Cf. *Memorabilia* iii, 5, 14 ff.

12. *Symposium* 8, 35.

13. This is not sarcastic: although Xenophon would not have bracketed himself with Socrates he would, I think, have claimed with some justice to be a perfectionist.

the citadel of Thebes, which Xenophon in a solemn passage[14] denounced as a deed of cynical perfidy that justly brought down divine retribution.

It would be interesting, if it were possible, to trace the fluctuations of Xenophon's feelings as the tide of fortune ebbed and flowed; but all that can be confidently affirmed is that for most of his life his loyalty was divided, and that on the whole he seems to have preserved a reasonable balance. Indeed if you consider the background of his early life – a childhood passed under the shadow of a long and bitter war; a youth spent fighting for a losing cause in a city torn by party struggles; the shock and humiliation of Athens' defeat; the atrocities of the Thirty and the civil war; the perils and stresses of the campaign in Asia; the shattering news of Socrates' death and his own banishment – if you consider all this you will not only find sympathy for his foibles; you will feel a kind of incredulous admiration for this man who came so near, if his account is honest, as it well may be, to his ideal of human excellence. And no doubt in all his many vicissitudes he drew comfort and confidence from his very real if simple piety, fostered (one may suppose) by Socrates' example.

How long and how well Xenophon knew Socrates is uncertain and matters little. He need not have heard and probably did not hear many of the conversations that he professes to report – but he must have heard some: there are several which seem much too realistic to be the product of hearsay and imagination. At any rate he came under the spell and adopted Socrates' outlook, so far as he was able. He was not a thinker but a practical man; and as soldier, sportsman and administrator he was primarily attracted by the Socratic con-

14. *Hellenica* v, 4, 1. Clearly he thought it marked the beginning of Sparta's slow decline.

cept of efficiency; but he was sincere also in his admiration and pursuit of moral goodness. Unfortunately he took himself rather too seriously. Socrates even in Plato's accounts sometimes sounds a little complacent, but nearly always saves himself by a touch of irony or absurdity; Xenophon's Socrates is obviously not without these redeeming qualities, but Xenophon himself is a natural hero-worshipper (witness his eulogies not only of Cyrus the Great but also of the mediocre Agesilaus), and when his enthusiasm is aroused he tends to orate with a sort of passionate *naïveté*[15] that embarrasses even sympathetic ears. These shocking pink passages – you can hardly call them 'purple' – should not be imputed to Socrates, who is unlikely to have indulged much in rhetorical devices. This leads us back to the question: how faithfully does Xenophon represent his friend and teacher?

Since the *Memoirs* (usually called by their Latin name, *Memorabilia Socratis*) were written with the avowed purpose of vindicating Socrates' memory, they cannot have existed in their present form before Socrates' death in 399. There is a sad lack of clear evidence, but most authorities would probably agree that shortly after this date several of Socrates' friends published books or pamphlets in defence of his life and teaching (one of these being Plato's *Apology*); that these provoked a counter-attack by the hostile Polycrates[16] and that either this or the earlier example of Plato, Antisthenes[16] and others, or perhaps his own spontaneous desire to pay tribute to a revered friend, prompted Xenophon to write down and publish both his personal impressions of Socrates' character and conduct and what he could remember of his conversation. The personal impressions are set out in *Memorabilia*, i, chs.

15. Cf. *Memorabilia* ii, 4, 5-7 iv, 4, 17.
16. See p.34, n.2. Antisthenes (see Glossary) was probably the first to write a Socratic dialogue, perhaps in Socrates' lifetime.

1 and 2[17] as a reply to the specific charges brought by the actual accusers or by Polycrates; there are other general appraisals, either introducing a conversation or group of anecdotes (*Memorabilia*, i, 3, 1–8; iv, 1) or summing up evidence already submitted (iv, 7–8). I have called these 'personal impressions' because that is what they purport to be; but obviously both they and the conversations may owe a good deal to other written sources, or to oral tradition, or to Xenophon's own imagination. He was certainly familiar with the views of Antisthenes, and besides other apparent allusions to Plato's dialogues we shall see that Xenophon's *Symposium* appears to comment upon Plato's. That Socrates was already a legendary figure in his lifetime would be a certain inference even without the evidence of Aristophanes and other comic poets; and that Xenophon was capable of invention is clearly shown by his *Cyropaedia* and *Oeconomicus*, of which the former contains large slices of pure fiction and the latter expresses the author's own ideas about the proper management of a household and estate. Add that many competent critics have impugned Xenophon's accuracy in his historical works; that he probably wrote the major part of the *Memoirs* at least ten or fifteen years after his last contact with Socrates; and that large sections of the text have at times been condemned as late interpolations: one cannot help asking whether this account of the man and his methods bears any relation to the facts.

Fortunately criticism is now rather more realistic than it was in the witch-hunts of the late nineteenth century, and inconsistencies – even quite glaring ones – are no longer held to be sufficient proof of multiple authorship.[18] Suspicion of

17. These two chapters may have been written originally as a separate work.

18. Critical studies of the Sherlock Holmes corpus have enlightened many English-speaking scholars.

Xenophon's text has generally been based on two kinds of inconsistency, (a) of thought and (b) of style. Some of the arguments in the *Memoirs* – especially those relating to the concept of Providence in i, 4 and iv, 3 – have been thought to betray Cynic and even Stoic influence, and therefore to be inappropriate if not impossible for Socrates and even for Xenophon. But this seems to be a mistaken view. We have seen that the views of Antisthenes were accessible to Xenophon; and the doctrine of divine providence was already familiar to Plato, and implicitly to the Socrates of the *Phaedo*: why not to the historical Socrates? It was quite in accordance with all that we can infer about his beliefs.[19] As for the argument from style, it is true that there are considerable variations in the *Memoirs*, but so there are in Xenophon's other works. The difference between the first two books of the *Hellenica*, in which he is consciously continuing the history of Thucydides, and the last five, in which he allows himself a much freer hand, is well known; and the *Cyropaedia*, like the *Memoirs*, exhibits many kinds of writing, from the chatty dialogue and lively narrative which sometimes almost recall Herodotus to pompous homilies and unseasonable displays of rhetoric. A third possible ground for suspicion, viz., the lack of artistic unity in the work as a whole, is evidence only of the curious fact that the discernment and orderliness of mind which made Xenophon a good tactician and administrator did not extend to his literary work. We may assume that the *Memoirs* is a compilation of papers written at different times over a period of some years; but the defects of the compilation are probably due to the author and not to some subsequent editor – though the latter alternative obviously cannot be excluded.

There is still the question of how genuine the reminiscences

19. He may not have worked out all the details as fully as Xenophon does, but that is another matter.

are, and to this there can be no simple answer. It is most unlikely that Xenophon was really an eavesdropper at some of these apparently private conversations. It may also be objected that even what he did hear or overhear could not have been reported accurately after the lapse of several years; but this objection may be less substantial than it seems. Memories were certainly much better in Xenophon's day than they are in ours, for two principal reasons: the comparative scarcity of books and writing materials, and the salutary practice of learning large quantities of poetry by heart at school. Moreover, a line of argument running through a discourse or conversation makes it much easier to remember. Since Socrates was obviously impressive and Xenophon equally impressionable, he may really have remembered the substance of a number of conversations with reasonable accuracy. At least there is no difficulty in supposing that he remembered what Socrates was like and what effect he had on his associates. He may even have compared notes with other Socratics; Phaedo was a native of Elis, not far away, and any visitor to Olympia could easily have paid a call at Scillus.

The *Symposium* or *Dinner-party* has been included in this volume for several reasons. It has a perfect right to be regarded as part of the *Memoirs*, even if it has a separate title. It shows Socrates in a lighter mood than anywhere else, except in his conversation with Theodote in *Memorabilia*, iii, 11. It is entertaining in itself and should help to refresh the reader (who may need refreshment by the time he reaches it). It is one of the two[20] earliest examples (Plato's *Symposium* being the other) of an important literary genre, and comparison of the two examples is as instructive as it is interesting. Finally, besides the jokes and leg-pulls and farcical paradoxes it con-

20. Plato's *Protagoras*, though not in form a symposium, has something of the same spirit; cf. Socrates' remarks at 347C–E.

tains some very important and neglected truths. Most of these features will reveal themselves with no more assistance than is offered in the introductions to each chapter, but a few general remarks may sharpen the reader's appreciation.

The question whether Plato's or Xenophon's *Symposium* came first has been much debated, but Professor K. J. Dover's article in *Phronesis*, x (1965), pp. 9–16 seems to decide the matter in favour of Plato. Moreover, Xenophon's treatment of the situation is much more understandable if it is regarded as conditioned by his predecessor's. Plato had prescribed Love as the theme for the whole evening, and had made each of his six speakers (seven if you count Alcibiades) discourse upon some aspect of the theme; and he had done this with such versatile invention that he left an imitator very little hope of finding anything fresh to say even about such a fertile subject, and no hope at all of finding enough to divide between Callias, his eight regular guests (nine if you count the bashful Autolycus), the gate-crasher Philippus and the Syracusan cabaret-manager. Xenophon ingeniously chose a subject – 'What I set most store by' – which could be handled with varying degrees of seriousness and prepare for Socrates' final speech. The result is not a great work of literary art but a clever and enjoyable, though uneven, piece of writing. Plato's brilliant parodies are replaced by something more like pastiche or straight forward imitation; there is character-drawing, but it is not very subtle; the dialogue is natural and often funny (except for the laboured witticisms of Philippus: had Xenophon really the penetration to realize that the professional joker is usually the least amusing?), although the speeches are apt to fall into artificiality. One may guess that Xenophon is (to some extent, at least) drawing upon actual experience. This does not, of course, mean that his report of the party is literally true. If the generally accepted date of his birth (about 430)[21] is right, he

21. Or even later; Delebecque argues persuasively for 426.

could not have been present at a dinner-party in 422,[22] and if he had been he would not have made much of the conversation. Besides, although he claims at the outset to have been present, he never speaks and is never mentioned: that little fiction is quickly forgotten. But much of the conversation may have been suggested by what he *had* heard at other similar parties; and if this is so, we have here a better picture of intelligent upper-class Athenian table-talk at the end of the fifth century than we are given by Plato's splendidly creative imagination. Or rather, this is true of the first part of the proceedings, in which the guests carefully avoid the obvious and show their ingenuity in making and supporting unexpected claims. This is the technique of the debater: the sort of thing that used to be heard at High Table or later in the Combination Room, and it is generally not meant to be taken at all seriously. But Xenophon intends to prepare his readers for Socrates' concluding discourse, and he does so rather neatly. First at the beginning of chapter 3 we have Charmides' brief observation that the combination of beauty and music stirs the emotions; in the next chapter Critobulus declares his infatuation with the beauty of Clinias, which leads to some serio-comic remarks on Love by Socrates and a little teasing by Charmides. Later in the same chapter comes a frank avowal of carnality by the Syracusan, and Socrates' defence of his claim to be a good procurer (in a non-physical sense) and his attribution of similar qualities to Antisthenes. In chapter 5 the beauty-contest between Socrates and Critobulus re-introduces the erotic motif in a jesting form. Finally, after discussion (some of it quite heated) of unrelated topics Socrates himself, by suggesting that graceful dances would give more pleasure

22. This must be the date if Autolycus' victory was at the Great Panathenaea; but of course the 'dramatic' date is not to be taken any more seriously than the chronological references in Plato's dialogues, which have caused much trouble to the literal-minded.

than acrobatic feats, leads up to his discourse on Love and the ballet-scene that – in a sense – illustrates it.

The distinction between Celestial and Common Love follows the example set by Pausanias in Plato's *Symposium* (see p. 19), but the treatment is quite different. Pausanias is surely a humbug defending his own form of homosexuality: 'It's all right so long as it's ennobling.' This is a familiar form of rationalization: so the parties to a treacherous and squalid act of adultery claim that theirs is no ordinary affair but a rare uplifting spiritual union; unfortunately there seems to be no limit to self-deception in this respect. Xenophon (who can be rather a Watson to Plato's Holmes) seems to think that Pausanias' attitude is submitted for approval, but it seems quite clear from *Republic*, 403A–C and *Laws*, 838E–839C that Plato regarded as shameful all sexual intercourse outside marriage, and *a fortiori* all homosexual intercourse; and there is no reason to suppose that Socrates thought otherwise. On the contrary, his attitude is shown clearly by Alcibiades' anecdote. But the implications of Plato's dialogue are admirably explained by Dr Hamilton in the introduction to his Penguin translation.

Xenophon has a simpler aim: his Socrates (in this respect perhaps more historical than Plato's) is trying to show what Love can be not for the philosopher but for the ordinary man. Where Plato passes from intellectual to mystical, Xenophon remains practical. Like Plato he speaks in terms of homosexual love, because the traditional seclusion of women made marriage for love improbable, and the realization in marriage of full mental and spiritual partnership virtually impossible.[23]

23. Things were improving by the end of the fifth century, thanks largely to Socrates and Euripides, but there was no question yet of intellectual equality. The husband must condescend and teach (cf. *Symp.* 2, 9, and Xenophon's own attitude, under the guise of Ischomachus, in the *Oeconomicus*). It was Plato who first recommended the same education for both sexes (*Rep.* 451E, 466C–D).

Plato's Pausanias assumes that both Common and Celestial Love are physical, the latter being redeemed by a generous attitude on the part of the lover and a desire for improvement on the part of the beloved. But this, although it seems to lift Celestial Love above the level of mere lust, is a fatally elastic criterion: who could fail to make it cover his own case? Xenophon's Socrates provides a clear-cut distinction: all carnal homosexuality is base and degrading. However, it does not follow (and Xenophon does not say) that Celestial Love is entirely psychical. Evidently there is a physical element in Callias' love, because we are shown the effect of Autolycus' remarkable beauty.[24] Indeed it should be obvious that there is a physical element in nearly all human relationships, inasmuch as the soul (or personality) is embodied. And this physical element can be, very often is, and no doubt often was in Xenophon's time, perfectly innocent – but it calls for ceaseless and most scrupulous self-control, as Socrates said (*Memorabilia*, i, 3, 8 ff.).

Love is indeed a great god: sex, if not quite so all-pervading as some psychologists believe (because for intelligent people there are other, and even some greater, interests in life) is a formidable instinct: if you don't control it, it will control you; and nothing rots the character more quickly than the hypocrisy that springs from indulgence in what, deep down inside you, you know to be wrong. For casual intimacy is the selfish exploitation of another person's body and soul: it is only in the lasting partnership of marriage that Common is transmuted into Celestial Love. This, although not stated in so many words, is the clear implication of the wedding-scene in the final chapter, and of the guests' reaction to it.

The translation would doubtless have benefited from wider criticism, but unfortunately most of my friends were already

24. *Symposium* i, 8–10.

so busy that it seemed unfair to invoke their aid. This has meant more work for the editor, Mrs Radice, to whom I am greatly indebted, above all for her patience. Valuable help and advice on particular points have also been given by Professor H. A. Harris, Mr J. S. Morrison, Dr Stephen Usher and my daughter Mary. The defects are my own.

H. T.

MEMOIRS OF SOCRATES

MEMORABILIA SOCRATIS

BOOK ONE

CHAPTER ONE

A defence of Socrates against the charge of heresy.[1] His only peculiarity was that, besides the normal methods of divination (i.e. ascertaining the will of the gods from oracles or from the interpretation of omens, etc.), he claimed often to receive a supernatural warning. Plato's account is similar (Apology 31C, 40A). To the materialist this will seem childishly absurd: others will recognize a real and not very uncommon experience. At any rate Xenophon has rightly fastened upon Socrates' religious convictions as the key to his character. He is also almost certainly right in insisting that Socrates' real interest was not in the world of nature but in human nature; Aristotle says the same (Metaphysics 987 b 1).

I HAVE often wondered what arguments Socrates' accusers can possibly have used to convince the people of Athens that he deserved execution. The indictment against him ran something like this – Socrates is a malefactor, firstly in that he does not recognize the gods recognized by the state but introduces the worship of other deities, secondly in that he corrupts the young.

With regard to the first charge, that he did not recognize the gods recognized by the state, on what evidence can they possibly have relied? Everyone could see that he sacrificed regularly at home and also at the public altars of the state; and he made no secret of using divination; in fact it was common gossip that Socrates claimed to have a 'divine sign'.[2] This, I imagine, was the chief reason for accusing him of introducing new deities. Yet he was no more heretical than any other

1. See note, p.12.
2. The Greek word is simply an adjective meaning 'supernatural'. Plato (*Apology*, 31D) makes Socrates describe it as a sort of voice which warns him against wrong courses of action.

people who believe in divination and follow the guidance of portents and omens and chance meetings and sacrifices. They do not suppose that the birds that they see or the people that they meet know what is the right course for those who want enlightenment; they believe that these things are simply means used by the gods to convey this information; and Socrates took the same view. But whereas most people say that it is the omen or encounter that dissuades or encourages them, Socrates asserted what he actually believed: he said that the 'divine sign' gave him a message. He often warned his associates to do this[3] or not to do that because he was inspired to do so by the 'divine sign', and those who took his advice benefited from it, while those who did not were sorry for it afterwards. Surely anyone would agree that Socrates did not want to seem either a fool or an impostor to his companions; and he would have been thought both if he had been palpably mistaken in making what he claimed to be divine revelations about the future. It seems obvious, then, that he would not have predicted the future if he had not been sure that his statements would come true; and who could base this trust on anything else than a god? And if he trusted in gods he surely must have believed in gods.

Besides, towards his intimate friends he adopted the following line: if an action was unavoidable, he advised them to carry it out as they thought best, but where the result was uncertain he sent them to consult an oracle whether action should be taken at all. He said that anyone who proposed to run a household or a state efficiently needed the help of divination. Skill in carpentry or metal-work or farming or government, or critical ability in these subjects, or proficiency in mathematics or domestic economy or military science – all these attainments he considered to be within the scope of human intellect; but he said that the most important aspects of these

3. According to Plato (see above) the voice never gave positive advice.

subjects the gods reserved for themselves, and none of them were revealed to mortals. A man who has sown a field well cannot tell who will reap the harvest; and a man who has built a house well cannot tell who will live in it. A general cannot tell whether it is to his advantage to hold his command, and a politician cannot tell whether it is to his advantage to be the head of the state. The man who has married a beautiful wife for his pleasure cannot tell whether she will cause him pain, and the man who has secured influential connexions in his native land cannot tell whether they will result in his banishment from it. To suppose that such consequences are all a matter of human judgement and contain no element of the supernatural was, he said, gross superstition; just as it was to consult oracles about questions which the gods had enabled us to decide by the use of our wits (e.g., supposing one were to ask whether it is better to engage a qualified or an unqualified driver for a carriage, or helmsman for one's ship); or to which the answers can be found by calculation or measuring or weighing. People who put this sort of question to the gods were, in his opinion, acting wrongly. He said that where the gods have given us power to act by the use of our intelligence, we ought to use it; but where the outcome is concealed from human eyes, we should try to discover it from the gods by consulting oracles; for the gods grant signs to those whom they favour.

Then again, Socrates was always in the public eye. Early in the morning he used to make his way to the covered walks and recreation grounds, and when the market-place became busy he was there in full view; and he always spent the rest of the day where he expected to find the most company. He talked most of the time, and anyone who liked could listen. But nobody ever saw Socrates do, or heard him say, anything that was irreverent or profane. He did not discourse about the world of nature, as most other philosophers did, inquiring into the constitution of the cosmos (as the sophists call it)[4] and the causes of the various celestial phenomena; on the contrary he pointed out the foolishness of those who concerned themselves with such questions. In the first place he inquired whether they proceeded to these studies only when they thought they had a sufficient knowledge of human problems, or whether they felt that they were right in disregarding human problems and researching on a superhuman plane. He expressed surprise that it was not obvious to them that human minds cannot discover these secrets, inasmuch as those who claim most confidently to pronounce upon them do not hold the same theories, but disagree with one another just like lunatics. 'Some lunatics,' he would say, 'don't even fear what is fearful, and others are terrified of things that aren't terrible; some don't scruple to say or do anything even in a crowd, and others feel that they can't even show themselves in public; some show no respect for temples or altars or anything else that is sacred, and others worship odd pieces of stone or wood, and animals. In the same way some of those who ponder about the world of nature think that reality is one,[5] and others that it is infinitely many;[6] some think that everything is always in motion,[7] and others that nothing can ever be moved;[8] some think that everything[9] comes to be and passes

4. The word was already applied to the ordered universe by philosophers before Xenophon was born. No doubt he attributes it to the sophists by way of disparagement.

5. The Eleatics, especially Parmenides.

6. The Atomists Leucippus and Democritus.

7. Heraclitus.

8. The Eleatics again, perhaps with special reference to Zeno and his paradoxes.

9. The antithesis *everything . . . nothing* is rather misleading. No Greek thinker seems to have imagined that body can be created out of nothing or completely annihilated: all assumed, more or less explicitly, a permanent corporeal substrate; but whereas most accepted that this was liable to every kind of modification, the Eleatics denied change altogether.

away, and others that nothing can come to be or pass away.'

He also raised this further question about them. 'Those who study human nature expect to achieve some result from their studies for the benefit of themselves or some other selected person. Do these students of the world above us expect that when they have discovered the laws that govern the various phenomena they will produce at will winds and rain and changes of season and any other such required effect? or have they no such expectation, contenting themselves with the mere knowledge[10] of how these various phenomena occur?'

That is how he spoke about people who occupied themselves with these speculations. He himself always discussed subjects of human interest, trying to find out the nature of piety and impiety, honour and dishonour, right and wrong, sanity and lunacy, courage and cowardice, state and statesman, government and the capacity for government, and all other subjects the knowledge of which he thought marked the really good citizen,[11] while those who were ignorant of them might fairly be called uneducated.

In so far as his views were not clearly known, it is no wonder that the jury formed a wrong estimate; but is it not extraordinary that they should have taken no account of what was common knowledge? On one occasion when he had been elected to the Council and had taken the councillor's oath, which included the clause 'I will act in accordance with the law', he was chosen to preside[12] in the Assembly. The people

10. He implies that useless knowledge ought not to be pursued. This is probably true; but uses are not always foreseeable.

11. Literally 'fine and good men'. See Introduction, p. 9.

12. In spite of this statement, echoed in iv, 4, 2, Socrates was probably not presiding at the time, and merely voted against the illegal motion (see Dodds on Plato, *Gorgias* 473E).

were bent on putting Thrasyllus and Erasinides[13] and all their colleagues to death by a single resolution, in defiance of the law; but Socrates refused to put the motion to the vote, although the people were angry with him and a number of influential men threatened him; he thought it more important to keep his oath than wrongfully to curry favour with the people and defend himself against intimidation.

He did not share the usual view about the interest that the gods take in human beings. Most people suppose that the gods know some things but not others; but Socrates believed that they know everything, both words and actions and unspoken intentions; and that they are present everywhere and give indications to people about all kinds of human affairs. So I cannot understand how the people of Athens were persuaded that Socrates was heretical in his religious beliefs, when he never said or did anything irreverent but on the contrary in his relationship to the gods said and did only what was recognizably consistent with the deepest reverence.

13. Two of the Athenian commanders at the battle of Arginusae in 406 B.C. Although victorious, they were prosecuted for negligence in rescuing the crews of sunken warships.

CHAPTER TWO

The charge of 'corrupting the young' was the most serious part of the prosecution's case. Xenophon's defence (which should be compared with that which Plato puts into Socrates' own mouth in the Apology) *tries to show that Socrates was neither an arch-sophist and perverter of morals (as Aristophanes portrayed him in the* Clouds) *nor an enemy of democracy (as he was evidently regarded in some left-wing circles) nor a tutor in crime to Critias and Alcibiades. The chapter has rather the air of a compilation, but it may well be an untidy arrangement of Xenophon's own notes.*

IT also seems extraordinary to me that any people should have been persuaded that Socrates had a bad influence upon young men. Besides what I have said already, he was in the first place the most self-controlled of men in respect of his sexual and other appetites; then he was most tolerant of cold and heat and hardships of all kinds; and finally he had so trained himself to be moderate in his requirements that he was very easily satisfied with very slight possessions. So if he himself was like this, how could he have made others irreverent or criminal or greedy or sensual or work-shy? On the contrary, he rescued many from this sort of state by inspiring them with a desire for goodness and offering them hopes that if they took themselves in hand they would become decent citizens. At the same time he never undertook to teach how this could be done; but by obviously *being* such a person he made those who spent their time with him hope that if they followed his example they would develop the same character.

He neither neglected the body himself nor commended others for doing so. He disapproved of over-eating followed by violent exercise, but he approved of taking enough exercise to work off the amount of food that the appetite accepts with pleasure; he said that this was quite a healthy practice and did not hinder the cultivation of the mind. He was certainly not foppish or ostentatious either in his clothing or in his footwear or in the rest of his daily life. Nor again did he make his associates money-lovers: he rid them of all other desires except for his company, and for that he charged no fee.[1] In exercising this restraint he considered that he was consulting his own independence; those who accepted a fee in return for their services he nicknamed 'self-enslavers', because they were bound to converse with those who paid the fee. He expressed surprise that a man who offered to teach goodness should demand to be paid for it and, instead of anticipating the greatest possible gain through obtaining a good friend, should be afraid that the person who has become a model of virtue will feel less than the deepest gratitude to his supreme benefactor. Socrates never made any such offer to anyone, but he believed that those of his associates who accepted the principles which he himself approved would be good friends all their life long to himself and to one another. How, then, could such a person have a corrupting influence upon the young? unless the cultivation of goodness is a form of corruption.

'But it is a fact,' said his accuser,[2] 'that he encouraged his associates to make light of constitutional practice by saying that it was foolish to appoint ministers of state by lot;[3] and that nobody would employ a candidate chosen by lot as a pilot or a carpenter or a musician or for any other such post; although if these posts are badly filled they cause far less harm than bad political appointments'; and he said that this sort of talk encouraged the young to despise the established constitution and made them violent. But I think that those who exer-

1. Unlike the sophists.
2. Probably not an actual prosecutor but Polycrates, a minor orator who wrote a pamphlet attacking Socrates.
3. See Introduction, pp. 11f.

cise reason and believe that they are capable of teaching their fellow-citizens what is for their good are most unlikely to become violent, since they know that violence involves enmity and danger, whereas persuasion produces the same results without danger and in a friendly spirit; because the victims of violence feel that they have been deprived, and are resentful, while those who have yielded to persuasion are appreciative of having received a kindness. So violence is not to be expected of those who exercise reason; such conduct belongs to those who have strength without judgement. I may add that anyone who ventures to use violence will also need not a few accomplices, while the man who can persuade will need none, because he will be sure of his power to persuade even if he is single-handed. Also such people are most unlikely to commit murder. Who would choose to kill a man rather than have him alive and acquiescent?

However, according to Socrates' accuser, Critias and Alcibiades, who had belonged to Socrates' circle, did more harm to their country than any other persons. Critias developed into the most avaricious and violent of all the oligarchs, and Alcibiades in his turn became the most dissolute and arrogant of all the democrats. For my part I shall not defend any wrong that these men did to the State; I shall merely explain how their connexion with Socrates came about.

These two men were by nature the most ambitious persons in all Athens, determined to have personal control over all State affairs, and to be famous above all others. They knew that Socrates lived quite contentedly on very slender resources, and that he was absolutely self-controlled in respect of all pleasures, and that he could do as he liked in argument with anyone who conversed with him. Given that they were aware of these facts, and were men of the kind that I have described, should one say that they courted Socrates' society out of admiration for his life and self-discipline, or because they thought that by associating with him they would acquire the highest efficiency in speech and action? My opinion is that if God had offered them the choice between living out their lives as they saw Socrates living his, and dying, they would have preferred to die. They showed as much by their conduct; because as soon as they felt superior to the rest of the company they broke away from Socrates and took up politics, the object for which they had courted his society.

Perhaps it might be objected that Socrates should not have taught his associates politics before he taught them self-discipline. I do not dispute this; but I observe that all teachers show their pupils how they themselves practise what they preach, and lead them on by reasoned argument. I know that Socrates in the same way made it clear to his companions that he was a good and honourable man, and excelled in discussing ethical questions and all other human problems. And I know that these men too were self-disciplined so long as they associated with Socrates; not because they were afraid of being fined or beaten by him, but because they thought for the time that it was best to behave so.

No doubt many professed philosophers[4] would say that a good man can never become bad, nor a self-disciplined man a bully, just as one who has learned any other subject can never become ignorant of it. But this is not my view of the matter. It seems clear to me that just as those who do not exercise their bodies cannot carry out their physical duties, so those who do not exercise their characters cannot carry out their moral duties: they can neither do what they ought to do nor avoid what they ought to avoid. That is why fathers keep their sons (even if they are right-minded) away from bad men, because they believe that the company of good people is a stimulus to virtue, while the company of bad men is the

4. Including Antisthenes.

ruin of it. Witness to this fact is borne by the poet[5] who says:

> Good company will edify you; bad
> Will rob you even of the wits you had,

and the one[6] who says

> But good men are by turns both base and brave.

And I can add my testimony to this. For I observe that just as epic poetry fades from the minds of those who fail to rehearse it, so those who neglect what their teachers tell them are liable to forget it. Now when a person forgets the advice he has been given, it means that he has also forgotten the influences that set his heart on self-discipline; and when he has forgotten these it is not surprising that he should forget self-discipline too. I observe also that those who have developed a taste for drinking, or have become involved in love affairs, are less capable of attending to what they ought to do and of abstaining from what they ought not to do. Often those who were able to control their spending before they were in love, after they have fallen in love can do so no more; and when once they have run through their money they no longer reject in disdain the sources of profit which they rejected before. Then how can it be impossible for one who was self-disciplined before to be undisciplined later, or for one who was formerly able to act rightly to be unable later? On the contrary it seems to me that every good and honourable capability needs to be exercised, and not least the capability of self-discipline; because the appetites that are implanted with the soul in the same body encourage it not to be self-disciplined, but to gratify both them and the body in the quickest possible way.

Critias, then, and Alcibiades, as long as they kept company

---

5. Theognis 35 f.
6. Unknown; quoted also by Plato, *Protagoras* 344D.

with Socrates, were able by his help to master their ignoble desires. But when they had parted from him Critias was banished to Thessaly[7] and attached himself to men who indulged more in law-breaking than in upright conduct, while Alcibiades on the other hand was courted for the sake of his beauty by many women of rank, and because of his prestige in the city and among the allies was pampered by many influential citizens and held in honour by the people, and enjoyed an easily-won supremacy; just as athletes who easily achieve supremacy in athletic competitions neglect their exercises, so he neglected himself. Well, when these men as a result of these experiences were exalted by their birth, elated by their wealth, puffed up with their power, and demoralized by various influences – is it any wonder that when they were corrupted for all these reasons and long separated from Socrates they became outrageous? Socrates' accuser holds him responsible for all their indiscretions: does he find nothing creditable in the fact that in their youth, when it was natural that they should be most irresponsible and undisciplined, Socrates made them behave decently? That is not how other cases are decided. If the teacher of a wind or string instrument or of some other art has made his pupils proficient, and they then attach themselves to other teachers and deteriorate, is the first teacher blamed for this result? If a man's son through attaching himself to some teacher becomes self-disciplined, and later through associating with somebody else becomes vicious, does the father blame the first teacher? Surely he gives him the greater credit in proportion as the son shows himself worse in the company of the latter. At any rate when fathers themselves look after their sons, if the sons go wrong the fathers are not blamed for it if they themselves have been impeccable in their conduct. Socrates ought to be judged in the same way. If he

7. In *Hellenica* ii, 3, 36 Xenophon makes Theramenes (a hostile witness) accuse him of encouraging peasants to revolt.

himself had done anything bad he might reasonably have been regarded as a depraved person; but if he was consistently scrupulous, how can he be justly held responsible for a fault which he did not possess?

However, even though he himself did nothing discreditable, if he had expressed approval of these men when he saw them behaving disreputably he would have deserved censure. Well, when he noticed that Critias was in love with Euthydemus and was trying to seduce him, like one seeking to gratify his sexual appetite, Socrates tried to dissuade him by insisting that it was crude and demeaning to solicit one's favourite, to whom one wishes to appear in a creditable light, importuning him like a beggar and entreating him to grant his favours, and that although they are far from honourable. And when Critias paid no attention to these protests and was not diverted from his purpose, Socrates is reported to have said, in the presence of several persons including Euthydemus himself, that Critias seemed to be suffering from pig's itch: he wanted to scratch himself against Euthydemus like a piglet scratching itself against a stone. This made Critias take a dislike to Socrates, so that when as one of the Thirty[8] he became a legislator along with Charicles he remembered it against Socrates and introduced a law against teaching an 'art of debate'. He did this out of spite towards Socrates, having no handle against him except misrepresenting him to the public by applying to him the usual layman's allegation[9] against all philosophers. I never heard Socrates do this myself, nor did I ever know anyone else claim to have heard him. He made his position quite clear. When the Thirty were putting to death many of the citizens (and those not the worst among them)

8. Often called the Thirty Tyrants: a group of oligarchs who seized power in 404 and earned detestation by their atrocious crimes.

9. 'Making the worse (appear) the better case'; cf. Aristophanes' *Clouds* 112 ff., Plato, *Apology* 19B.

and were inciting many others to do wrong, Socrates observed on one occasion that it seemed extraordinary to him that a man appointed to look after a herd of cattle who made them fewer and worse than they were before should not admit that he was a bad herdsman, and still more extraordinary that a man appointed as a political leader who was making the citizens fewer and worse than they were before was not ashamed and did not consider himself a bad political leader. This was reported to Critias and Charicles; they summoned Socrates and called his attention to the law and forbade him to converse with the young. Socrates asked them if he was allowed to ask for information about anything in their proclamation that he did not understand. They said he could.

'Well,' said he, 'I am prepared to obey the laws; but in order that I may not unconsciously offend through ignorance, I want you to make this point clear to me. When you tell me to abstain from the art of debate, is it because you think it conduces to correctness or to incorrectness of speech? If to correctness, clearly I shall have to refrain from speaking correctly; and if to incorrectness, clearly I shall have to try to speak correctly.'

Charicles was annoyed with him and said 'As you are so dense, Socrates, we issue you this warning, which is easier to grasp: not to converse with the young at all.'

'Well, then,' said Socrates, 'to prevent any misunderstanding, give me a definition of the age up to which one should regard people as young.'

Charicles replied 'As long as they are considered too immature to serve on the Council; on the same principle you are not to converse with men below the age of thirty.'

'Not even if I am buying something,' asked Socrates, 'and the seller is below the age of thirty; can't I even ask what the price is?'

'Yes, of course you can ask that sort of question,' said Charicles. 'But you know, Socrates, most of the questions you like to ask are ones to which you know the answers. That is the kind you must stop asking.'

'Am I not to reply either, then,' said Socrates, 'when a young man asks me something, if I know the answer – like "where does Charicles live?" or "where's Critias?"?'

'Yes, of course you can answer that kind,' said Charicles.

Critias interposed, 'The people you will have to keep off, Socrates, are the cobblers and carpenters and smiths.[10] They must be worn out by now with all your talk about them.'

'Then must I also keep off the topics that they lead to,' said Socrates, 'morality and piety and so on?'

'Certainly,' said Charicles, 'and from herdsmen. Otherwise you had better take care that you don't decrease the number of the herd yourself.'

This made it plain that their hostility to Socrates was due to their having been told of his remark about the cattle.

So much for the association of Critias with Socrates and the relations between them.

I myself should deny that anyone can be seriously influenced by a person of whom he disapproves; and it was not because they approved of him that Critias and Alcibiades associated with Socrates while they did associate with him, but because from the very first they had set out to be supreme in the state. Even while they were still in Socrates' company they tried to converse with the leading politicians in preference to anybody else. There is a story that when Alcibiades was still under twenty he had the following conversation about the laws with Pericles, who was his guardian and the head of the state.

'Tell me, Pericles,' he said, 'could you explain to me what "law" is?'

'Most certainly,' said Pericles.

10. Socrates used to support his arguments by analogies drawn from trades and professions; cf. iv, 4, 5 and Plato, *Gorgias* 490D–491A.

'Then please do so,' said Alcibiades. 'I hear people being praised for being law-abiding, and I presume that nobody can rightly win this praise if he does not know what "law" is.'

'Well,' said Pericles, 'it's not at all a difficult object that you're seeking, Alcibiades, if you want to find out what law is. When the people, meeting together, approves and enacts a proposal stating what should or should not be done, that is a law.'

'On the assumption that good actions should be done, or bad ones?'

'Good ones, of course, my boy, not bad ones.'

'Supposing that instead of the whole people a small section of it (as happens where there is an oligarchy) meets and enacts what ought to be done, – what is that?'

'Everything that the ruling party in the state enacts, after deliberating what should be done, is called a law.'

'Then supposing a despot, being in power in the state, enacts what the citizens are to do, is that a law too?'

'Yes, even the enactments of a despot in power are called laws.'

'And what is violence and lawlessness, Pericles? Isn't it when the stronger party compels the weaker to do what he wants by using force instead of persuasion?'

'So I believe,' said Pericles.

'Then anything that a despot enacts and compels the citizens to do instead of persuading them is an example of lawlessness?'

'I suppose so,' said Pericles. 'I retract the statement that what a despot enacts otherwise than by persuasion is law.'

'And if the minority enacts something not by persuading the majority but by dominating it, should we call this violence or not?'

'It seems to me,' said Pericles, 'that if one party, instead of persuading another, compels him to do something, whether by enactment or not, this is always violence rather than law.'

'Then if the people as a whole uses not persuasion but its superior power to enact measures against the propertied classes, will that be violence rather than law?'

'You know, Alcibiades,' said Pericles, 'when I was your age I was very clever too at this sort of thing; I used to practise just the same sort of dialectical ingenuity that I observe you practising now.'

'I wish I could have met you when you were at the height of your powers, Pericles,' said Alcibiades.

Well, as soon as they thought that they were a match for the politicians, they stopped associating with Socrates – because, apart from their general lack of sympathy with him, whenever they came into his company they had the annoyance of having their mistakes exposed – and took up politics, which was the very object for which they had attached themselves to Socrates.

But Crito was Socrates' constant companion, and so were Chaerephon and Chaerecrates and Hermogenes and Simmias and Cebes and Phaedondas and others, who associated with him not because they wanted to become politicians or barristers but because they wanted to be good and honourable men and to be able to behave properly towards their family and servants and relatives and friends, their city and their fellow-citizens. Not one of these men at any period of his life did anything wrong, or was accused of doing so.

But Socrates, according to his accuser, taught children to treat their fathers with contempt[11] by claiming to make those who associated with him wiser than their fathers, and asserting that it was legal to put even one's father in confinement after first getting him certified; using this as evidence that it was lawful for the ignorant to be kept under restraint by the wise. Actually Socrates thought that anyone who imprisoned

11. Cf. Aristophanes, *Clouds* 1321 ff.

people on the ground of ignorance might fairly be confined himself by those who understood what he did not. Such reflections led him often to examine the difference between ignorance and madness; and he considered that whereas for mad people to be confined would be an advantage both to themselves and to those who were fond of them, the right thing for those who lacked necessary knowledge would be to learn from those who had it.

Socrates' accuser said that he lowered the regard of his associates not only for their fathers but also for their other relatives, by saying that it is not their relatives that help the victims of disease or litigation, but doctors in the one case and competent advocates in the other. He also accused Socrates of saying that it was no good having friends who were loyal unless there was a prospect of their being actually able to help you; and of asserting that the only friends who deserved to be esteemed were those who knew what was right and could make it clear to others. In this way, he said, Socrates, by prevailing on the young to believe that he was the wisest of men and best qualified to make others wise, so influenced his associates that nobody else had any position in their eyes by comparison with himself.

I know that he expressed these views both about fathers and other relatives and about friends; and what is more, that he said that when the soul, which is the one and only seat of the intelligence, has departed, people lose no time in carrying out and putting away the body of the person dearest to them. He used to say that even in life, although the body is our most precious possession, everyone is ready to give up any part of it that is useless or unprofitable, either removing it himself or getting someone else to do it. People cut their own nails and hair and corns, and allow surgeons to amputate and cauterize with consequential pain and suffering, and feel bound to show them gratitude and pay a fee; and they spit out phlegm from their mouths as far as they can, because its presence there does them no good and is much more likely to harm them. It was not with the object of instructing his friends to bury their fathers alive or cut themselves to pieces that Socrates stated these facts; by showing that what is without intelligence is without value he was appealing to people to take pains to be as intelligent and helpful as possible, so that if a person wished for the regard of father or brother or anyone else he might not rely on the relationship and take no trouble, but try to be of service to those whose regard he wished to obtain.

Another charge against Socrates was that he used to pick out the most mischievous lines of the most famous poets and by using their evidence, taught his associates to be criminals and autocrats. The line of Hesiod

> No work is shame, but idleness is shame[12]

he is supposed to have explained as meaning that the poet bids us shrink from no kinds of work, not even such as are wicked or discreditable, but to do even these for the sake of gain. Actually when Socrates had agreed that to be a worker was beneficial to a man and a good thing, while to be an idler was harmful and a bad thing, in other words that to work was good and to be idle was bad, he used to add that only those who performed a good action were working and were good workers, while those who played dice or performed any other kind of worthless and punishable action he denounced as idlers.[13] On this basis 'no work is shame, but idleness is shame' would be quite correct.

He was also accused of constantly quoting the passage from Homer[14] which says that Odysseus

---

12. *Works and Days* 309; cf. Plato, *Charmides* 163B.
13. Cf. iii, 9, 9.
14. *Iliad*, ii, 188 ff., 199 ff.

When 'twas a prince or noble that he met,
Stood by him and with courteous speech restrained him:
'Sir, you astound me. It becomes you not
In craven fashion thus to spread dismay.
Hold fast yourself, and stay the other folk.' . . .
But when again he saw a man of the host
And found him bawling, with his staff he smote
And chid him thus: 'Fie! keep you still, and hear
Your betters speak, unwarlike, feeble man,
Of no account in fighting or debate.'

This he interpreted (it was alleged) as meaning that the poet
upheld the beating of commoners and poor people. But that
was not what Socrates meant. If it had been he would have
thought that he ought to be beaten himself. What he did say
was that any persons who could neither say nor do anything
useful, who were incapable, if the need arose, of helping the
army or the state or even the citizen body, ought to be placed
under every kind of restraint (especially if they are audacious
too), even if they happen to be very rich. No; on the contrary Socrates was obviously a friend of the people and well
disposed towards all mankind. Although he had many admirers, both native and foreign, he never charged any of them
a fee for his company, but shared his resources unhesitatingly
with everyone. Some people after getting some scraps of wisdom from him free sold them to the others at a high price,
and were not as democratic as he was, because they refused
to converse with those who could not pay. But Socrates, even
in the eyes of the world at large, brought greater honour to
his city than the celebrated Lichas did to Sparta. Lichas used
to give a dinner to the foreigners who visited Lacedaemon for
the festival of the Gymnopaedia,[15] but Socrates spent his life

15. So called because at it boys danced naked. It was a major festival
which attracted many visitors. Lichas is no doubt the same man who
got into trouble with the judges at the Olympic Games in 420 B.C.
(Xenophon, *Hellenica* iii, 2, 21; Thucydides v, 50).

conferring the highest benefits at his own expense upon all who wanted them, for he never let his associates go without improving them.

Since Socrates was as I have described him, in my opinion he deserved to be honoured by the state rather than executed. Consideration of the law would lead one to the same conclusion. According to law, death is the penalty for conviction as a thief or pickpocket or cutpurse or housebreaker or kidnapper or temple-robber; but Socrates was the last man on earth to commit these crimes. In his public life he was never guilty of involving his country in an unsuccessful war, or in sedition or treason or any other calamity; and in his personal dealings he never deprived anyone of a benefit or got anyone into trouble, and he was never even accused of any such action. How, then, could he be liable to the indictment? So far from being an atheist, as was alleged, he was obviously the devoutest of men; and so far from corrupting the young, as he was accused of doing by his prosecutor, he obviously rid his associates of any wrong desires that they had and urged them to set their hearts on the finest and most splendid form of excellence, which makes both states and households well administered. By acting in this way he surely deserved high honour at the hands of his country.

CHAPTER THREE

Further examples of Socrates' piety and of his attitude towards food, drink and sex. The last subject is illustrated by a reported conversation between Socrates and Xenophon himself. This is lively enough to be a genuine reminiscence, but since Xenophon's name never occurs again in this work one may suspect that it is introduced here to give the memoirs an air of authenticity. Socrates' views on sex are stated more fully in Symposium, *ch. 8.*

I SAID above that in my opinion he actually benefited his associates, partly by practical example and partly by his conversation. I shall record as many instances as I can recall.

As regards religion, anyone can see that Socrates' behaviour accorded exactly with the Pythia's[1] advice to those who inquire what they ought to do about sacrifices or showing respect to ancestors or any other such observance. The Pythia replies that they will show proper piety if they act in accordance with the law of the land. Socrates both acted on this principle himself and urged others to do so; and he thought that those who acted otherwise were either over-scrupulous or irresponsible.

He prayed to the gods simply to give him what was good, recognizing that they know best what is good for us. He thought that to pray for gold or silver or unlimited power or anything of that sort was just like praying for a throw of dice or a battle or anything else with an obviously unpredictable sequel. He thought that in offering small sacrifices to the gods from small resources he was in no way falling behind those who offered ample ones from ample resources. He said that it

1. The Pythia (so called from Pytho, the name of the surrounding district) was the inspired priestess who gave oracular responses at the shrine of Apollo at Delphi.

was a poor thing for the gods if they took more pleasure in great sacrifices than in small ones, because then they would often be better pleased with the offerings of the wicked than with those of the good; and for human beings life would not be worth living if the offerings of the wicked pleased the gods better than those of the good. On the contrary he believed that the gods appreciated most the honours paid to them by the most devout people. He also was a strong supporter of the line[2]

Offer thine utmost to the immortal gods,

and he said that it was a sound maxim to offer one's utmost to friends and strangers and in all other departments of life. If he thought that he was receiving any direction from the gods he could no more have been persuaded to act against it than if someone had tried to persuade him to accept a blind guide who didn't know the way in preference to one who could see and did know it. And he denounced the folly of others who acted against the direction of the gods through avoiding the disapproval of men. He himself disregarded all human opinions in comparison with the advice of the gods.

He disciplined both his mind and his body by a way of life which would enable anyone who followed it (in the normal course of events) to live with confidence and security, and to have no difficulty in meeting its expenses. In fact he was so economical that I doubt whether anyone could work so little as not to earn enough for Socrates' needs. He took only so much food as he could eat with pleasure, and he was so ready for a meal when he came to it that his appetite was sauce enough. Any drink was agreeable to him, because he only drank when he was thirsty. If he ever accepted an invitation to dinner he very easily resisted what costs most people the greatest effort, viz., the temptation to fill oneself beyond repletion. Those who could not resist this he advised to avoid

2. Hesiod, *Works and Days* 336.

anything that impelled them to eat when they were not hungry or drink when they were not thirsty; for that, he said, was what ruined stomachs and heads and characters. He used to say jokingly that he believed Circe[3] turned Odysseus' comrades into pigs by entertaining them with this kind of fare; and that the reason why Odysseus was not turned into a pig was partly the prompting of Hermes and partly the fact that he was self-controlled and refrained from partaking of the dishes beyond the point of repletion. Such were the views that he expressed on this subject, humorously but seriously.

He urged resolute avoidance of sexual relations with beautiful people, because it was not easy for one who became involved with them to preserve self-control. Indeed on one occasion when he had discovered that Critobulus the son of Crito had kissed the handsome son of Alcibiades he said to Xenophon in Critobulus' presence 'Tell me, Xenophon: didn't you think that Critobulus was the sort of person to be more sober than reckless and more prudent than thoughtless and foolhardy?'

'Yes, indeed,' said Xenophon.

'Well, now you must look on him as a thorough hot-head and desperado. He would somersault over sword-points[4] and jump into a furnace.'

'Why,' said Xenophon, 'what have you seen him do that you have passed such an unkind judgement on him?'

'Isn't it a fact,' said Socrates, 'that he dared to kiss Alcibiades' very handsome and attractive son?'

'Well, really,' said Xenophon, 'if that's the type of a foolhardy act, I think I might face such a risk myself.'

'Very rash of you,' said Socrates. 'What good do you think you would do yourself by kissing him? Don't you realize that you would instantly be a slave instead of a free man, and

---

3. The famous enchantress of Aeaea: see Homer, *Odyssey* x, 135 ff.
4. Cf. *Symposium* 2, 11.

spend a lot of money on harmful pleasures, and have no time to take an interest in anything of real value, and be forced to exert yourself for ends that not even a lunatic would bother about?'

'Good heavens!' said Xenophon, 'what a sinister effect a kiss has, according to you!'

'Does that really surprise you?' said Socrates. 'Don't you know that spiders not a quarter of an inch long by the mere contact of their mouths distract people with pain and drive them crazy?'

'Yes, of course,' said Xenophon, 'because they inject something in the act of biting.'

'You *are* dense,' said Socrates. 'Do you assume that beautiful people inject nothing in the act of kissing, just because you can't see it? Don't you realize that this creature which they call the bloom of youth is even more dangerous than the spiders I spoke of? They produce their effect by contact, but this needs no contact; if one looks at it, even from quite a distance it can inject a kind of poison that drives one crazy. No; I advise you, Xenophon, when you see a beautiful person, to take to your heels as fast as you can; and I advise you, Critobulus, to go away for a year. That may give you just enough time to recover.'

In the same way he thought that those who are not proof against sexual attraction should confine their relations to such as their conscience would only tolerate where there was real physical need, and not otherwise. He himself was obviously so well schooled in this respect that he could avoid the most beautiful and attractive people more easily than others could avoid the ugliest and most unattractive.

This, then, was his attitude towards food, drink and sex; and he considered that in this way he would obtain no less satisfaction and would suffer much less discomfort than those who devoted a large part of their energy to these objects.

CHAPTER FOUR

Socrates did not merely convict of ignorance; he gave positive guidance, as in the conversation which follows. Some have thought that the Argument from Design as presented here has a post-Aristotelian flavour; but the outlook seems perfectly Socratic. The similar passage in Book iv, ch. 3 is open to more suspicion.

If this Aristodemus is the same as the informant of Apollodorus in Plato's Symposium (described there as a little man and one of Socrates' greatest admirers), Socrates' guidance would seem to have been effective.

IF anybody thinks (judging from some of the spoken and written accounts of him) that Socrates, though excellent at setting people on the road to goodness, was incapable of leading them to their goal, I invite him to consider not only the way in which Socrates used to question and refute (by way of correction) those who thought they knew everything, but also the way in which he used to spend the whole day in conversation with the members of his circle; and then to decide whether Socrates was capable of making his companions better men.

I shall relate first a conversation about religion which I once heard between him and Aristodemus the Midget. Socrates had learned that this man neither sacrificed to the gods nor practised divination, and went so far as to scoff at those who did so. 'Tell me, Aristodemus,' he said, 'have you ever admired any people for their artistry?'

'Yes,' he replied.

'Tell us their names,' he said.

'Well, in epic poetry the man I have most admired is Homer, and in dithyrambic[1] Melanippides, and in tragedy

52

Sophocles, and in sculpture Polycleitus, and in painting Zeuxis.'

'Which do you think is more admirable – the artist who creates senseless and motionless images, or the one who creates things that are alive and intelligent and active?'

'The one who creates live things, by far; provided that they are products of design and not of chance.'

'Some things have no purpose so far as we can tell, and others are obviously useful for some end. Which class do you assign to chance and which to design?'

'Those which are useful should be products of design.'

'Then don't you think that it was for their use that the creator provided men with the various sense-organs – eyes to see what is visible and ears to hear what is audible? Take the case of smells: what good would they be to us if we weren't supplied with noses? And how should we perceive sweet and bitter tastes, and all the pleasures of the palate, if the tongue had not been fashioned in us to distinguish them? And apart from these, don't you feel that there are other things too that look like effects of providence? For example, because our sight is a delicate thing, it has been shuttered with eyelids which open when we have occasion to use it, and close in sleep; and to protect it from injury by the wind, eyelashes have been made to grow as a screen; and our foreheads have been fringed with eyebrows to prevent damage even from the sweat of the head. Then our hearing takes in all sounds, yet never gets blocked up. And the front teeth of all animals are adapted for cutting, whereas the molars are adapted for masticating what is passed on to them. And the mouth, through which the things

1. A form of choral lyric connected with the worship of Dionysus and very popular in the fifth and early fourth centuries. Melanippides of Melos, Sophocles, Polycleitus of Argos, and Zeuxis of Heraclea in S. Italy were all active in the fifth century, Zeuxis being the youngest by twenty years or so.

that animals like are admitted, is situated close to the eyes and nose, whereas the outlets for excrement, which is disagreeable, are directed as far as possible away from the sense-organs. Are you in real doubt whether such provident arrangements are the result of chance or of design?'

'No, indeed,' he said; 'looked at in this way they seem very much like the contrivances of some wise and benevolent craftsman.'

'And the implanting of the instinct to procreate, and the implanting in the female parent of the instinct to rear her young, and in the young so reared an intense desire to live and an intense fear of death?'

'These provisions, too, really seem like the contrivances of someone who has determined that there shall be living creatures.'

'Do you believe that you have some intelligence?'

'Go on asking questions and you will get your answer.'

'Do you suppose that there is nothing intelligent anywhere else, knowing as you do that what you have in your body is only a small portion of all the earth there is, and only a little water out of a vast volume of it, and that your share of each of the other elements of which your body is composed is minute in proportion to the whole? Do you really believe that by some lucky chance you have appropriated Mind for yourself; that it alone exists nowhere else; and that these vast masses of infinite multitude are regulated – according to you – by a kind of unintelligence?'

'I protest; I can't see who controls them as I can see that the processes of manufacture that go on around us are controlled by the craftsmen.'

'You can't see your own mind either, although it controls your body. On that principle you can say that you do nothing by design and everything by chance.'

Aristodemus said, 'I assure you, Socrates, it isn't that I think little of the deity; I regard it as too magnificent to need my service.'

'Then,' said Socrates 'the more magnificent the object that deigns to serve you, the more you ought to esteem it.'

'You can be sure,' he said, 'that if I thought the gods took any interest in human beings I shouldn't neglect them.'

'So you don't think they take any interest? Well, in the first place man is the only creature that they have set erect; and his erect carriage enables him both to see farther in front of him and to observe better what is above him, and to be less liable to injury of the eyes, ears and mouth. Then to all other terrestrial creatures they have given feet, which only supply locomotion; but to man they have also given hands, which are the principal agents of our superior happiness. Again, while all animals have a tongue, the human tongue alone is so made that by touching different parts of the mouth at different times it can produce articulate sounds and enable us to communicate with one another as much as we like. And don't forget that whereas to other animals they have granted the pleasures of sex for a limited period of the year, for us they provide them continuously as far as old age.

'Now God was not content with merely caring for the body; what is far more important, he also endowed man with soul in its highest form. What other animal, in the first place, has a soul that is aware of the existence of the gods, who have set in order the greatest beauty on the grandest scale?[2] What kind of creature except man worships the gods? What soul is better able than man's to make provision against hunger or thirst, cold or heat; to relieve disease or cultivate bodily strength or take pains to acquire knowledge, or to keep in memory all that it has heard or seen or learned? Isn't it quite manifest to you that, compared with other creatures, men live like gods, naturally supreme both in body and in soul?

2. The heavenly bodies.

A person with the mind of a man but the body of an ox would not be able to do what he wanted; and it is no advantage to have hands without intelligence. You are lucky enough to possess both these priceless gifts; how can you think that the gods have no concern for you? What do you expect them to do before you believe that they care about you?'

'Send advisers, as you contend that they do,[3] to tell me what to do and what not to do.'

'When they reply by means of divination to some inquiry made by the people of Athens, do you not believe that the message is intended for you as well? nor when by sending portents they give warning to the whole of Greece or to all mankind? Are you the one exception that they deliberately ignore? Do you suppose that the gods would have implanted in man the belief that they can do good and harm, if they were really unable? and that we men could have been deceived all this time and never realized the fact? Can't you see that the human institutions which have the longest history and the greatest wisdom – I mean civilized communities and nations – are the most religious, and that the most judicious age-groups are the most regardful of the gods?

'My good friend,' he went on, 'get it into your head that your own mind, which is inside you, controls your body as it wills; and in the same way you must believe that the intelligence which is in the universe disposes all things just as it pleases. If you accept that your vision has a range of several miles, you must not suppose that the eye of God lacks the power to see everything at once; and if you accept that your mind can take thought about affairs both here and in Egypt and in Sicily, you must not suppose that the wisdom of God is incapable of taking thought for all things at the same time. Indeed if you make the experiment of doing services to the

3. Cf. i, 1, 2-10.

gods to see whether they will be willing to advise you about events concealed from human foresight – just as by doing services or favours to men you discover who are willing to repay them, and by seeking advice you find out who are clear-headed – you will discover that the divine nature is so infinitely great and potent that it can see and hear everything, and be present everywhere, at the same time, and take care of everything at the same time.'

It seemed to me that by speaking in this way he made his associates abstain from irreverent and wrong and discreditable actions not only in public but also when they were by themselves, for the simple reason that they had made up their minds that none of their actions could ever escape the knowledge of the gods.

CHAPTER FIVE

The form of the following exhortation to self-discipline, which is addressed not to an individual but to a group, rather suggests a 'diatribe' or moral discourse such as the Cynics used for general edification; but since the sentiments are quite appropriate to Socrates there is no real ground for doubting Xenophon's attribution.

IF self-control is a good and honourable quality for a man to possess, let us consider whether Socrates gave any impulse towards it by homilies of the following kind.

'Gentlemen, supposing that war had broken out, and we wanted to elect a man under whose leadership we were most likely to save ourselves and subdue our enemies, should we choose someone who had no power of resistance against appetite or wine or sexual desire or hard work or sleep? How could we possibly expect that such a person would either save us or overcome the enemy? Or suppose that we have reached the end of life and want to entrust someone with the education of our sons or the guardianship of our un-married daughters or the safe keeping of money: are we likely to regard a moral weakling as worthy of our confidence? Should we entrust livestock, or management, or the supervision of labour to an employee of weak character? Should we be prepared to accept a person of this kind in the capacity of agent or buyer, even as a free gift? But if we would not put up with even an employee of weak character, surely it is proper to guard against incurring this defect oneself. It is not the case that a weak-willed man benefits himself by harming others, in the way that clever financiers are supposed to enrich themselves by taking money from others; no, he injures others, but he injures himself much more, because to ruin not only one's own home but also one's own body and

58

soul is to do oneself the greatest injury of all. And who would appreciate the company of such a person at a social function if he saw him caring more about the food and wine than about his friends, and paying more attention to street-walkers than to his companions? Surely every man ought to regard self-control as the foundation of moral goodness, and to cultivate it in his character before anything else. Without it who could either learn anything good or practise it to a degree worth mentioning? Or who could escape degradation both of body and of soul if he is a slave to his appetites? I assure you it seems to me that a free man ought to pray that he may never happen upon a slave of this kind, while a man who is a slave to such pleasures ought to pray to the gods that he may find good masters; for that is the only way in which such a person can be saved.'

While expressing these sentiments Socrates showed himself to be even more self-controlled in practice than in theory. He overcame not only his physical appetites but also the attraction of money; because he thought that the man who accepts money indiscriminately is setting up a master over himself and submitting to a peculiarly disgraceful form of servitude.

CHAPTER SIX

Socrates defends his way of life and his policy as a teacher against the criticisms of Antiphon the sophist. This man has generally been distinguished from Antiphon the first of the Attic orators (about ten years older than Socrates), a man of great literary and political ability who was prominent in the oligarchic revolution of 411 (Thucydides viii, 68); but a good case has been made[1] for identifying the two. The question should probably be left open.

The conversation is reported (or invented) to contrast the philosophic with the sophistic outlook. The philosopher's aim is not self-gratification but contentment; not material success but moral betterment. To sell one's wisdom is as squalid as to sell one's favours; and to show others how they can best serve their country is a more effective form of patriotism than playing a part in politics oneself.

IT is only fair to Socrates not to leave unrecorded the conversation that he had with Antiphon the sophist. On one occasion this man, wishing to transfer Socrates' associates to himself, went up to him in their presence and said:

'Socrates, I always thought that people ought to become happier through the study of philosophy, but it seems to me that you have experienced the opposite effect. At any rate you lead the sort of life that no slave would put up with if it were imposed upon him by his master. You eat and drink the worst possible food and drink, and the cloak that you wear is not only of poor quality but the same for summer and winter; and you never wear shoes or a tunic. Then you never accept money, the receipt of which is cheering and the possession of which enables people to live more generously and agreeably. So if you are going to affect your associates in the same way

1. By J. S. Morrison in *Proceedings of the Cambridge Philological Society*, 1961.

as the teachers of other occupations, who turn out pupils after their own pattern, you should regard yourself as a teacher of misery.'

Socrates replied, 'You seem to have got it into your head that I live such a miserable life, Antiphon, that I really believe you would rather die than live as I do. Come on then; let us see what hardship you have detected in my way of life. Is it that those who accept payment are bound to produce the result for which they are paid, whereas I, since I don't accept it, am not compelled to converse with a person if I don't want to? Or do you depreciate my diet on the ground that it is less wholesome and sustaining than yours? or that my means of subsistence are harder to procure than yours, because they are rarer and more costly? or that you enjoy your provisions more than I do mine? Don't you know that the more a man enjoys eating the less he needs a stimulus for his appetite, and the more he enjoys drinking the less he craves for a drink that he hasn't got? As for cloaks, you know that people change them because of cold or hot weather, and they wear shoes to prevent things from hurting their feet and so impeding their movements. Well, have you ever known me stay indoors more than anybody else on account of the cold, or compete with anyone for the shade on account of the heat, or fail to walk wherever I wanted to because my feet were sore? Don't you know that those who are physically weakest by nature, if they train with a particular end in view, become better able to achieve that end, with less effort to themselves, than the strongest athletes who neglect their training? and if that is so, don't you think that I, who am always training myself to put up with the things that happen to my body, find everything easier to bear than you do, with your neglect of training? As for my not being a slave to my stomach, or to sleep, or to lechery, what better reason for it can you imagine than that I have other more pleasant occupations, which cheer me not

only when I am engaged upon them but also as giving me
ground for hoping that they will benefit me always? Besides,
you must be aware of this, that those who think they are
having no success are not happy, while those who feel that
their farming or seafaring or any other occupation that they
have is going well, are cheered by the consciousness of success.
Now then, do you suppose that all these feelings give as much
pleasure as the thought that one is becoming better one's self,
and acquiring better friends? Well, I have this belief all the
time. And then, if one's friends or the state needs help, which
has more leisure to attend to this duty – the man who passes
his time as I do now, or the one whom you regard as fortunate? Which could more readily go on military service; the
man who can't live without an expensive diet, or the one who
is content with what he has? And which would be sooner re-
duced to surrender in a siege: the one whose requirements are
most difficult to obtain, or the one who is satisfied with whatever comes most readily to hand? It seems to me, Antiphon,
that you identify happiness with luxury and extravagance;
but I have always thought that to need nothing is divine, and
to need as little as possible is the nearest approach to the divine;
and that what is divine is best, and what is nearest to the divine
is the next best.'

On another occasion when Antiphon was talking to Socrates
he said, 'You know, Socrates, I think that you are an honest
man, but not at all a wise one. And it seems to me that you are
beginning to realize this yourself; at any rate you don't charge
anyone for admitting him to your company; and yet take the
case of your cloak or your house or any other item of your
property: if you thought that it was worth money, so far from
giving it away, you wouldn't even accept a price lower than
its value. So obviously if you thought that your company was
worth anything, you would charge a fee for it no less than
its value. Therefore honest you may be, since you don't de-

ceive with a view to your own advantage; but wise you cannot be, if your knowledge is worthless.'

To this Socrates replied, 'In our society, Antiphon, the
same rules with regard to what is creditable and what is not
are thought to apply equally to the disposal of physical attrac-
tions and of wisdom. A man who sells his favours for a price to
anyone who wants them is called a pimp; but if anyone forms
an attachment with someone whom he knows to be a good
and honourable lover, we regard him as perfectly respectable.
In just the same way those who sell wisdom at a price to anyone who wants it are called sophists; but if anyone, by im-
parting any edifying knowledge that he possesses, makes a
friend of one whom he knows to be naturally gifted, we consider that he is behaving as a good and honourable citizen
should behave. As for myself, Antiphon, I take as much pleasure in good friends as other people take in a good horse or
dog or bird – in fact I take more; and if I have anything good
to teach them I teach it, and I introduce them to any others
from whom I think they will get any help in the quest for
goodness. And in company with my friends I open and read
from beginning to end the books in which the wise men of old
have written down and bequeathed to us their treasure; and
when we see anything good we take it for ourselves; and we
regard our mutual friendship as great gain.'

When I heard him say this it certainly seemed to me that he
was a fortunate man himself, and that he was leading his
hearers on towards honour and goodness.

On another occasion Antiphon asked him how it was that
he expected to make others politicians when he himself did
not take part in politics, if indeed he was capable of doing so.
Socrates retorted: 'Which would be the more effective way
for me to take part in politics – by doing so alone, or by making it my business to see that as many persons as possible are
capable of taking part in them?'

CHAPTER SEVEN

The contrast between the sincerity of the philosopher and the super-ficiality of the sophist recalls Socrates' exhortations against imposture and pretence of every kind.

LET us also consider whether in discouraging his associates from pretence he encouraged them to apply themselves to goodness;[1] for he always said that there was no better road to distinction than that by which one could become really good at the pursuit at which one wished to seem good. He used to demonstrate the truth of this statement in the following way.

'Let us consider,' he said, 'what a man ought to do if he wants to be thought a good musical performer although he is not. Surely he should imitate good performers in respect of the outward accessories of their art. First, as they possess imposing paraphernalia and take round with them a large retinue, he must do the same. Secondly, as there are many who express admiration of them, he must provide himself with plenty of admirers. But actual playing he must never attempt; otherwise he will immediately be exposed as a laughing-stock and not merely a bad performer but an impostor. Now if he spends a lot of money and gets no benefit from it, and has besides a bad reputation, surely his life will be laborious and unprofitable and ridiculous. Similarly, supposing that someone should wish to be regarded as a good general or a good pilot without actually being one, let us consider what would happen to him. If he really wanted to be thought capable of such a line of conduct, and could not convince people, wouldn't his position be distressing? and still more wretched if he did convince them, because obviously if a man who did not know his job was appointed as a pilot or as a general he would destroy

1. See Introduction, pp. 7f.

those whom he least wished to destroy, and the consequences for himself would be shameful and disastrous.'

On the same principle he showed that it did one no good to be thought rich or brave or strong if one was not such in reality, because people who were in this position were faced with obligations that were beyond their powers; and if they could not perform them although they seemed to be capable of doing so, they would get no sympathy. It was no slight deception, he said, even to deprive another person by persuasion of a sum of money or an article of value, but it was the grossest deception of all for a good-for-nothing person to convey the false impression that he was capable of directing the state. In my opinion by conversations of this kind he discouraged his associates even from making pretensions.

BOOK TWO

CHAPTER ONE

Most of the conversations in Book II show Socrates giving advice about personal relationships or solving personal problems, but the first chapter deals with wider moral issues. Socrates urges the exercise of self-control by showing that this quality is necessary for a prospective ruler. To say that one has no desire to rule is a feeble objection, because in general the subject is evidently less happy than the ruler; and to say that one is content to be neither ruler nor subject but a resident alien is no better, because aliens are peculiarly exposed to ill-treatment and even to loss of liberty. On the other hand the effort involved in working for a worth-while end is not only tolerable but actually rewarding; whereas a life of ease and self-indulgence saps the vigour of body and mind. Socrates supports this doctrine by quoting from the poets and by reproducing Prodicus' story of the Choice of Heracles. This passage, although undeniably relevant, is unlikely to have formed part of a real conversation; it seems to have been introduced partly by way of ornament, to gild the philosophic pill, and partly to exhibit the writer's (presumably Xenophon's) virtuosity. It is in fact a lively piece of writing and seems to have been famous in antiquity; a Latin version of the opening sentence is to be found in Cicero, De Officiis, i, 118.

Prodicus of Ceos was a distinguished sophist, contemporary with Socrates; he was interested in the correct and precise use of words. He is one of the speakers in Plato's Protagoras, and is mentioned with rather ironical respect in several other dialogues. There is a reference to his 'Choice of Heracles' (which perhaps comes from a longer work called 'Horae') in Plato's Symposium 177B.

For Aristippus see the Glossary.

IT seems to me that Socrates also encouraged his associates to practise self-control with regard to food and drink and sex and sleep and heat and cold and physical exertion by discourses like the one which follows. When he observed that one of them was rather undisciplined in these respects he said:

'Tell me, Aristippus: if you had to take charge of two young men and educate them, one to be capable of governing and the other not even to aspire to it, how would you educate each of them? Shall we consider this problem, starting with the basic question of their food?'

Aristippus replied, 'It certainly seems to me that food is the starting-point; one can't even live without taking food.'

'So it's natural that both of them should feel the desire to partake of food when the right time comes.'

'Yes, it is.'

'Which of them should be practised in choosing to press on with an urgent duty rather than gratify his appetite?'

'Emphatically the one who is being educated to govern, so that the business of the state may not be neglected under his government.'

'Then similarly when they want to drink, the same one must be endowed with the ability to restrain himself when he's thirsty.'

'Certainly.'

'Which should we endow with self-control as regards sleep, so that he can go to bed late and get up early and stay awake in an emergency?'

'The same one ought to have this too.'

'What about self-control in matters of sex, so that he may not be prevented by that sort of thing from acting in an emergency?'

'The same one ought to have this too.'

'What about not shirking hard work, but willingly putting up with it? which should we endow with this quality?'

'We should give this too to the one who is being educated for government.'

'What about acquiring any kind of knowledge that is conducive to defeating one's opponents – to which would this faculty be more appropriate?'

'Far more, of course, to the one who is being educated for government. None of the other qualities is any good without this sort of knowledge.'

'Don't you think that a person so educated would be less likely to be caught by his opponents than other creatures? Isn't it true that some of these are lured on by their greed, and are often attracted to the bait, in spite of their timidity, by their craving for food, and so get caught; while others are trapped by means of drink?'

'Quite true,' he said.

'And isn't it true that others are trapped because of their lasciviousness, as for example quails and partridges are attracted by the cry of the female because of their desire and expectation of sexual intercourse, and losing all count of the risks rush into the hunting-nets?'

He agreed that this was true too.

'Don't you think that it's shameful for a man to be affected in the same way as the stupidest of creatures? I am thinking of the way in which adulterers walk into the snare, although they know that an adulterer is in danger not only of incurring the penalty threatened by the laws, but of having a trap set for him and, if he is caught, of suffering physical violence. When the adulterer is liable to all these serious and shameful consequences, and there are plenty of means to relieve his sexual appetite with impunity, nevertheless to rush headlong into the paths of danger – isn't that the very acme of infatuation?'

'So it seems to me.'

'As most of the essential human activities – such as those which relate to warfare and farming, and not the least important of the rest – are carried out in the open air, don't you think that it is extremely casual for most people to be untrained to endure cold and heat?'

He agreed to this too.

'Then do you think that the future ruler ought also to practise taking these things lightly?'

'Certainly.'

'Then if we rate those who are self-controlled in all these respects as fit to govern, shall we rate those who are incapable of such conduct as not even claiming fitness to do so?'

He agreed again.

'Very well, then: now that you know the rating of both types, I suppose you have considered to which class you would rightly assign yourself?'

'I have indeed,' said Aristippus, 'and I certainly don't put myself in the class of those who want to govern. In fact, considering that it's a serious task to provide for one's own needs, it seems to me to be quite crazy not to be content with this but to pile on top of it the task of supplying the needs of the rest of one's fellow-countrymen as well. And when a person has to do without a great many things that he wants himself, surely it's the height of folly, by assuming responsibility for his country, to render himself liable to prosecution if he doesn't carry out all his country's requirements. States claim the right to treat their ministers as I treat the slaves in my own household. I expect my servants to make lavish provision for me, but not to touch any of it themselves; and in the same way states think that their ministers ought to provide them with as many benefits as possible without participating in any of them personally. So if there are any people who want to have a lot of trouble themselves and cause it to others, I would educate them in your way and set them in the category of potential rulers; but I rank myself among those who want their lives to be as easy and pleasant as possible.'

Socrates said, 'Would you like us to consider this question too: which have the more pleasant life, the rulers or the subjects?'

'By all means.'

'Well, in the first place, of the peoples that we know, in Asia[1] the Persians are rulers and the Syrians and Phrygians and Lydians are subjects. In Europe the Scythians are rulers and the Maeotians subjects. In Africa the Carthaginians are rulers and the Libyans subjects. Which of these do you think have the pleasanter life? Or take the Greeks, to whom you belong yourself: which seem to you to have the pleasanter life – the conquerors or the conquered?'

'But, you know,' said Aristippus, 'I don't assign myself to the slave category either. It seems to me that there is a middle path which I am trying to follow: the path not through rule nor through servitude but through liberty, which is the surest road to happiness.'

'Well,' said Socrates, 'if this path of yours which avoids rule and servitude does not lead through mankind either, there may perhaps be something in what you say; but if while living among men you expect neither to rule nor to be ruled, and don't intend to defer willingly to authority, I presume you can see that the stronger know how to make the weaker suffer both collectively and individually, and to treat them as slaves. Don't you realize that there are people who cut the corn that others have sown, and chop down the trees that others have planted, and put every kind of pressure upon inferiors who refuse them deference, until they finally prevail on them to prefer slavery to war against a stronger power? And in private life too, don't you know that the bold and powerful reduce the timid and powerless to slavery, and then exploit them?'

'But I have an escape, you know,' he said. 'To avoid being treated in this way, I don't confine myself to a nationality at all: I am a stranger in all countries.'

Socrates replied, 'Now that really is a clever stroke; because

1. I.e., Asia Minor. For the various peoples see Glossary.

ever since Sinis and Sciron and Procrustes[2] were killed nobody has done any more harm to strangers! All the same, at the present time those who enjoy citizenship in their several countries both make laws to protect themselves against harm, and in addition to their so-called intimate friends make others also to give them help, and put fortifications round their cities and acquire arms to keep off aggressors, and besides all this procure external allies as well. And with all these assets they still incur harm. As for you, who have none of them, and spend a great deal of time in the streets, where most injuries are sustained – you who, whatever country you visit, are in a weaker position than any of the citizens, and a natural victim for intending wrongdoers – do you still imagine that you would not be harmed, because you are a stranger? Is your confidence based on official assurances of safety on entering and leaving the country? or on the belief that you are the sort of person who would be useless as a slave to any master? because who would care to have in his house a man who refuses to do any work and enjoys the most expensive diet?

'Now let us consider another point: what sort of treatment slaves of this kind receive. Isn't it true that their masters discipline their wantonness by starvation, and stop them from stealing by locking up any place or receptacle from which anything can be removed, and prevent them from running away by putting them in fetters, and drive out their idleness by beating them? Or what steps do you take when you dis-

2. Three notorious brigands. Sinis operated on the Isthmus of Corinth: he used to bend down two pines and tie one end of a wayfarer to each; the trees when released tore the victim in two. Sciron waylaid travellers on the cliff road above Megara, making them wash his feet and kicking them, while thus occupied, into the sea. Procrustes tortured visitors to his house in Attica, lengthening them (by racking or hammering out) or curtailing them (by chopping off the extremities) to make them fit one or other of his two beds. All three were given a taste of their own medicine by the Athenian hero Theseus.

cover that one of your house-slaves is behaving in this sort of way?'

'I punish him with the utmost severity until I have made him submit. But look here, Socrates, about these people who are being educated in the art of ruling, which you seem to regard as happiness: how are they any better off than those who suffer through force of circumstances, if they are going to be hungry and thirsty and cold and sleepless and to suffer every other kind of hardship voluntarily? I don't see that there is any difference between having the same skin flogged voluntarily and having it flogged involuntarily, or in general that there is any difference between having the same body harassed by all these trials voluntarily and having it harassed involuntarily, except that anyone who submits to painful experiences deliberately is a fool into the bargain.'

'Come, come, Aristippus,' said Socrates, 'don't you think that voluntary sufferings of this kind are preferable to involuntary ones from this point of view; that the man who is hungry or thirsty of his own free will can eat and drink when he wants to, and similarly in the other cases, whereas the man who suffers through force of circumstances can't stop when he wants to? And then the man who undergoes hardship voluntarily is encouraged in his efforts by the prospect of success, as, for example, hunters enjoy their exertions because they have a prospect of catching the animals that they are hunting. This sort of reward for effort is trivial; but when people devote their energy to acquiring good friends or worsting their enemies, or becoming physically and mentally efficient and managing their households well and benefiting their friends and serving their country, surely we must suppose that they find pleasure in working for these ends, and enjoy life, contented with themselves and praised and envied by others. Again, easy tasks and momentary pleasures (as we are told by the experts in physical education) cannot produce physical

fitness or develop in the mind any knowledge worth mentioning; whereas sustained application enables us to achieve
results that are good and honourable, so good men tell us.
Hesiod[3] says somewhere:

> Evil is easily to find, and freely;
> Smooth is the road, and very near she dwells.
> But sweat the gods have set upon the way
> To goodness: long and steep is the path to it
> And rough at first; but if thou reach the summit
> Thereafter is it easy, hard though it be.

'Epicharmus[4] testifies the same in the line

> Pain's the price the gods require us pay for all our benefits.

'He also says in another place

> Rascal, do not crave for comfort, lest the lot you have be hard.

'The same view of moral goodness is also set out by the
sophist Prodicus in the story of Heracles[5] which he recites to
large audiences; it runs like this, so far as I remember. When
Heracles was setting out from childhood towards manhood,
at the age when the young become independent and let it be
seen whether they are going to approach life by the path of
goodness or by the path of wickedness, he went out to a quiet
spot and sat down considering which way he should take.
While he was sitting there he thought he saw two women

3. *Works and Days* 285 ff.
4. A Syracusan (?530–440 B.C.) who wrote farcical comedies seasoned
with moral maxims and apophthegms. The lines quoted here are 36 and
37 in Diels-Kranz, *Vorsokratiker*.
5. Heracles, better known by his Latinized name Hercules, was
revered from early times, because of his 'labours', as a benefactor of
mankind and a pattern of courage and endurance; he was later credited
with other virtues (e.g. wisdom and self-control) which are not conspicuous in the stories told about him. For Prodicus see the introduction
to this chapter.

approach him. Both were tall, but one of them was handsome in appearance, with a natural air of distinction, clean-limbed and modest in expression and soberly dressed in a white robe; while the other was well-developed to the point of fleshiness and sensuality, made up to have a complexion too pink and white to be real, and with a carriage more upright than was natural, with a brazen expression, and robed in a way that revealed as much as possible of her charms. She kept on eyeing herself, and watching to see whether anyone was looking at her, constantly glancing at her own shadow. When they got nearer to Heracles the former of the two continued to advance in the same way, but the other, wishing to forestall her, ran up to him and said:

'"Heracles, I see that you can't make up your mind which way of life to adopt. If you take me as your friend, I will lead you by the easiest and pleasantest road; you shall not miss the taste of any pleasure, and you shall live out your life without any experience of hardship. In the first place you will not be concerned with wars or responsibilities; you shall spend your time considering what food or drink you can find to suit your taste, or what smell or touch; which lover's society will gratify you most; how you can sleep most comfortably; and how you can achieve all these objects with the least trouble. And if there is ever any suspicion of a shortage of any of these benefits, you need not fear that I shall involve you in any physical or mental effort or distress in procuring them; you shall enjoy the fruits of other people's labours, and you shall refrain from nothing from which you can derive any advantage; because I authorize my followers to benefit themselves from all quarters."

'When Heracles heard this he asked, "What is your name, madam?" She replied, "My friends call me Happiness, but people who don't like me nickname me Vice."

'Meanwhile the other woman came forward and said "I

too have come to meet you, Heracles, because I know your parentage and I have carefully observed your natural qualities in the course of your education, and this knowledge makes me hope that, if you will only take the path that leads to me, you may become a very effective performer of fine and noble deeds, and I may win much greater honour still, and brighter glory for the blessings I bestow. I will not delude you with pleasurable anticipations; I shall give you a true account of the real facts, exactly as the gods have ordained them. Nothing that is really good and admirable is granted by the gods to men without some effort and application. If you want the gods to be gracious to you, you must worship the gods; if you wish to be loved by your friends, you must be kind to your friends; if you desire to be honoured by the state, you must help that state; if you claim to be admired for your fine qualities by the whole of Greece, you must try to benefit Greece; if you want your land to produce abundant crops, you must look after your land; if you expect to make money from your livestock, you must take care of your livestock; if you have an impulse to extend your influence by war, and want to be able to free your friends and subdue your enemies, you must both learn the actual arts of war from those who understand them, and practise the proper way of applying them. And if you want to be physically efficient, you must train your body to be subject to your reason, and develop it with hard work and exercise."

'Here Vice (says Prodicus) broke in. "Do you realize, Heracles," she said, "what a long and difficult road to enjoyment this woman is describing to you? I will put you on a short and easy road to happiness."

'"Impudent creature!" said Virtue. "What good have you to offer, or what do you know of pleasure, you who refuse to do anything with a view to either? You don't even wait for the desire for what is pleasant; you stuff yourself with everything before you want it, eating before you are hungry and drinking before you are thirsty. To make eating enjoyable you invent refinements of cookery, and to make drinking enjoyable you provide yourself with expensive wines, and rush about searching for ice in summer. To make going to sleep pleasant you provide yourself not only with soft blankets but with spring mattresses;[6] because it is not work but boredom that makes you want to go to bed. You force the gratification of your sexual impulses before they ask for it, employing all kinds of devices and treating men as women. That is the sort of training that you give your friends – exciting their passions by night, and putting them to sleep for the best part of the day. Although you are an immortal you have been turned out by the gods, and you are despised by decent men. You are denied the hearing of the sweetest of all sounds – praise of yourself – and you are denied the seeing of the sweetest of all sights; for you have never contemplated any act of yours · that was admirable. Who would trust your word? Who would supply your demands? What sane person would have the face to join your devotees? When they are young they are puny in body, and when they get older they are foolish in mind; maintained in their youth in effortless comfort, but passing their old age in laborious squalor, disgraced by their past actions and burdened by their present ones, because in their youth they have run through all that was pleasant, and laid up for their old age what was hard to bear.

'"I associate both with gods and with good men, and no fine action, human or divine, is done independently of me. I am held in the highest honour both among gods and among men of the right sort. I am a welcome fellow-worker to the craftsman, a faithful guardian to the householder, a kindly

6. The Greek word probably refers to some rocking device, but the sense is uncertain.

protector to the servant, an efficient helper in the tasks of peace, a staunch ally in the operations of war, and the best partner in friendship. My friends can enjoy food and drink with pleasure and without effort, because they abstain until they feel a desire for them. Their sleep is sweeter than the sleep of the easy-living, and they neither are vexed when they have to give it up, nor make it an excuse for neglecting their duty. The young enjoy being praised by their elders, and the older people are happy in the respect of the young. They recall their past achievements with pleasure, and rejoice in their present successes; because through me they are dear to the gods, loved by their friends, and honoured by their country. And when their appointed end comes they do not lie forgotten in obscurity, but flourish celebrated in memory for all time.

'"There, Heracles," she said, "child of good parents:[7] if you work hard in the way that I have described you can possess the most beatific happiness."

'That is roughly how Prodicus describes the education of Heracles by Virtue; except that he actually dressed up the sentiments in language still more splendid than I have used now. At any rate, Aristippus, you had better think this over and try to take some account of the factors that will affect the life that lies in front of you.'

7. Zeus and Alcmene, wife of Amphitryon.

CHAPTER TWO

Lamprocles is reproved for losing patience with his mother – presumably Xanthippe, whose reputation fits the description. She may have been Socrates' second wife (see Diogenes Laertius ii, 26), but the evidence is sadly confused. She appears briefly in Plato's Phaedo 60A, and is mentioned by implication (note the plural 'women') at 116B. One thing is certain: she had much provocation. A husband who is a logician and a moralist; who spends all day and much of the night talking with his men friends; who is too high-principled to charge a fee or indeed to earn any money worth mentioning; who cares nothing for appearances or public opinion; who is tireless in argument and always right, and well-meaning on the top of it – such a husband might ruin any woman's temper.

All the same, the conversation shows some awareness of a mother's trials, and it is probably the first treatment of the subject in prose. Socrates was a great admirer of Euripides, who was the first writer to show a profound interest in the woman's point of view. Xenophon himself would be sympathetic; to judge from his self-portrait in the Oeconomicus (for Ischomachus' views are pretty obviously Xenophon's) he was a kind and considerate if rather patronizing husband.

Incidentally the conversation is calculated to show the absurdity of supposing that Socrates taught disrespect for parents.

ONCE when Socrates noticed his eldest son Lamprocles getting angry with his mother he said, 'Look here, my boy, you know that there are some people who are called ungrateful?'

'Yes, of course,' said the boy.

'Are you clear about what it is that people do to earn this name?'

'Yes, I am,' he said. 'People are called ungrateful when they have been well treated and could show gratitude in return, but don't.'

'Then you think that ingratitude is regarded as wrong?'

'Yes, I do,' he said.

'Have you ever considered this question: whether perhaps ingratitude is wrong if it is shown towards friends but right if it is shown towards enemies, in the same way that it is considered to be wrong to enslave one's friends but right to enslave one's enemies?'

'Yes, indeed,' he said, 'and I think that anyone who has received a favour either from a friend or from an enemy and doesn't attempt to show gratitude is morally wrong.'

'Well, then, if that is so, ingratitude must be downright wickedness.'

Lamprocles agreed.

'Then the greater the favours that a person receives without showing gratitude in return, the more wicked he is?'

He admitted this too.

'Well,' said Socrates, 'whom can we find that enjoy greater benefits than children receive from their parents? Their parents have brought them into existence from non-existence, and have enabled them to see all the beauty and share in all the good things that the gods provide for mankind – privileges which we consider so priceless that anyone would do anything rather than part with them, and civilized states have made death the penalty for the greatest crimes, on the presumption that there could be no stronger deterrent from wrongdoing.

'You don't imagine that people have children just for sexual satisfaction; the streets and brothels are full of potential suppliers of that need. Besides, you can see that we look out for the sort of women who will make the best mothers, and then unite with them to beget our children. The husband both supports his wife and provides for the children that are to be born everything that he thinks will be an asset to them in life; and he provides it as fully as he can. The wife conceives and carries this burden, bearing the weight of it and risking her life and giving up a share of her own nourishment; and after all her trouble in carrying it for the full time and bringing it to birth, she rears it and cares for it, although the child has never done her any good and does not know who his benefactor is. He cannot even indicate what he wants; his mother's attempts to supply what will be good for him and give him pleasure depend upon her powers of guessing; and she goes on rearing him for a long time, putting up with drudgery day and night, without knowing whether she will receive any gratitude.

'And it is not merely a matter of rearing children. When they seem to be capable of learning, their parents teach them themselves whatever they can teach that is valuable for life; but if they think that there is anything that is better taught by somebody else, they incur the expense of sending their children to that person. They leave nothing undone in their anxiety to see that their children's development is as perfect as possible.'

To this the lad replied, 'But really, even if she has done all this and a great deal more besides, nobody could put up with her temper.'

'Which kind of ferocity do you think is harder to bear – a wild beast's or a mother's?'

'A mother's,' he said, 'if she's like mine.'

'Has she ever injured you by biting or kicking, as a good many people have suffered before now from wild animals?'

'Oh no,' he said, 'but she says things that one wouldn't want to hear every day of one's life.'

'And how much trouble,' said Socrates, 'do you think you have given her by your peevish cries and behaviour day and night ever since you were a baby, and how often have you worried her by your illnesses?'

'Well,' said Lamprocles, 'I have never said or done anything to her to make her ashamed of me.'

'Look here,' said Socrates, 'do you think it is harder for you to listen to the things that she says than it is for actors in a play when they go all out to abuse each other?'

'As they don't imagine that the speaker who accuses them intends to punish them, or that the one who threatens them intends to injure them, I suppose they take it quite lightly.'

'But *you* get angry, although you know quite well that what your mother says to you is said not only without any unkind intention but actually out of a desire for your especial benefit? Or do you imagine that your mother is ill-disposed towards you?'

'Oh, no,' he said, 'I don't think that.'

'So,' said Socrates, 'although this mother of yours is well-disposed towards you and does her very best to see to it that you get well when you are ill and that you shan't lack anything that you need; and besides all this is constantly praying to the gods for blessings upon you and paying her vows on your account, you say that she is hard to put up with? In my opinion, if you can't bear a mother like that, you can't bear what is good for you. Tell me,' he went on, 'do you think that there is anyone else who claims your respect? or are you prepared to make no attempt to please anybody, and to obey neither your superior officer nor any other authority?'

'Of course not,' said he.

'Well then,' said Socrates, 'do you want to be pleasant to your neighbour, so that he may give you a light for your fire when you need it, and both contribute to your success, and give you prompt and friendly help if you meet with any misfortune?'

'Yes, I do,' he said.

'Take the case of a fellow-traveller or fellow-voyager, or anyone else that you might meet: would it make no difference to you whether he became your friend or your enemy, or do you think that you ought to concern yourself with the goodwill even of people like these?'

'I do think so,' he said.

'So you are prepared to concern yourself with these people, and yet see no need to show consideration for your mother, who loves you more than anyone else does? Don't you know that the state cares nothing for any other kind of ingratitude, and prescribes no penalty for it, but turns a blind eye when beneficiaries fail to repay a favour; but if anyone shows no consideration for his parents, the state imposes a penalty upon him, disqualifies him, and does not allow him to hold public office, on the presumption that the sacrifices could not be performed on behalf of the state with proper piety if he performed them, nor any other act be well and duly carried out if he were the agent? And what is more, if anyone fails to tend the graves of his dead parents, even this becomes the subject of a state inquiry when candidates for office are having their conduct scrutinized.

'So if you are wise, my boy, you will beseech the gods to pardon any disregard that you have shown towards your mother, for fear that they may set you down as ungrateful and refuse to do you good; and at the same time you will take care that your fellow-men don't observe you neglecting your parents, and all lose respect for you, so that you stand revealed as destitute of friends; because if they once got the notion that you were ungrateful to your parents, nobody would expect gratitude in return for doing you a kindness.'

CHAPTER THREE

Chaerecrates is urged to become reconciled to his brother Chaerephon. The dialogue serves as a bridge leading from the special relation of child and parent to the more general relations between friend and friend. The argument is chiefly notable for its insistence upon the necessity of being ready to take the initiative in order to achieve a reconciliation.

For Chaerecrates and Chaerephon see the Glossary.

ON another occasion Chaerephon and Chaerecrates, two brothers with whom Socrates was well acquainted, were having a quarrel. Socrates became aware of this, and when he saw Chaerecrates he said:

'Tell me, Chaerecrates, surely you aren't one of those who think that possessions are more useful than a brother, although they are not endowed with sense and he is, and they need protection whereas he can give it, and what is more they are several while he is only one? It is extraordinary, too, that anyone should regard brothers as a liability because he doesn't possess their property as well as his own, and not regard his fellow-citizens as a liability on the same ground. Since in the one case people can reason that it is better to have a secure sufficiency by living in a group than to have precarious possession of all their fellow-citizens' property by living alone, it's curious that they fail to realize the same fact in the case of their brothers. And they buy house-slaves (if they can afford it) to help them with the work, and make friends, showing that they feel the need for support; and yet they show no interest in their brothers – as if they expected their fellow-citizens to be friendly, but not their brothers. Then again it's a powerful incentive to affection to have been born of the same parents and brought up together; even animals develop a kind of strong attachment for members of the same litter. Besides, the rest of mankind have a greater respect for those who have brothers, and are less likely to attack them.'

Chaerecrates replied, 'Well, Socrates, if the quarrel weren't a serious one, very likely it would be right to bear with one's brother and not shun him for petty reasons. As you say, a brother is an asset if he behaves as he should; but when he is deficient in every respect and the exact opposite of what he ought to be, why should one attempt the impossible?'

'Tell me, Chaerecrates,' said Socrates, 'is Chaerephon as incapable of getting on with anybody as he is with you, or are there some people with whom he gets on quite well?'

'That's precisely my ground for disliking him, Socrates,' he replied. 'He can be agreeable to other people, but in all his associations with me, in word and in deed, he's more of a liability than an asset.'

'Well,' said Socrates, 'a horse is a liability to a person who tries to manage it without having enough knowledge. Perhaps in the same way a brother is a liability when one tries to manage him without knowledge.'

'How can I not have the knowledge to manage a brother,' said Chaerecrates, 'when I know how to speak and behave civilly to those who are civil to me? But when a man does his best to annoy me by what he says and does, I can't speak or behave civilly to him, and I'm not going to try, either.'

'That's a queer thing to say, Chaerecrates,' said Socrates. 'If you had a trained sheep-dog which was friendly to the shepherds but resented it when you came near, you would pay no attention to its bad temper – you would try to win it over by kindness; you say that your brother would be a great asset to you if he treated you properly; you admit that you know how to behave and speak civilly, yet you don't attempt to find a way to make him as well disposed towards you as possible.'

'I'm afraid, Socrates,' said Chaerecrates, 'that I'm not

enough of a genius to make Chaerephon behave properly to me.'

'I assure you,' said Socrates, 'so far as I can see, you needn't employ any subtle or novel method on him; I think you could prevail on him to have a high regard for you by using means which you understand yourself.'

'If you have detected that I am the unconscious possessor of some magic formula,'[1] he replied, 'you can't tell me too quickly.'

'Very well, then,' said Socrates, 'if you wanted to prevail upon one of your acquaintances to invite you to dinner whenever he was holding a celebration, what would you do?'

'Obviously I should begin by inviting him when I was celebrating.'

'And if you wanted to induce one of your friends to take care of your property when you were away from home, what would you do?'

'Obviously I should first try to take care of his when he was away.'

'And if you wanted to make a foreigner give you hospitality when you visited his country, what would you do?'

'Obviously I should first give him hospitality when he came to Athens. And if I wanted him to be eager to achieve the object of my visit for me, obviously I should have first to do the same for him.'

'So you know all the magic spells that influence human conduct, and have kept your knowledge dark all this time! Why do you hesitate to begin? Are you afraid that it will look bad if you treat your brother well before he treats you well? Surely it is considered to be extremely creditable to take the lead in harming one's enemies and benefiting one's friends. If I had thought that Chaerephon was likelier than you to take the lead towards friendliness I should have tried to persuade

1. Literally 'love-charm'.

him first to try to win you over; but as it is I think that you are more likely to take the lead in achieving this result.'

Chaerecrates said, 'It is preposterous, Socrates, and not at all like you, to urge me, the younger brother, to take the lead. Why, the universal practice is just the opposite – that the older should take the lead in everything that is said or done.'

'Surely not,' said Socrates. 'Isn't it customary in all countries for the younger to make way for the older, and to stand up when he approaches, and to show respect for him by giving him the most comfortable seat, and to allow him to speak first? Don't hold back, my dear fellow,' he said, 'but try to pacify him, and he will very soon respond. Don't you see what a noble and generous nature he has? Low types of humanity are most likely to be won over by a gift; but the best way to influence a gentleman is by courtesy.'

Chaerecrates said, 'Supposing that I do what you recommend, and he shows no improvement?'

'In that case,' said Socrates, 'you will simply run the risk of demonstrating that you are a good and affectionate brother, and he is a bad one who doesn't deserve to be treated kindly. But I don't suppose that anything of the sort will happen. I think that when he once realizes that you are challenging him to this kind of contest he will be very keen to outdo you in kindness both spoken and practical. At the moment your attitude towards each other is like this: as if two hands which God created to cooperate with one another were to give up doing this and turn to hindering one another; or as if two feet designed by Providence to help each other were to neglect their duty and get in each other's way. Wouldn't it be great folly and perversity to use for our disadvantage what was intended for our benefit? And yet, so far as I can see, brothers were intended by God to be more helpful to one another than hands or feet or eyes or any other natural pairs with which he has supplied mankind. If the hands were required to perform two operations more than six feet apart simultaneously, they could not do it; and the feet could not even reach two points six feet apart simultaneously; and the eyes, which are supposed to have the greatest range, could not see both front and back at the same time of two objects at a lesser distance still. But a pair of brothers, if they are on good terms, can carry out two simultaneous operations at a great distance, to their mutual advantage.'

CHAPTER FOUR

Socrates deplores the carelessness shown by most people in the cultivation of friends. The thought is not original, and the tone is rather querulous; but the denunciation of illogicality in conduct is quite Socratic. On the other hand the rhetorical paragraph which ends the chapter (with a feeble climax) seems to be contributed by Xenophon – unless it is a later addition.

I ONCE heard Socrates expressing views about friendship which I thought would be extremely helpful to anyone for the acquisition and treatment of friends. He said that although he often heard it stated that a good and sure friend was the best of all possessions, he noticed that most people gave their attention to anything rather than the acquisition of friends. He saw that they took pains to acquire houses and lands and slaves and cattle and furniture, and tried to preserve what they had; but in the case of a friend, who according to them was the greatest blessing, most of them never considered either how to acquire one or how to retain those that they had. Indeed, he observed (he said) that some people, when their friends and servants were ill, called in the doctor and scrupulously made all the other provisions for the health of their servants, but neglected their friends; and that when friends and servants died, they grieved over their servants and felt a sense of loss, but in the case of their friends considered that they were none the worse; and that they allowed none of their other possessions to lack attention and supervision, but neglected their friends when they needed care.

Further, besides all this, he observed (he said) that most people knew the extent of their other possessions, even if they were very numerous, but as for their friends, few as they were, they not only did not know how many they had, but when they tried to furnish an inventory in answer to inquiry, they revised their opinion of those whom they had previously reckoned as friends; which showed how much they thought of friendship!

Yet if we compare a good friend with any other possession, it must be obvious that the friend is far superior. What horse or vehicle is as valuable as a staunch friend? What slave is as loyal and trusty? What other possession is so entirely service-able? A good friend sets himself to supply all his friend's de-ficiencies, whether of private property or of public service. If it is required to do someone a good return, he lends vigor-ous support; if some fear is causing anxiety, he comes to the rescue; sometimes sharing expense, sometimes joining in action; sometimes helping to persuade, sometimes using com-pulsion; equally effective in cheering on the successful and in retrieving failure. A friend is just as much a benefactor to a man as are the hands that work for him, the eyes that see for him, the ears that hear for him and the feet that carry him. Often one friend supplies for another something which that other has failed to do or see or hear or carry out himself. And yet although some people try to cultivate trees for the sake of their fruit, most are indolent and negligent in taking care of the most productive of all possessions – what we call a friend.

CHAPTER FIVE

The relative value of friends is discussed in a way which seems cold-blooded, but it may reasonably be claimed that the discussion is calculated to provoke serious thought.

The English values are of course only rough equivalents: they assume that a mina is worth £50 and a talent £3,000, which is probably too little; but it is really impossible to fix a 'rate of exchange' which will fit all circumstances, and for the purpose of this chapter only the relative values matter.

ONE day I heard another discourse of his which I thought stimulated anyone who heard it to examine himself and see what he was worth to his friends. Socrates saw that one of his associates was neglecting a friend who was distressed by poverty, and he questioned Antisthenes,[1] in the presence of the neglectful person and of several others.

'Antisthenes,' he said, 'do friends have values, in the same way that domestic slaves do? For instance, one slave, I suppose, is worth £100, and another not as much as £25, and another £850 and another £500; and they say that Nicias the son of Niceratus bought a silver-overseer for £3,000. What I am trying to discover is whether friends have their values too, like domestic slaves.'

'Yes, indeed,' replied Antisthenes; 'at any rate I would rather have A as my friend than £100, while I wouldn't rate B higher than £25; and I would choose C in preference to £500, and I would spend any amount of money and effort to obtain the friendship of D.'

'Very well, then,' said Socrates, 'if the facts are as you say, it would be well for a man to examine himself and see what he really is worth to his friends, and to try to be worth as

1. For Antisthenes and Nicias see the Glossary.

much as possible to them, so that his friends may be less likely
to let him down. You see,' he said, 'I have often heard one
person say that a friend has let him down, and another say that
a man who he thought was his friend has given him up for
£50; and that is why I am investigating the whole question.
I am inclined to think that, just as one offers a bad slave for
sale and disposes of him for what he will fetch, in the same
way there is a temptation to sell a bad friend when one can
get a price greater than his value. But in my experience there
is no more question of giving up a good friend than of selling
a good slave.'

CHAPTER SIX

Socrates shows Critobulus what qualities one should look for in a friend, and how friendship is to be won. There is no true friendship except between good men; and the problem really resolves itself into making oneself as good as one can, so as to merit the regard of others.

There is some sound psychology here, and much common-sense; indeed if Socrates' advice were followed the world would no doubt be a much better place. But the reader may feel that Xenophon's report is unduly prolix.

For Critobulus see the Glossary.

I THOUGHT that the following conversation quickened one's wits to estimate what sort of friends it was worth while to make.

'Tell me, Critobulus,' said Socrates, 'if we wanted a good friend, how should we set about our search? Should we first look for a man who can control his desires for food and drink and sex and sleep and idleness? because the man who is a slave to these can't do his duty either to himself or to a friend.'

'No, of course not,' said he.

'So you think that one should keep away from the man who is governed by his desires?'

'Certainly,' said he.

'Well, now,' said Socrates, 'if a man is extravagant and can't meet all his expenses, but is always appealing to his neighbours; and if when he gets a loan he can't repay it, and when he doesn't get one he bears a grudge against the person who refused it: don't you think that this man too is a difficult sort of friend?'

'Yes, indeed,' said he.

'So one should keep away from him too?'

'Yes, one should.'

'What about the good businessman who is bent on making a great deal of money and consequently drives a hard bargain, who enjoys receiving money but is reluctant to part with it?'

'In my view,' he said, 'this one is even worse than the last.'

'What about the man who has such a passion for making money that he has no time for anything that won't turn to his own profit?'

'He should be avoided too, in my opinion; he will be no use to anyone who associates with him.'

'What about the trouble-maker who wants to stir up a lot of bad feeling against his friends?'

'He certainly should be given a wide berth too.'

'And supposing that someone, although he has none of these defects, accepts any amount of kindness and never thinks of repaying a good turn?'

'He would be no use either. But tell me, Socrates, what sort of person shall we try to make our friend?'

'Presumably one who has the opposite qualities – who is self-controlled with regard to physical pleasures, and who proves to be good at managing his own affairs, reliable in his dealings with others, and eager not to fall short in doing services to his benefactors, so that it is an advantage to associate with him.'

'How can we test these qualities before we commit ourselves, Socrates?'

'We don't judge sculptors on the evidence of their claims, but if we see that a man's earlier works are well executed, we assume that his future works will be of high quality too.'

'You mean that anyone who has evidently treated his past friends well will obviously do good to his subsequent friends too.'

'Yes,' said Socrates, 'because in the case of horses if I see that someone has treated them well in the past, I assume that he is likely to treat other horses well too.'

'Very good. But when a man seems worthy of one's friendship, how should one set about making friends with him?'

'First of all,' said Socrates, 'you must consider the will of the gods,[1] and see whether they advise you to make friends with him.'

'Well, then, supposing that we decide to make friends with someone and the gods raise no objection, can you tell me how to capture him?'

'Not, of course, by chasing him, like a hare; nor by snaring him, like a bird, nor by force, like an enemy – it's hard work catching a friend against his will. And it's difficult, too, to keep him shackled like a slave. That sort of treatment is more likely to make enemies than friends.'

'But how are friends made?'

'They say that there are incantations which those who know them can use to win the friendship of anyone that they like; and drugs too, which can be used by those who understand them to make them loved by anyone that they like.'

'Then how can we find out about them?'

'You have heard from Homer the incantation that the Sirens[2] uttered over Odysseus: it begins something like this:

   Come hither, famed Odysseus, great glory of the Greeks.'

'Did the Sirens utter this incantation over all their other victims too, to keep them from getting away?'

'No; they kept it for those who were eager for recognition of their bravery.'

'What you are saying amounts practically to this: that in each case one should use an incantation of such a kind that the hearer won't think that he is being praised sarcastically.'

1. Cf. i, 1, 6–9.
2. *Odyssey* xii, 184.

'Yes; you would repel people and incur dislike instead of friendship if you praised a man by calling him handsome and tall and strong when he knew that he was short and ugly and weak.'

'Do you know any other incantations?'

'No; but I have heard that Pericles[3] knew a great many, which he used to utter over the state and so won its affection.'

'How did Themistocles[4] win its affection?'

'Not by incantation, certainly, but by conferring some benefit upon it.'

'I suppose you mean, Socrates, that if it were our intention to secure a good friend, we ought to make ourselves good both in word and in deed.'

'Did you think,' asked Socrates, 'that it was possible for a bad man to acquire good friends?'

'Well, yes,' said Critobulus, 'because I have seen bad speakers on friendly terms with good orators, and incompetent commanders intimate with men of great military ability.'

'Do you also know, in the case that we are considering, any persons who can make useful friends although they are useless themselves?'

'No, certainly not,' said he. 'But if it is impossible for a bad man to make good and honourable friends, the question immediately presents itself: is it possible for a man who has shown himself good and honourable to be a friend, by that very fact, to those who are the same as himself?'

'What is bothering you, Critobulus, is that you often see men who act honourably and shun anything discreditable, but instead of being friends, they quarrel and treat each other worse than if they were good for nothing.'

'And it isn't only individuals that do this,' said Critobulus.

3. See Glossary.
4. See Glossary.

'Even states that have the highest regard for honourable dealing and the least tolerance of anything base are often hostile in their attitude to one another. These considerations make me very despondent about the acquisition of friends. On the one hand, I see that bad people can't be friends with one another; how can you make friends of those who are ungrateful or careless or grasping or untrustworthy or uncontrolled? It seems to me that bad men are altogether more naturally inclined to be enemies than friends to one another. Then again, as you say, it is equally impossible that bad men should be suitable for friendship with men of high character; for how can evil-doers become friends of those who loathe that sort of conduct? And finally if even those who practise goodness quarrel about pre-eminence in the state and are mutually envious and hate one another, who are there still left to be friends? And in what class of men shall we find trust and goodwill?'

'Well, Critobulus,' said Socrates, 'this is rather a complex problem. By nature human beings have certain tendencies towards friendliness. They need one another, they feel pity, they benefit from cooperation; and realizing this they are grateful to one another. They also have hostile tendencies. When they have the same opinions about things beautiful and pleasant, they fight for their possession; when they disagree, they take opposite sides. Rivalry and passion also make for hostility. The desire to over reach is a cause of ill-feeling, and envy arouses hatred. Nevertheless friendliness finds a way through all those obstacles and unites men of all-round excellence. Their moral goodness makes them prefer to enjoy moderate possessions without effort rather than win vast fortunes by means of war, and enables them when hungry and thirsty to share their food and drink without a pang, and to control their pleasure in the sexual attraction of beauty in such a way as not to cause improper annoyance. It enables them not only to suppress greedy instincts and be content with a lawful share of wealth, but even to assist one another. It enables them to compose differences not only without annoyance but even to their mutual advantage; and to keep their tempers from rising to a degree that they will later regret. It rids them completely of envy, since they give their own goods into the possession of their friends, and regard their friends' property as their own.

'It must surely follow from this that in the sharing of political privileges too, men of all-round excellence not only do not hinder but actually help one another. People who desire political distinction and authority in order that they may have licence to embezzle money and employ force and have a good time are likely to be unscrupulous and wicked and incapable of cooperation with others; but if a person wishes for political distinction to protect himself from injustice and be able to give legitimate help to his friends, and by holding office to try to do some good to his country, why shouldn't he be able to cooperate with others like himself? Will he be less able to help his friends in company with men of all-round excellence? or will he be more incapable of benefiting his country if he has the assistance of such men? Why, even in athletic contests it is obvious that if the strongest were allowed to band together against the weaker, they would win all the events and carry off all the prizes. In athletics this is not allowed, but in public life, where men of all-round excellence have most influence, there is no objection to a man's combining with anyone that he likes in order to benefit the state. So surely it is a good thing that a man should prepare himself for public life by acquiring the best friends, and use them as partners and helpers in his activities rather than as opponents.

'Then again it is obvious that if you are at war with anyone you will need allies, and you will need more of them if you are opposed by men of all-round excellence; besides, you must treat those who are prepared to be your allies well, so that they may be willing to put their hearts into it; and it is far better to benefit the best, who are few, than the worse, who are many, because bad people demand much more in the way of services than good ones.

'Don't lose heart, Critobulus,' he went on, 'but try to make yourself a good man; and when you have succeeded you can set about hunting for people of all-round excellence. Perhaps even I myself might be able to lend you a hand in the search, on account of my loving nature. When I take a fancy to anyone it's terrible how completely I throw myself into getting them to reciprocate my friendship or passion or craving for their society, as the case may be. I can see that you will feel the same need when you set your heart on making friends with people. Well, don't keep me in the dark about your aspirations; thanks to my efforts to please those who please me, I think I'm not without experience in capturing people's affections.'

'As a matter of fact, Socrates,' said Critobulus, 'I have been anxious for this sort of instruction for a long time, especially to find out whether the same technique will serve with people who are good in character as with those who are beautiful in body.'

'Well, Critobulus,' said Socrates, 'my technique doesn't include prevailing upon beautiful persons to stay by laying hands upon them. I am convinced that that is why men fled from Scylla,[5] because she laid hands upon them; whereas it is said of the Sirens that because they never laid hands upon anyone but always sang their enchanting songs from a distance, everyone stayed to hear their singing and was charmed by it.'

'If you've got a good method of making friends, tell me what it is,' said Critobulus; 'I promise I won't lay hands upon them.'

5. She had no proper hands; see Glossary.

'Then will you also refrain from laying your lips upon theirs?' asked Socrates.

'Don't worry!' said Critobulus; 'I won't lay my lips upon anyone else's either – except in the case of a beautiful person.'

'There you go, Critobulus!' said Socrates; 'you have said just the opposite of what you ought. Beautiful people don't put up with that sort of thing; whereas ugly ones actually take pleasure in inviting it, because they think that they are called beautiful in virtue of their character.'

'You can rest assured,' said Critobulus, 'that if I kiss the beautiful I shall kiss the good even more. Now tell me how to capture friends.'

'Well, then, Critobulus,' said Socrates, 'when you want to become friendly with someone, will you let me inform him that you admire him and are eager to be his friend?'

'Inform away,' said Critobulus. 'Nobody that I know of objects to being complimented.'

'And if I further inform him,' said Socrates, 'that because of your admiration you are kindly disposed towards him, you won't consider that I am misrepresenting you?'

'No,' he said; 'I myself feel a kindness towards anyone whom I imagine to be kindly disposed towards me.'

'Very well, then,' said Socrates; 'I shall be allowed to say this about you to any persons whom you wish to make your friends. If you will grant me further permission to say of you that you really care about your friends, and delight in nothing so much as in good friends, and rejoice no less in your friends' fine achievements than in your own, and delight no less in your friends' good fortune than in your own, and never weary in contriving that your friends may have good fortune; and that you believe that the best quality in a man is to outdo his friends in acts of kindness, and his enemies in acts of hostility: then I think that I should be a very efficient helper for you in winning good friends.'

'Why do you talk to me like this,' asked Critobulus, 'as if it wasn't open to you to say whatever you like about me?'

'It certainly is not, for the reason that I once heard Aspasia[6] give. She said that good match-makers[7] were expert at joining people together in matrimony by giving true reports of their good qualities, but refused to sing their praises falsely; because the victims of such deception hated both each other and the woman who arranged the match. Well, I too have been convinced that she was right, and so I don't consider that I am entitled, in praising you, to say anything that is not true.'

'I see, Socrates,' said Critobulus, 'you are the sort of friend who will cooperate provided that I myself have some aptitude for the making of friends; otherwise nothing would induce you to use your imagination in saying something to help me.'

'Which do you think would be the better way of helping you, Critobulus,' asked Socrates; 'by praising you falsely, or by persuading you to try to be a good person? If the answer isn't clear to you from this point of view, look at it from another. Suppose that I wanted to put you on friendly terms with a ship-owner and praised you to him falsely by asserting that you were a good navigator, and suppose that he believed me and entrusted his ship to you although you knew nothing about navigation: are you optimistic enough to expect that you wouldn't destroy both yourself and the ship? Or suppose that by making a false public declaration I prevailed upon the state to entrust itself to you, as to a man of military and legal and political ability: what do you think the consequences would be for yourself and the state? Or suppose that I were to persuade some of our citizens privately by false representations to give you charge of their property, as an able and

6. See Glossary under Pericles.

7. These were a feature of Athenian social life. Free-born women were much secluded before (and even after) marriage; it was a man's world; and marriages were generally arranged with professional help.

scrupulous administrator: when it came to the test wouldn't you both ruin them and expose yourself to ridicule? No, Critobulus: if you want to be thought good at anything the shortest and safest and most reputable way is to try to make yourself really good at it. If you consider the virtues that are recognized among human beings, you will find that they are all increased by study and practice. That, Critobulus, is the way in which I think we ought to proceed; but if you incline to some other opinion, tell me what it is.'

'No, Socrates,' said Critobulus, 'I should be ashamed to oppose your point of view; if I did, what I said would be neither honourable nor true.'

CHAPTER SEVEN

In this and the following chapters Socrates is shown giving sound practical advice to people in difficulties. First Aristarchus, unable to support a houseful of refugee relatives, is told to find them gainful employment: he does so, and the result is both a financial and a psychological success. Obvious? Perhaps; but Socrates' solution is not yet always adopted even in this country and century. In fifth/fourth-century Athens free women seem normally to have made clothes only for use in their own homes, not for sale. It would be interesting to know how Aristarchus marketed the clothes made by his household.

WHEN his friends had difficulties, if they were due to ignorance he tried to remedy them by giving good advice, and if to deficiency, by teaching them to help one another as much as they could. I will relate what I know about him in this connexion also.

One day he saw Aristarchus[1] looking gloomy. 'You look as if you were weighed down by something, Aristarchus,' he said. 'You ought to share the burden with your friends. Perhaps even we can relieve you a little.'

Aristarchus replied, 'Yes, indeed, Socrates, I am in serious difficulty. Since the civil war broke out, and large numbers withdrew to Piraeus,[2] so many deserted sisters and nieces and female cousins have gathered together under my roof that there are fourteen free persons in the house. We can get nothing from our farm, because it is in the hands of our opponents; and nothing from our house properties, because

1. Otherwise unknown.
2. The port of Athens, four miles from the city; always a democratic stronghold, it was used by Thrasybulus in 403 B.C. as a base for his successful counter-revolution against the Thirty.

the town is practically deserted. There is no buyer for one's furniture, and one cannot even raise a loan from anywhere; I think you would sooner find money by looking for it in the streets than get it by borrowing. It is painful, Socrates, to let one's family die by inches; and it is impossible to feed so many in such difficult circumstances.'

When Socrates had heard this story he said, 'Tell me, how is it that Ceramon,[3] who has to feed a large household, not only is able to provide what is necessary for himself and them, but has so much to spare that he is actually rich, while you in feeding a large household are afraid that you will all die of want?'

'Surely because he is feeding slaves and I am feeding free persons.'

'Do you think,' said Socrates, 'that the free persons in your house are better than the slaves in Ceramon's?'

'In my opinion,' he said, 'the free persons in my house are the better.'

'Isn't it a shame, then, that he should be well off because he has the worse household, while you who have a much better one are in need?'

'Yes indeed,' said he, 'because he is supporting artisans, while I am supporting people with a liberal education.'

'Does "artisans" mean people who know how to make or do something useful?'

'Certainly.'

'Is porridge useful?'

'Very.'

'What about bread?'

'No less so.'

'What do you say about men's and women's coats and shirts and cloaks and tunics?'

'They are all very useful too.'

3. Otherwise unknown.

'Well, then,' said Socrates, 'don't your relations know how to make any of these things?'

'On the contrary, I imagine that they know how to make all of them.'

'Then don't you know that from one of these trades – grain-dealing – Nausicydes[4] supports not only himself and his servants, but also a large number of pigs and cattle, and has so much to spare that he often carries out public services to the state? And that from baking Cyrebus both maintains his household in comfort and lives luxuriously, while Demeas of Collytus[5] keeps himself by making cloaks, and Meno by making blankets, and most of the Megarians[6] by making tunics?'

'Yes,' he said, 'because these people buy and keep foreign slaves, so that they can compel them to do whatever work is convenient, but I am dealing with free people and relations.'

'Do you really think,' said Socrates, 'that because they are free and related to you they ought to do nothing but eat and sleep? What is your view about other free people? Do you find that those who live in this way have a better time, and do you regard them as happier, than those who concern themselves with things that they know are useful to life? Does it strike you that idleness and indifference help people to learn what they ought to know, and to remember what they have learnt, and to gain physical health and strength, and to acquire and keep what is useful to life, whereas energy and diligence are no help at all? Did these female relations of yours learn the arts which you say they understand because they regarded them as practically useless and had no intention of practising them? Wasn't it just the opposite? Didn't

4. Mentioned also by Aristophanes, *Ecclesiazusae* 426. The other characters are otherwise unknown.

5. The north part of the city of Athens.

6. Megara adjoined Attica on the S.W.

they mean to take them seriously and get some benefit from them? Which is the more sensible conduct for a human being – to do no work at all, or to occupy oneself usefully? and which is the more honourable – to work, or to ponder about the necessaries of life without working? As things are, I suppose, there is no love lost between you; you feel that they are imposing upon you, and they can see that you are annoyed with them; consequently there is a danger that the ill-feeling will grow and the former goodwill decline. But if you encourage them to work, you will feel friendly towards them, when you see that they are doing something for you, and they will like you when they realize that you are pleased with them; and as you both remember former kindnesses with greater pleasure, you will increase the gratitude aroused by them, with the result that the relations between you will become cordial and intimate. Now if these women were faced with an occupation that was dishonourable, they might fairly choose to die first; but as it is, the kinds of work at which they are competent are apparently those which are considered to be most honourable and appropriate for a woman; and everybody does most easily and quickly and pleasurably and well what he understands. So don't hesitate,' he concluded, 'to suggest to them a course of action that will benefit both you and them. They will probably be glad to comply.'

'Upon my word,' said Aristarchus, 'your advice strikes me as being really good, Socrates. Up till now I haven't been anxious to borrow, because I knew that when I had spent what I got I shouldn't be able to pay it back; but now I feel I can bring myself to do it so as to meet the initial outlay for the work.'

As the result of this conversation capital was obtained and wool purchased. The women began work before breakfast, and went on until supper-time; and they were cheerful instead of gloomy. Instead of eyeing each other askance, the two parties regarded each other with pleasure: the women felt for Aristarchus the affection due to a guardian, and he grew fond of them for their practical help. In the end he went to Socrates and joyfully told him the whole story, adding that he himself was now criticized as being the only person in the house who did not work for his keep.

'You should tell them the story about the dog,' said Socrates. 'They say that in the days when animals could talk the sheep said to its master, "I don't understand your conduct. To us, who provide you with wool and lambs and cheese, you give nothing except what we get from the earth; but to the dog, who provides you with nothing of this kind, you give a share of your own food." The dog heard this and said, "Quite right, too; I am the person to whom you owe security from being stolen by men and carried off by wolves. If I didn't watch over you, you wouldn't even be able to graze for fear of being killed." In the light of this argument, they say, even the sheep conceded the dog his privileges. So you should tell your women-folk that you take the place of the dog in guarding them and taking care of them; and that it is through you that they are unmolested and can live and work safely and happily.'

CHAPTER EIGHT

Socrates advises Eutherus to give up heavy manual work before his health fails, and to seek a post as steward of a large estate. In reply to objections he points out that all service entails some sacrifice of freedom and some acceptance of responsibility, but insists that – given a little patience – whole-hearted service to a reasonable employer offers the best prospect of security and happiness.

Eutherus is otherwise unknown.

SEEING another old friend one day, after a long time, Socrates said, 'Where do you spring from, Eutherus?'

'At the end of the war, Socrates,' he replied, 'I came back from abroad, but just now I come from near by. Since we were deprived of our foreign property, and my father left me no property in Attica, I have been forced to take up my residence here and to earn a bare livelihood by manual labour. It seems better to do this than to appeal to someone for help, especially as I have no security on which to borrow.'

'And how long do you suppose your constitution is capable of supporting you by working for hire?' said Socrates.

'Not very long, certainly.'

'Besides,' said Socrates, 'as you get older, obviously your expenses will increase, and nobody will be willing to pay you for your manual labour.'

'That's true,' said he.

'Then you had better apply yourself at once to the sort of occupation that will still be suitable for you when you are older. You should approach some owner of a large estate who needs assistance in managing it; so that by superintending the work and helping to get in the produce and taking care of the property you may both confer benefit on him and receive it in return.'

'I should find it hard to give up my freedom, Socrates,' he said.

'But in the political sphere the fact that a man holds an official position and manages public affairs makes him regarded not as servile but as liberal-minded.'

'As a general principle, Socrates,' he said, 'I don't at all like being responsible to anybody.'

'But, Eutherus,' said Socrates, 'it is not at all easy to find an occupation in which one cannot be called to account. It is difficult to do anything faultlessly; and it is difficult, even with a faultless performance, not to incur ill-judged criticism; indeed even in respect of the work that you say you are now doing, I am surprised that you find it easy to get through it without incurring blame. So you must try to avoid censorious people and seek the company of good-natured ones; if a job is within your power, you must put up with it; if it is not, you must avoid it; and whatever you do, you must give it your best and keenest attention. If you take this advice I think that you will incur the least risk of blame, you will have the best prospect of finding a remedy for your difficulties, and you will live with the least trouble and anxiety and with the amplest provision for your old age.'

CHAPTER NINE

On Socrates' advice Crito provides himself with a protector against attempts to extort money from him by threats. The term 'blackmail', used in the translation, gives the right general sense but no hint of the actual procedure, viz., prosecution, or the threat of it. There was no public prosecutor at Athens; any citizen could act (or pose) as the champion of law and morality by bringing an action against an alleged wrongdoer; and since the reward for a conviction was often a proportion of the fine exacted or the property confiscated, prosecution became a kind of profession. Those who followed it were called 'sycophants' (a curious word which has shifted its meaning more than once). Some attempts were made to discourage vexatious litigation, but they were not very successful; and since prosecutors were not required to confine themselves to proving a specific charge, but were allowed to attack any aspect of the defendant's life and character, even innocent people often preferred to pay the sycophant not to prosecute rather than have their reputation systematically blackened. To such people (represented here by Crito and his friends) the sycophant was a blackmailer.

Archedemus is hardly likely to have been the prominent democrat who impeached Erasinides after Arginusae (p. 32; cf. Hellenica i, 7, 2). The name was fairly common. Observe that he was not paid a salary but received gifts in reward for his services, thus preserving his amateur status and ranking not as an employee but as a friend.

I KNOW that he once heard Crito complain what a difficult thing life in Athens was for a man who wanted to mind his own business. 'At this very moment,' he said, 'some people are bringing an action against me, not because they have any grievance against me but because they believe that I would rather pay a fine than have trouble.'

Socrates said, 'Tell me, Crito; do you keep dogs to protect your sheep from wolves?'

'Indeed I do,' he replied. 'It pays me better to keep them.'

'Then wouldn't you keep a man who was willing and able to protect you from anyone who tried to injure you?'

'I should be glad to,' he said, 'if I weren't afraid that he might turn on me myself.'

'Well,' said Socrates, 'can't you see that it is much more pleasant to benefit by the goodwill of a man like yourself than by incurring his enmity? You may be sure that there are people in this city whose greatest ambition would be to enjoy your friendship.'

Immediately after this conversation they discovered Archedemus, a person of considerable rhetorical and practical ability, but poor, because he was not the sort to make money indiscriminately; he was a man of strict principles, and adept at extracting money from blackmailers. So whenever Crito was getting in crops of corn or olives or wine or wool or any other useful agricultural product he used to give a percentage to Archedemus; and whenever he gave a dinner he invited him; and showed him every consideration of this kind. Archedemus regarded Crito's house as a haven of refuge, and treated him with great respect. He very soon found out that one of the people who were blackmailing Crito had a number of crimes against him and a number of enemies, so he summoned him to face a public trial at which it was to be decided what punishment or penalty he must suffer. Since the black-mailer was conscious of a good many misdeeds, he did every-thing he could to rid himself of Archedemus; but Archedemus refused to be shaken off until the man abandoned his attack on Crito and gave him (Archedemus) a sum of money.

When Archedemus had carried out this and other similar operations, many of Crito's friends, seeing that he had got such a good sheep-dog, wanted to station their flocks near him so that they might share the benefit of him; in other words, they begged Crito to extend the protection of Archedemus to themselves as well. Archedemus was pleased to gratify his patron, and not only Crito but his friends too were left in peace. If any of Archedemus' enemies taunted him with toadying to Crito in return for benefits received, he said, 'Which is the more discreditable – to cultivate the friendship of honest men by returning their kindness, and so fall out with the bad; or to alienate good and honourable men by trying to injure them, and by collaborating with the bad to try to make them your friends and put them in the place of the good?'

From this time on Archedemus was one of Crito's friends and was highly esteemed by the rest of them.

CHAPTER TEN

Diodorus (otherwise unknown) is urged to take as much trouble to secure a good friend as he would to retain a useful servant. Once again the attitude of mind seems rather coolly calculating, but it is logical enough; besides, the reader should be aware by this time that Xenophon's Socrates, like Plato's, often speaks with his tongue in his cheek, or at least with a twinkle in his eye.

I KNOW that Socrates had the following conversation with one of his companions, Diodorus.

'Tell me, Diodorus,' he said, 'if one of your house-slaves runs away, do you see to it that you get him safely back again?'

'Yes, indeed,' he said, 'and I invite the help of others by offering a reward for his recovery.'

'Well,' went on Socrates, 'if one of your house-slaves is ill, do you look after him and call in doctors to guard against his dying?'

'I certainly do.'

'And if one of your acquaintances who is much more useful to you than your house-slaves is in danger of dying of want, don't you think you should see to it that he is saved? You must surely know that Hermogenes[1] is not insensitive, and that he would feel ashamed if he didn't return your kindness. Also to have an assistant who is willing and loyal and reliable and able to carry out instructions – and not only that, but capable of independent action and foresight and planning – this is surely worth a good many house-slaves. Now economic experts say that when you can purchase something valuable at a low price, you ought to buy it; and at the present

1. See Glossary.

time, owing to circumstances, it is possible to acquire good friends very reasonably.'

Diodorus said, 'You are quite right, Socrates. Tell Hermogenes to come and see me.'

'Certainly not!' said Socrates. 'To my mind it's no more proper for you to summon him than it is to go to him yourself; and it's no more to his advantage to have the business completed than it is to yours.'

So Diodorus went to see Hermogenes; and with a small outlay he acquired a friend who made it his business to look out for every opportunity to help Diodorus and make him happy.

BOOK THREE

The first five chapters are almost entirely concerned with the qualities, aims and duties of army officers, although the fifth moves on to consider how Athens could recover her military prestige. There is no reason why Socrates should not have discussed these subjects; but since Xenophon was an experienced soldier and certainly had views of his own about every aspect of the art of war, one may surmise that (like Plato) he took a Socratic theme and wrote his own variations on it. He must be responsible for at least the more technical points raised in the following discussions.

CHAPTER ONE

The first conversation lays down the principle that it takes more than a knowledge of tactics to make a general. This was especially true in a Greek state like Athens. Here there was an annually elected board of ten strategi, *who were not only naval and military commanders but ministers of state, with duties and powers covering the whole range of warfare and defence. Such men clearly ought to be fairly versatile.*

The arrangement of the chapter is careless. Instead of trying to show why tactics is not enough, Socrates declaims a catalogue of contrary qualities without explaining why they are necessary, and then goes back to concede the importance of tactics in the narrow sense of troop-arrangement, with an implication of good discipline. This leads to the discrimination of good and bad troops and the recognition of special aptitudes; but instead of drawing any general conclusion from what has been admitted Socrates suddenly asks whether the lecturer explained how to suit formations to circumstances, and on hearing that he did not, very rightly advises his friend to go back and demand more instruction.

A real conversation might well exhibit just this sort of inconsequentiality; but what we have here is surely neither verbatim reporting nor subtle artistry but a written record of untidy thinking on Xenophon's part.

I SHALL now describe how Socrates used to help people with honourable ambitions by making them apply themselves to the objects of those ambitions.

One day he heard that Dionysodorus[1] had come to Athens and was offering to teach the art of generalship. So he said to

1. Probably the brother of Euthydemus in Plato's dialogue of that name (273c). They came from Chios to Thurii and later to Athens. They professed a wide range of theoretical and practical knowledge.

one of his companions who he knew was eager to attain the rank of general in the state, 'You know, my boy, it's a poor thing for one who wants to be a general in the state to neglect the opportunity of instruction when it's available. Such a person would be more justly liable to public prosecution than one who undertook to make statues without having learned how to do it; because in the perils of war the whole state is entrusted to the care of the general, and the good effects of his success and the bad effects of his failures are likely to be equally far-reaching. So a man who did his best to get himself elected to this office without troubling to learn how to discharge it would surely deserve to be penalized.'

By using arguments like these Socrates persuaded his friend to go and take lessons. When he came back after completing the course, Socrates began to tease him.

'You know, gentlemen,' he said, 'how Homer describes Agamemnon as "majestic".[2] Don't you think that our friend here seems more majestic now that he has learned how to be a general? A man who has learned to play a musical instrument is a musician even if he is not playing it; and one who has learned how to cure disease is a doctor even if he is not practising. In the same way from now on our friend will always be a general, even if nobody appoints him; whereas the untrained person is neither a general nor a doctor, even if his appointment is unanimous. However,' he continued, 'in case one of us serves under you as a captain or a colonel, we ought to have a better grasp of military studies; so tell us where he began to teach you the art of generalship.'

'At the same point that he stopped at,' said the young man. 'He taught me tactics and nothing else.'

'But that is only a fractional part of the general's business,' said Socrates. 'A general must be able to get together the resources for making war, and to provide supplies for his men;

2. *Iliad* iii, 169 f.

he must be inventive and executive, persevering and brilliant, both friendly and harsh, both straightforward and subtle, a good protector and a good thief, lavish and rapacious, generous and grasping, steady and aggressive; and a man must have a great many other qualities, natural and acquired, if he is to be a good general. Still, it is a fine thing to be a tactician. An orderly army is far superior to a disorderly one, just as the materials of a house – bricks and stones, timber and tiles – are no good at all when dumped at random, but when they are arranged as they are combined in a building, with those which will neither rot nor disintegrate, the stones and the tiles, underneath and on top, and with the bricks and timber in between, then the result is a valuable possession – a house.'

'That's a close parallel, Socrates,' said the young man, 'because in war too you should post the best troops in front and in the rear, and the worst in between, so that they may be led on by the one lot and pushed forward by the other.'

'That's all right if the lecturer has taught you how to distinguish the good from the bad; but if he hasn't, what have you gained from your lessons? He might as well have told you to arrange the finest silver in front and the back, and the worst in between, without explaining to you how to tell fine from base metal.'

'He certainly didn't teach us that,' said he; 'so we shall have to distinguish good and bad for ourselves.'

'Then why not consider how we can avoid making blunders about them?'

'I should like to,' said the young man.

'Well, then,' said Socrates, 'supposing that we had to carry off some silver, wouldn't it be sound tactics to give the first place to those who were fondest of silver?'

'Yes, I think so.'

'What about facing danger? Should we put the most ardent lovers of glory in the front rank?'

'They are certainly the people who are willing to take risks in order to earn praise. Of course they aren't hard to identify; they are conspicuous in any company, and so they would be easy to pick out.'

'Tell me,' said Socrates, 'did he only teach you how to arrange your troops, or did he also explain how and in what circumstances you should employ each formation?'

'No, not at all,' said he.

'But there are many situations which call for quite different arrangements and movements of troops.'

'He certainly didn't clearly distinguish them,' said he.

'Then surely you ought to go back and ask him more questions,' said Socrates. 'If he knows his subject and has a conscience, he will be ashamed to send you away with gaps in your knowledge, after taking your money.'

CHAPTER TWO

Socrates argues that the primary concern of the general is the welfare of his men and of the people generally. The doctrine that government is for the benefit of the governed is of course Platonic (cf. Republic 342E, 345C–D), but Xenophon liked to think of the ideal ruler as a shepherd or father; he applies these images often to Cyrus in the Cyropaedia, *and no doubt felt that they fitted himself also.*

ONE day Socrates met a man who had just been appointed general.

'Why do you think Homer called Agamemnon "shepherd of the people"?[1] Was it because it is the shepherd's duty to see to it that his sheep are safe and have their food, and that the purpose for which they are kept is achieved, and in the same way it is the general's duty to see that his soldiers are safe and have their food and that the purpose for which they are serving is achieved – this purpose being to improve their fortune by defeating the enemy? Or what did he mean by praising Agamemnon in this way

> Both, a good king and a stout warrior?[2]

Was it that he would be a stout warrior not if he just personally contended bravely with the enemy, but if he caused the whole army to do so; and a good king not if he merely directed his own life well, but if he also brought happiness to his subjects? Because a king is chosen not to take good care of his own interests but to secure the well-being of those who chose him; and all peoples go to war with one object only, to secure the best possible living conditions for themselves; and they appoint generals for the single purpose

1. *Iliad* ii, 243.
2. *Iliad* iii, 179; cf. also *Symposium* 4, 6.

of leading them to this goal. So it is the duty of a general to realize the aims of those who appointed him as such; because it is not easy to find a nobler purpose than this, or a baser one than its opposite.'

By investigating in this way what is the ideal of a good general he eliminated all other considerations and left the quality of securing the happiness of his followers.

CHAPTER THREE

This discourse about the duties of a cavalry commander must owe a good deal to Xenophon's personal knowledge. It is unlikely that Socrates had any special interest in the subject, whereas it is almost certain that Xenophon and at least one of his sons served in the Athenian cavalry; moveover the views expressed below can be closely paralleled in the first two chapters of Xenophon's Hipparchicus, *a treatise on the duties of a cavalry officer.*

I KNOW that he also once had the following conversation with someone who had been appointed to a cavalry command. 'Could you tell us, young man,' he said, 'why you set your heart on becoming a cavalry officer? I presume that it wasn't that you wanted to ride at the head of the cavalry, because that is the privilege of the mounted archers – at least they ride ahead of even the cavalry commander.'

'That's true,' he said.

'And it wasn't publicity that you wanted either: even lunatics get that in its widest form.'

'That's true too.'

'Well, then, is it because you think that you might improve the efficiency of the cavalry while it is in your charge, and that if any need for mounted troops should arise you might do our country some service as their commander?'

'Yes, indeed.'

'A very fine thing, too,' said Socrates, 'if you can do this. The command for which you have been chosen is, I suppose, over both horses and riders.'

'Yes, it is.'

'Come along, then: first tell us how you propose to improve the horses.'

'But I don't think that is my job: each man ought to look after his own horse.'

'Well,' said Socrates, 'suppose that you find some of them turning out their horses with such bad feet or legs, or in such poor condition, or so under-fed, that they can't keep up with the rest; while others are so fresh that they won't keep their places, or such kickers that you can't get them into position at all; what will be the good of your cavalry? or how will you be able to do your country any service if your troopers are mounted like that?'

'You're right,' said he, 'I will do my best to look after the horses.'

'Well, now, what about the horsemen? Won't you try to improve their quality?'

'Yes, I will.'

'Won't you begin by making them better at mounting their horses?'

'I ought to, certainly, because then if one of them fell off he would stand a better chance.'

'And next, if you have to risk an engagement, will you order them to draw the enemy on to the sandy ground where you are accustomed to exercise, or will you try to carry out your training in the sort of country in which campaigns are fought?'

'That would be better, certainly.'

'Next, will you make a practice of unseating as many of them as possible?'

'That would be a good idea, too.'

'Is it your intention to make your troopers stouter warriors by whetting their courage and rousing their anger against the enemy?'

'If it isn't, I will try to make it so now,' he said.

'Have you given any thought to the question of discipline?

because without it there is no use in horses or horsemen, however good and warlike.'

'True,' he said. 'But how can one best direct them towards
it, Socrates?'

'You know, I'm sure, that in every situation people are
readiest to obey those whom they consider to be best informed.
In illness they pay most attention to the man who they think
has most medical knowledge; and on board ship the passen-
gers pay most attention to the man whom they regard as the
most experienced sailor; and in farming most attention is
paid to the man who is regarded as the most experienced
farmer.'

'Quite so.'

'Then presumably in the case of horsemanship too the man
who clearly knows best what ought to be done is most likely
to receive the willing obedience of the rest.'

'Then if I am obviously better than any of them, will that
be enough to make them obey me?'

'Yes, provided that you also inform them that obedience
to you will be both more honourable and more salutary for
them than disobedience.'

'How shall I teach them that?'

'Much more easily, I assure you, than if you had to teach
them that bad conduct is better and more profitable than
good conduct.'

'Do you mean,' said he, 'that besides all his other duties a
cavalry officer ought to cultivate the ability to speak in
public?'

'Did you suppose that he had to exercise his command in
silence? Haven't you noticed that all the ideals that tradition
has taught us – ideals to which we owe our knowledge of how
to live – are learned through discourse? and that any other
fine accomplishment that anyone acquires is acquired by
means of discourse? and that the best teachers make the most

use of discourse? and that those who have the profoundest knowledge of the most important subjects are the most brilliant debaters? Or again, haven't you noticed that when a chorus is chosen to represent this city of ours, like the one which is sent to Delos,[1] no chorus from anywhere else can match it; and no other city can muster a display of manhood like ours?'

'That's true,' he said.

'But it's not so much in quality of voice, or in physical size and strength that Athenians are superior to the rest, as in the love of honour, which is the keenest incentive to noble and honourable actions.'

'That's true too,' he said.

'Then don't you think that if our cavalry was taken seriously the Athenians would be far superior here too, both in their provision of equipment and horses, and by their discipline and readiness to venture against the enemy, if they thought that by doing so they would win praise and honour?'

'Very likely.'

'Then don't hesitate any longer,' said Socrates, 'but try to induce your men to adopt a course which will benefit both you and, through you, the rest of our people as well.'

'All right,' said he, 'I will certainly try.'

1. See Glossary. The 'chorus' would be a company of singers and dancers to compete at the festival.

CHAPTER FOUR

Conversation with an unsuccessful candidate for election as a general reveals that in this sphere organizing and administrative ability are quite as important as the more soldierly qualities.

Socrates (or Xenophon) seems to be considering the strategus more as a minister than as a commander in the field. To compare him with a choregus is unrealistic. A choregus was simply a rich citizen who accepted responsibility for providing and training a chorus for a dramatic or choral performance; he needed no special knowledge provided that he could hire experts to supply it. On the other hand a man with no administrative or military ability would hardly have been elected strategus; and if he had been it is very doubtful whether he could have carried out his duties satisfactorily through hired agents. The comparison with a major-domo or steward, which is not very adroitly substituted in section seven, is perhaps valid for administrative duties; but this too entirely disregards military expertise. In fact the analogies are pushed too far; but whether the culprit is Socrates or Xenophon or some zealous interpolator is a baffling problem.

Nicomachides is otherwise unknown.

ONE day he saw Nicomachides coming away from the elections, and asked him, 'Who have been elected as generals, Nicomachides?'

'Why, naturally, Socrates,' he replied, 'the people of Athens, being what they are, have not elected me, although I am worn out with active service as a major and a colonel, and have received all these wounds from the enemy' – as he spoke, he drew back his clothes and exhibited the scars – 'but they have chosen Antisthenes,'[1] he said, 'who has never served

---

1. Clearly not the philosopher but a businessman.

as a foot-soldier and has won no distinction in the cavalry, and knows nothing except how to pile up money.'

'Surely it's a good thing,' said Socrates, 'if he will be able to provide his men with supplies.'

'Merchants can pile up money too,' said Nicomachides, 'but that doesn't qualify them to be generals.'

Socrates said, 'But Antisthenes is set on winning, which is an appropriate quality for a general. Don't you see that every time that he has been *choregus*[2] he has won with all his choruses?'

'Yes,' said Nicomachides, 'but it's one thing to have charge of a chorus, and quite another to have charge of an army.'

'All the same,' said Socrates, 'although Antisthenes had no experience of singing or of training a chorus, he succeeded in finding the best people for his purpose.'

'So in his capacity as general,' said Nicomachides 'he will find other people to work out his tactics and to do the fighting.'[3]

'Well,' said Socrates, 'if he is as good at searching out and selecting the best agents in his military operations as he is in training his choruses, he will probably be successful in this case too. Besides, he would naturally be prepared to spend more to win a military victory with the whole nation than to win one in a choral competition with the help of his tribe.'[4]

'Do you mean, Socrates, that a good chorus-trainer would also make a good general?'

'I mean that when a man is given a post of responsibility,

2. See the chapter introduction.

3. This is sarcastic.

4. The citizen population of Athens was divided into ten *phylae* or 'tribes', and each of these tribes appointed its own *choregus* for the choral competitions at the great festivals.

if he finds out what is needed and is able to supply it, he can fill that post efficiently, whether it relates to a chorus or a household or a state or an army.'[5]

'I must say, Socrates,' said Nicomachides, 'I never thought that I should hear you say that good managers of households[6] would make good generals.'

'Come along, then,' he said, 'let's consider their respective duties, so that we may see whether they are the same or there is some difference.'

'By all means.'

'Isn't it the duty of both of them to make their subordinates obedient and tractable?'

'Certainly.'

'What about assigning the various tasks to those who are qualified to perform them?'

'That too.'

'Then I suppose it is appropriate for both to punish the bad and give credit to the good.'

'Quite so.'

'And surely it is proper for both to make their subordinates well disposed towards them?'

'That too.'

'Do you think that it is in the interest of both to win allies and helpers, or not?'

'Certainly,' said he.

'Shouldn't both be conservative of their possessions?'

'Very much so.'

'Then shouldn't they both be careful and industrious about all their duties?'

'All these qualities are equally applicable to both; but fighting is not.'

5. See above, p. 129.
6. This is a shift of ground.

'But surely both make enemies?'[7]

'That is so, certainly.'

'Isn't it in the interest of both to get the better of them?'

'Quite; but you're leaving something out of account: if fighting becomes necessary, what will be the good of house-hold management?'

'Surely then it will be more valuable than ever. The good manager, knowing that nothing brings so much profit and gain as defeating one's enemies in battle, and nothing so much loss and ruin as being defeated, will eagerly seek and prepare what is conducive to victory, and will carefully note and guard against what tends towards defeat; and if he sees that his preparations offer hope of victory, he will vigorously fight; and – not least in importance – if he is unprepared, he will avoid an engagement. You mustn't despise household managers, Nicomachides. The difference between the care of private and the care of public affairs is only one of degree; in all other respects they are closely similar, especially in that neither can dispense with human agency, and the human agents are the same in both cases. Those who look after public affairs employ just the same agents as in managing their private properties; and if people understand how to use these agents, they carry out their duties successfully, whether public or private, but if they do not, then they come to grief in either case.'

7. The awkward fact that a military commander needs theoretical knowledge, practical experience, and personal qualities not usually available to the civilian is neatly evaded. However, since Xenophon picked up most of his 'generalship' in conflict with mediocre commanders and inferior troops, it is possible that he really thought it was largely a matter of common sense.

CHAPTER FIVE

*This chapter seems to express Xenophon's own dream of a return to
the glories of the Periclean age. Such feelings might have been
shared by any patriotic Athenian; but the manner of their expression,
and in particular the criticisms of army discipline and the scheme for
frontier defence, are more appropriate to a soldier than to a philosopher, and the allusion to Mysian and Pisidian guerrilla tactics
would hardly have occurred to Socrates without some prompting.*

*Xenophon's conflicting loyalties are considered in the Introduc-
tion, pp. 12–14.*

ONE day Socrates was talking to Pericles the son of the
famous Pericles.

'You know, Pericles,' he said, 'I have hopes that if[1] you are
appointed as a general our city will become more efficient and
renowned in warfare, and will conquer its enemies.'

Pericles replied, 'I should like it to be as you say, Socrates;
but I can't make up my mind how it could happen.'

'Would you like to discuss the subject, then,' said Socrates,
'and try to discover where the possibility really lies?'

'Yes, I should,' he said.

'Very well, then: you know that the Athenians are no
fewer in number than the Boeotians?'[2]

'Yes, I know that.'

'Do you think that there would be more examples of
physical perfection in Boeotia than in Athens?'

'To my mind we aren't inferior in this respect either.'

'And which people do you suppose is better disposed
towards its own citizens?'

1. He was elected in 406 B.C. See Glossary.
2. Boeotia was the state next to Attica on the N.W. Thebes was its
most powerful city.

'I should say the Athenians. A good many of the Boeotians resent the aggressiveness of the Thebans; but I don't see anything of that sort at Athens.'

'Besides, the Athenians have a greater thirst for glory and warmth of feeling than any other race; and these are no slight incentives to take risks for the sake of honour and their country.'

'In this respect too the Athenians are above criticism.'

'Then again, no people can claim more or greater ancestral exploits than the Athenians; and consequently many of them are inspired by this example to cultivate valour and show themselves stout fighters.'

'All this that you say is true, Socrates. But you can see that ever since the disaster to the Thousand with Tolmides at Lebadia,[3] and the other one with Hippocrates at Delium,[4] the prestige of Athens has been low in relation to Boeotia, and the confidence of Thebes high in relation to Athens; so that the Boeotians, who used not even to dare to face the Athenians in their own territory without the support of the Spartans and the other Peloponnesians, are now threatening to invade Attica on their own account; while the Athenians, who used to wreak havoc in Boeotia, are afraid that the Boeotians will ravage Attica.'

'I realize that this is so,' said Socrates; 'but it seems to me that our city is now more amenably disposed towards a good ruler. Confidence induces carelessness and indifference and disobedience, but fear makes people more inclined to be attentive and docile and disciplined. You can see an illustration of this in what happens on board ships. When there's

3. A town in the west of Boeotia near which the Athenian general Tolmides was defeated and killed in 447 B.C. (Thucydides i, 113).

4. A town in Boeotia where Athens suffered a heavy defeat in 424 B.C. (Thucydides iv, 89-101). Socrates showed great courage in the retreat (Plato, *Symposium* 221A, *Laches* 181B).

nothing to fear, the crew are completely unruly; but so long as they are afraid of storm or enemy they not only carry out all instructions but wait for the next order in perfect silence, like members of a chorus waiting for their cue.'

'Well,' said Pericles, 'assuming that they are at their most docile now, it would be the right moment to say how we can encourage them to set their hearts again upon their former valour and renown and happiness.'

'If we wanted them to claim property that was in the possession of others, the best way of inciting them to lay hands upon that property would be by proving to them that it belonged to them by inheritance; and since we want them to make it their object to excel in valour, we must similarly show them that this has been their special characteristic from of old, and that if they cultivated it seriously they could be the most powerful nation in the world.'

'How can we teach them this lesson?'

'I suppose by reminding them of the stories that they have been told about the exploits of their earliest recorded ancestors.'

'Do you mean the contest of the gods which Cecrops[5] and his advisers were allowed to decide because of their goodness?'

'Yes, and the birth and rearing of Erechtheus,[6] and the war that broke out in his time against the inhabitants of all the adjoining mainland;[7] and the war against the Peloponnesians

5. The legendary first king of Athens. The contest was for the post of tutelary deity of the city. Poseidon offered as his gift a spring of water on the Acropolis, but Athena outbid him with the olive-tree.

6. A legendary king of Athens (cf. Homer, *Iliad* ii, 547; *Odyssey* vii, 80 f.). The present Erechtheum seems to hav ereplaced an older shrine shared by him with Athena.

7. According to Isocrates, *Panegyricus* 19 ff., the immediate enemy was the neighbouring town of Eleusis; but possibly a general attack by the Thracians is meant.

in the days of the Heraclidae,[8] and all the campaigns under Theseus;[9] in all of which our ancestors showed themselves plainly to be the best men of their generation. Or again, the feats accomplished later by their descendants not much before our time:[10] either striving unaided against an enemy who was master of the whole of Asia and of Europe as far as Macedonia, who possessed vaster armies and resources and had carried out greater operations than any previous nation; or sharing the leadership by land and sea with the Peloponnesians; who are also reputed to have far surpassed the other people of their time.'

'So it is said.'

'And that is why, in spite of the many migrations that have taken place in Greece, they remained in their own country;[11] often answering appeals for arbitration from those disputing about their rights,[12] and often giving sanctuary to the victims of oppression.'[13]

'I can't understand, Socrates,' said Pericles, 'how it was that our country ever deteriorated.'

Socrates replied, 'You know how athletes sometimes, when they have enjoyed unchallenged superiority, through sheer lack of enterprise become no match for their opponents? My

8. When Eurystheus king of Argos made war on Athens for harbouring the children of his old enemy Heracles (Euripides, *Heraclidae*, Herodotus, ix, 27).

9. E.g. against the Amazons and Centaurs (cf. the Parthenon frieze).

10. In the Persian Wars.

11. The Athenians claimed to be the original inhabitants of Attica; cf. Herodotus i, 56; vii, 161; Thucydides i, 2; ii, 36; Isocrates, *Panegyricus* 166.

12. The justification for this claim is not clear, but Pausanias (iv, 5, 1 f.) says that the Messenians wanted to refer their quarrel with Sparta to the Areopagus.

13. E.g. to the Heraclidae (see above, n. 8), to Adrastus and the widows of the 'Seven against Thebes' (Euripides, *Supplices*), and to Oedipus (Sophocles, *Oedipus Coloneus*).

belief is that in the same way the people of Athens were so far supreme that they became negligent, and that their deterioration is due to this.'

'Well, then,' said he, 'what can they do now to recover their former excellence?'

Socrates replied, 'I don't think that the answer is anything abstruse. If they rediscovered their ancestors' way of life and followed it no worse than they did, they would prove to be just as good men as they were. Alternatively, if they took as their model the present leaders[14] of the Greek world and followed the same way of life, then with similar application to the same activities they would become no worse than their models, and with closer application they would actually surpass them.'

'You imply that our country is a long way from the ideal of conduct. Are the Athenians ever likely to equal the Spartans in showing respect for their elders when they despise anyone older than themselves, beginning with their fathers?[15] or in developing their bodies, when they not only care nothing for physical fitness themselves but jeer at those who do care about it? Will they ever have as much obedience to authority, when they pride themselves on despising authority? Will they ever have as much unanimity, when so far from working together for their common interest they are more envious and abusive towards one another than towards the rest of the world, and quarrel more in their discussions, both private and public, than any other people; and bring the greatest number of actions[16] against one another, and prefer to gain in this way at each other's expense rather than by cooperation, and

14. The Spartans. For Xenophon's attitude towards them see Introduction pp. 13 f.

15. Cf. the anecdote in Cicero, *De Senectute* 63.

16. The litigiousness of the Athenians is pungently satirized by Aristophanes in his *Wasps*.

while treating public duties as no personal concern of theirs, at the same time fight over them, and take the greatest delight in the qualities that fit them for such a purpose? As a result of this a great deal of harm and mischief is developing in our city, a great deal of mutual enmity and hatred is growing in the hearts of our people; and for this reason I for my part am in constant dread that some intolerable disaster will fall upon our city.'

'Really, Pericles,' said Socrates, 'you mustn't imagine that the Athenians are suffering from such incurable depravity as that. Don't you see how well-disciplined they are in the navy, and how punctiliously they obey the officials at athletic meetings, and how, when they are members of a chorus, they yield to nobody in following the directions of their trainers?'

'Yes, that's the strange thing, you know,' he said, 'that people like these should obey their superiors, while the infantry and cavalry, who are supposed to be the pick of the population in general excellence, should be the most unruly.'

Socrates said, 'But the Council of the Areopagus,[17] Pericles: isn't it composed of men of tried character?'

'Yes, indeed.'

'Do you know any other body that tries cases and conducts all its other business better, or more in accordance with law and honour and justice?'

'I have nothing to say against them.'

'Then you mustn't despair of the Athenians as being disorderly.'

'But on military service, where there is the greatest need

17. A hill just to the west of the Acropolis at Athens, meeting-place of an ancient council. This was originally administrative, but when magistrates began to be elected by lot in 487 B.C. it gradually lost its importance, retaining only prestige and jurisdiction in cases of homicide. It was recruited from ex-magistrates of proved integrity.

for self-control and discipline and obedience, they give no thought to any of these qualities.'

'Perhaps,' said Socrates, 'that is because in this sphere they have the least expert direction. Don't you see that in the case of musicians and singers and dancers nobody without expert knowledge attempts to give directions, and similarly with boxers and wrestlers? The authorities on all these subjects can point to the source from which they learned the arts for which they are responsible; but the great majority of military commanders are self-taught. However, I don't imagine that you are that sort of person. I expect that you can tell me when you began to learn generalship just as easily as when you began to learn wrestling. I expect that besides keeping a stock of stratagems that you have inherited from your father, you have amassed a great many from every source from which you could learn anything useful for the art of war. And I expect that you are constantly on your guard against inadvertent ignorance of anything that is useful to this end; and that if you become aware that there is something of this sort that you don't know, you seek out the experts in the subject, grudging neither presents nor favours, in order to learn from them what you don't know, and have the help of qualified persons.'

Pericles replied: 'You can't deceive me, Socrates. Your reason for saying all this is certainly not that you think that I *do* take these things seriously; you are trying to show me that one *ought* to take them seriously if one aspires to be a general. As a matter of fact I quite agree with you.'

'Have you noted the fact, Pericles, that our frontier is protected by high mountains[18] running down into Boeotia, through which the approaches into our territory are narrow and steep; while the land between is an unbroken chain of rugged heights?'

18. The ranges of Cithaeron and Parnes.

'Yes, indeed,' said he.

'Well, now, have you heard that the Mysians and Pisidians,[19] who occupy strongholds in the territories of the king of Persia, are able, though only lightly armed, not only to preserve their independence but to do the Persians a good deal of damage by raiding their country?'

'Yes, I have heard that too.'

'Don't you think that if the young and active age-groups of the Athenian army were equipped with lighter arms and occupied the mountains that screen our frontiers they would both be able to harass our enemies and form an effective defence for our people against invasion?'

'I think that all these are useful suggestions too,' said Pericles.

'Well, then,' said Socrates, 'if you approve of them, give them a trial, my good friend. If you can put any of them into practice, it will be to your credit and the benefit of your country; and if you can't, you will neither harm your country nor bring discredit upon yourself.'

19. The Mysians lived in N.W. Asia Minor, the Pisidians towards the south, round the Taurus mountains. They are mentioned together in *Anabasis* iii, 2, 23 as thorns in the side of Persia.

CHAPTER SIX

Glaucon, Plato's elder brother, is warned that if he wants to distinguish himself in politics he must first acquire a great deal of specialized knowledge and do some hard thinking about it.

This is one of the best dialogues in the book. The characters are neatly sketched and well contrasted. The vain and impetuous Glaucon starts off confidently enough, but Socrates' awkward questions soon make him shuffle, and although he tries to recover his poise by a sweeping criticism, his ignorance and evasiveness are quickly exposed. Socrates, as usual, is cruel only to be kind; he is determined to show the young man how ill-equipped he is for his chosen task, but the object is not to mock but to prepare him for enlightenment.

Glaucon is the most prominent character, after Socrates, in Plato's Republic, *where he appears as a very intelligent young man. Even if we allow for some fraternal partiality it would seem that he benefited from Socrates' elenchus.*

WHEN Glaucon the son of Ariston was trying to become a popular orator, because he was set on being the head of the state, although he was not yet twenty years old, none of his friends and intimates could stop him; he was always getting dragged off the public platform and laughed at. The one person who prevailed upon him was Socrates, who was kindly disposed towards him for the sake of two persons, Charmides,[1] the son of Glaucon,[2] and Plato. Socrates happened to meet him, and he first won his attention by addressing him in the following way:

'Glaucon,' he said, 'have you made up your mind to become the head of our state?'

1. See Glossary.
2. Grandfather of the younger Glaucon.

'Yes, I have, Socrates.'

'And a fine thing too, upon my word; I don't know that there is any higher human ambition. Clearly if you succeed in it you will have the power to obtain your own desires, and be able to help your friends; you will gain distinction for your family and extend the power of your country; and you will win a name for yourself first in our city, and then in Greece, and perhaps even, like Themistocles, among foreign powers. And wherever you are, every eye will be fixed upon you.'

This description appealed to Glaucon's vanity, and he was glad to remain where he was. Socrates then went on:

'It's obvious, isn't it, Glaucon, that if you want to be held in honour you must help your country?'

'Certainly.'

'Well, then,' said he, 'please don't make a secret of it, but tell us where you will start to benefit your country.'

Glaucon made no reply, as if he were considering for the first time where he should start.

'If you wanted to make the family of a friend more important, you would try to make it wealthier. On the same principle I suppose you will try to make your country wealthier.'

'Yes, of course.'

'Wouldn't it be wealthier if its revenues were increased?'

'Naturally.'

'Tell me, then: what are our country's present revenues derived from, and what do they amount to? No doubt you have looked into this, so that you may make up any of them that are inadequate and supply any that are lacking.'

'Actually,' said Glaucon, 'I haven't looked into that.'

'Well,' said Socrates, 'if you have left that aside, tell us what the country's expenditure is. You must be planning to curtail any extravagance.'

'Actually,' said Glaucon, 'I haven't had time for that yet either.'

'Then we will defer the question of making the country wealthier. You can't very well look after the expenditure and revenues if you don't know what they are.'

'But, Socrates,' said Glaucon, 'it is possible to enrich one's country from the resources of its enemies.'

'Yes, indeed, perfectly possible,' said Socrates, 'if you are stronger than they are. If you are weaker, you are likely to lose even what you have already.'

'That is true.'

'So before you start considering on whom to make war you ought to know the strength both of your own country and of her opponents, so that if your country is the stronger you may encourage her to undertake the war, and if she is weaker you may persuade her to be cautious.'

'Quite right,' said he.

'Then tell us first what our country's land and sea forces are, and then do the same for the enemy's.'

'Well, really,' he said, 'I couldn't tell you off-hand.'

'If you've got a written note, fetch it; I should very much like to hear the answer.'

'Actually,' he said, 'I haven't got a note of it yet either.'

'Very well, then,' said Socrates, 'we will put off our military discussion too, in the first instance. Probably you haven't yet had time to go carefully into the matter, because of its magnitude, besides your being so newly in office. But of course I'm sure that you have already given your attention to the defence of our territory, and know how many guard-posts are well placed and how many are not, how many of the garrisons are adequate and how many are not. And you will recommend the strengthening of those that are well placed and the abolition of those that are superfluous.'

'Actually I shall recommend abolishing the lot,' said Glaucon, 'because they are so badly manned that the produce of the land gets stolen.'

'But if the guard-posts are abolished,' said Socrates, 'don't you think that it will be open to anyone to help himself freely? By the way, have you found this out by personal inspection, or how do you know that the posts are badly manned?'

'I assume it,' he said.

'Shall we wait to discuss this subject too until we have got beyond assumptions and know the facts?'

'Perhaps that would be better,' said Glaucon.

'Then there are the silver mines,'[3] said Socrates. 'I know that you haven't visited them so as to be able to account for the decline of revenue from them.'

'No, I haven't.'

'As a matter of fact,' said Socrates, 'they say that it's an unhealthy district; so when you have to state your views about it this excuse will cover you.'

'You're making fun of me,' said Glaucon.

'But there's another problem that I'm sure you haven't neglected but investigated: how long can the country be fed on home-produced corn, and how much extra does it need per year?[4] You wouldn't like your country to incur a shortage of this kind without your realizing it; you would wish to be able to advise from personal knowledge about essential supplies, and so to give her help and security.'

'That's an enormous task you're suggesting,' said Glaucon, 'if one is to be obliged to look after that sort of thing.'

'But surely,' said Socrates, 'a man could never manage even his own household properly unless he knows all its deficiencies and supplies them by looking after them all. As our city consists of more than ten thousand houses, and it would be

3. At Laurium near Cape Sunium at the southern extremity of Attica. They furnished a great part of Athens' wealth.
4. About one third of the corn supply was imported.

difficult to look after so many households simultaneously, why don't you first try to look after one, your uncle's?[5] It needs it. And if you can cope with that, you can try your hand on more; but if you can't do any good to one, how can you do good to many? If a man can't carry one hundred-weight, surely it's obvious that he shouldn't even try to carry more than one.'

'Well,' said Glaucon, 'I would do something for my uncle's household if he would follow my advice.'

'So although you can't persuade your uncle,' said Socrates, 'you expect to be able to make the whole population of Athens, including your uncle, follow your advice? Take care, my dear Glaucon, that your craving for distinction doesn't take you in the opposite direction. Can't you see how risky it is to say or to do things that you don't know about? Consider the rest of your acquaintances, those whom you know to be the sort of people who obviously say and do things that they don't know about; do you think that they are more admired or despised for this sort of conduct? And then consider the case of those who know what they are saying and what they are doing. In my opinion you will find in every sphere of action that esteem and admiration are reserved for those who are best informed, while ignominy and contempt are the lot of the most ignorant. So if you really want to be esteemed and admired in the state, try to ensure as far as possible that you know about the things that you want to do. If you have this advantage over the rest when you try your hand at politics, I shouldn't be surprised if you realized your ambition quite easily.'

5. The reference is to Charmides.

CHAPTER SEVEN

Plato's uncle Charmides is urged to exercise his talents in public life. There is no reason for him to be shy: if he can give good advice in private he can do the same in public.

Here Socrates' (or Xenophon's) logic seems to be better than his psychology. Most people would agree that to give advice to an individual (especially when requested) is vastly different from proposing or attacking a line of policy at a public meeting. Perhaps this ought not to be so; but that is not much comfort to a sensitive person. On the other hand the average Athenian in Xenophon's day must have been much more accustomed to public speaking than his modern English counterparts, and the children of well-to-do parents received regular lessons in rhetoric; so perhaps Charmides was only making excuses.

WHEN he saw that Charmides, the son of Glaucon,[1] though a person of influence and much more capable than the active politicians of that time, was hesitant to enter public life and handle his country's affairs, he said, 'Tell me, Charmides; supposing that there was somebody capable of winning championship contests[2] so as to gain honour for himself and enhance his country's reputation in the Greek world, and supposing that he refused to compete, what sort of man would you think he was?'

'Obviously soft and unenterprising.'

'And supposing that there was somebody who, though capable of handling his country's affairs in such a way as to raise its prestige and win honour himself, was hesitant to do so; wouldn't he reasonably be regarded as unenterprising?'

'Probably,' he replied. 'But why do you ask me that?'

1. The elder, grandfather of Glaucon the younger.
2. At the great athletic festivals.

'Because I think you are failing to use your administrative ability, and that in a sphere where you are bound as a citizen to take part.'

'In what kind of activity,' said Charmides, 'have you studied my ability so thoroughly that you now bring this condemnation against me?'

'In your relations with public men. When they consult you I notice that you give them good advice, and when they make mistakes your criticism is fair and right.'

'It's not the same thing, Socrates,' he said, 'to talk to a person privately and to debate in public.'

'All the same,' said Socrates, 'a man who can count counts just as well in public as by himself; and the best private performers of music are also those who are most successful in public.'

'But don't you realize that shyness and nervousness are part of human nature, and that they come out much more in public gatherings than in individual contacts?'

'Yes; and I am anxious to open your eyes. You are neither overawed by the cleverest people nor afraid of the most powerful, and yet you are too modest to speak in front of the silliest and weakest. Whom are you shy of? the dry-cleaners or the shoemakers or the carpenters or the smiths or the farmers or the merchants or the shopkeepers in the market, whose business it is to buy at a cheaper rate and sell at a dearer one? because all these go to make up the Assembly. What difference do you think there is between what you are doing and a professional champion's being afraid of amateurs? You converse easily with our leading statesmen, some of whom look down on you, and you are far better qualified than the professional politicians; yet you shrink from speaking in front of people who have never troubled their heads about politics or formed a poor opinion of you – because you are afraid of being laughed at!'

'Well, but,' said Charmides, 'don't you think that the members of the Assembly often laugh at those who advocate the right policy?'

'Yes, and so do the others.[3] That's why I am surprised that although you can easily deal with the one class, you imagine that you will be quite incapable of facing the other. My good man, don't depreciate yourself, or make the usual mistake. Most people when they are set upon looking into other people's affairs never turn to examine themselves. Don't shirk this responsibility, but make a greater effort to take yourself seriously; and don't neglect public affairs if you can better them in any way, because if they are well conducted it will benefit not only the rest of the citizen body but your personal friends, and not least yourself.'

3. The politicians.

CHAPTER EIGHT

Interest is now focused upon moral values, aesthetics and various human activities and attitudes of mind. In the following chapter Socrates parries an attempt by Aristippus to trap him into a contradiction, and expounds the doctrine that the terms 'good' (agathos) and 'beautiful' (kalos) are properly used only with reference to function, and so used are convertible. He then applies this doctrine to the practical planning of a house.

The meanings of these Greek words as applied to people have been discussed already (Introduction, p. 9). Here it may be enough to say that, even when they are used with this limited reference, the two words, although they often overlap, are not absolutely convertible: agathos tends to mean 'of good quality', 'dependable', 'efficient', appealing to the judgement; kalos to mean 'delightful', 'admirable', appealing to the senses or emotions.

Socrates argues that neither term can be used absolutely: a thing is good or beautiful only if it serves its proper purpose. There is much truth in this; a truth that is often overlooked; but so far from being the whole truth it is only a part of an aesthetic problem much too large to be discussed here. What he goes on to say, that the fact that two things are beautiful does not imply that they are alike, if their purposes are different, might seem to be a semi-paradox levelled at Plato's Theory of Forms, and particularly at Diotima's description (Plato, Symposium 210) of the soul's approach to absolute Beauty. But although Xenophon may sometimes (it is hard to be sure) attempt to 'correct' Plato, there is no contradiction here: Xenophon's Socrates – in this context one might say the historical Socrates – has pretty certainly never heard of the Forms; he has not even advanced far enough in the practice of abstraction to detect a common characteristic that makes all these dissimilar objects perfectly adapted for their dissimilar ends. And no wonder, because that characteristic is purely conceptual – mathematical, if *you like – certainly not visual, and therefore extremely hard to apprehend when one is talking on a practical level about visible objects.*

For Aristippus see the Glossary.

ARISTIPPUS was once trying to argue Socrates down in return for the defeats that he had suffered in the past. Socrates, whose object was to benefit the people listening, answered not like a man who is guarding against getting his argument tangled up, but like one who is fully convinced that he is doing his duty. Aristippus asked him whether he knew anything that was good, intending, if Socrates mentioned anything such as food or drink or money or health or strength or courage, to prove that it was sometimes bad. But Socrates knew that if anything annoys us what we need is something to stop it, and he replied in the most effective way:

'Are you asking if I know something good for fever?'

'Of course not.'

'For ophthalmia?'

'No, not that either.'

'For starvation?'

'No, nor starvation either.'

'Well, really, if you are asking me whether I know anything good that is good for nothing, I don't, and what's more I don't want to.'

Another time Aristippus asked him whether he knew anything beautiful.

'Yes indeed, plenty of things.'

'Well then, are they all alike?'

'On the contrary, they are as unlike as they can be.'

'How can a thing be beautiful if it is unlike what is beautiful?'

'Why, because a man who is a beautiful runner has another unlike him who is a beautiful wrestler; and a shield which is beautiful for defence is totally unlike a dart which is beautiful for throwing hard and fast.'

'You are giving me just the same sort of answer as when I asked you if you knew anything good.'

'Do you really imagine that "goodness" and "beauty" are different? Don't you know that things are always good and beautiful by the same standards? In the first place goodness is not "good" for some things and "beautiful" for others; secondly, people are called "beautiful" and "good" on the same ground and with the same ends in view; and people's bodies are obviously beautiful and good in relation to the same end; and everything else that we use is considered to be beautiful and good in accordance with the same standard, viz. the end for which it is serviceable.'

'Then is a dung-basket beautiful?'

'Certainly: and a golden shield is ugly, if the one is well and the other badly constructed for carrying out its function.'

'Do you mean that the same things are both beautiful and ugly?'

'Certainly, and what's more, both good and bad. Often what is good for starvation is bad for fever, and vice versa; and what is beautiful for running is ugly for wrestling, and vice versa. Everything is good and beautiful in so far as it's well adapted for its purpose, and bad and ugly in so far as it's ill adapted.'

Similarly in maintaining that a beautiful house is one that serves its purpose well Socrates seemed to me to be teaching the principle that building should satisfy practical requirements. He approached the question in this way:

'If a man is to have the sort of house that he needs, ought he to contrive to make it as pleasant and convenient as possible to live in?' When this was admitted: 'Isn't it pleasant to have a house which is cool in summer and warm in winter?' When they agreed to this too: 'Well, in houses that have a south aspect in winter the sun shines into the verandas, while in summer it passes over our heads and over the roof and casts a shade. So, if this is the desired effect, one should build the south side higher, so as not to shut off the winter sun, and the north side lower, to avoid exposure to the cold winds. In short, the most pleasant and most beautiful residence is likely to be that which offers at all seasons the most agreeable retreat for the owner and the safest repository for his possessions. Frescoes and decorations deprive us of more amenities than they supply.' As for temples and altars, he said that the most suitable site for them was one that was at once conspicuous and off the beaten track; it was pleasant for passers-by to say their prayers at the sight of a shrine, but it was also pleasant to approach it in a reverent frame of mind.

CHAPTER NINE

A scrappy selection of Socrates' views on various subjects – the cardinal virtues (wisdom, courage, temperance and justice), madness and ignorance, envy, leisure, knowledge as the qualification for rule, and efficiency.

At first sight there is little here to arouse enthusiasm or even interest, but the whole chapter repays careful reading. The section on courage clearly recognizes and states the general truth (obvious but often disregarded) that the high development of any quality demands both natural aptitude and assiduous practice. 'Temperance' is a poor translation of sophrosyne, but this is an old difficulty: the Greek word implies a healthy state of mind which is neither erratic in its judgement nor inclined towards excess. Other renderings such as 'moderation', 'sobriety' and 'self-control' seem equally unsatisfactory, because sophrosyne is primarily a mental quality; it is often, as here, identified or at least associated with wisdom (cf. Plato, Protagoras 332–3; Laws 710A); so perhaps 'prudence', although a smug word to modern ears, may be the best solution.

Socrates held that virtue is knowledge, i.e. that in order to act rightly it is only necessary to understand what needs to be done and to know how to do it (this doctrine has been discussed in the Introduction, p. 8). Here, challenged by a paradox to account for wrong conduct, he lays the blame on faulty judgement. Clearly this may often be the right diagnosis, but in our experience there are two much commoner causes: weakness of will and self-deception. Perhaps Socrates himself was not much affected by these.

How far Xenophon intends to distinguish knowledge from wisdom is not clear. At any rate the argument to equate justice with wisdom is obscure as it stands; perhaps it may be clarified thus:

Just acts, i.e. acts done through virtue, are good and honourable.
Good and honourable deeds are done only by those who know how,
   i.e. by the wise or in other words through wisdom.

But good and honourable deeds are done through virtue.

Therefore wisdom = virtue.

At best the argument seems to rest on an equivocation: for there is no guarantee that wisdom and virtue are related to good actions in the same way, and in fact they are not.

Next a superficial difficulty about madness and ignorance – if they are both opposed to wisdom, are they identical? – is cleared up by Socrates with some common-sense remarks, and his analysis of envy is straightforward enough; but the discussion of leisure calls for some explanation. A man is at leisure if he has nothing serious to do; if he is just amusing himself he can always turn to something useful. But if he is seriously engaged he cannot be said to be at leisure to turn to something lighter, and if he does so turn he is doing wrong. In spite of the moral judgement the point of interest here is probably terminological rather than ethical. No doubt Socrates would have admitted that recreation is sometimes necessary or at least justifiable.

His insistence upon knowledge as the essential qualification for a ruler is reasonable in itself, but its piquancy is increased by the fact that since the year 487 B.C. the archons (nominally the highest ministers of the state: the word means 'ruler') had been elected by lot, and had no special qualifications at all – an arrangement which Socrates regarded, with some justice, as inefficient.

Finally Socrates takes advantage of the fact that 'efficiency' and 'success' are expressed by the same word or phrase in Greek to stress the difference between 'success' as the direct consequence of good work, and 'good luck' as something fortuitous, unearned and probably undeserved. Socrates' interest in efficiency has already been noted (Introduction pp. 7f).

ON another occasion he was asked whether courage was a matter of teaching or a natural gift. 'I think,' he said, 'that just as one body is born with more endurance than another for facing hardship, so one soul is naturally endowed with greater fortitude than another for facing danger; because I observe that people who are brought up among the same laws and customs differ greatly in courage. At the same time I imagine that every natural disposition can be developed in the direction of fortitude by instruction and application. It's obvious that the Scythians and Thracians[1] would never dare to take shields and spears and fight it out with the Spartans; and it is evident that the Spartans would refuse to join mortal combat either with light shields and darts against the Thracians or with bows and arrows against the Scythians. My personal experience is that similarly in all other cases people both differ in natural capacity and improve greatly by the help of application. From this it clearly follows that everyone, whether his natural ability is above or below the average, ought to study and exercise any qualities for which he wishes to earn recognition.'

He did not distinguish wisdom from temperance, but judged that the man who recognizes and puts into practice what is good and honourable, and the man who knows and guards against what is disgraceful, are both wise and temperate. When somebody asked him if he thought that those who understood what they ought to do but did the opposite were wise and dissolute, he replied, 'No more than I think them both unwise and dissolute. I presume that everyone acts by choosing from the courses open to him the one which he supposes to be most expedient. So I think that those who act wrongly are neither wise nor temperate.'[2]

He used to say that not only justice but all the other moral virtues were wisdom. Just actions and any others proceeding from a virtuous motive were good and honourable; those who knew how to do them would choose to do nothing else, and those who did not understand them could not do

1. See Glossary.
2. I.e., all errors of conduct are errors of judgement. See Introduction, p. 8.

them, and if they tried to, failed. Thus it was the wise that performed good and honourable actions: those who were not wise could not, and if they tried to, failed. So, since just actions and all other good and honourable deeds were all done from a virtuous motive, obviously both justice and all the other moral virtues were wisdom.

He also said that madness was contrary to wisdom; yet he did not think that mere lack of knowledge was madness; but to be ignorant of oneself, and to form opinions about, and think that one comprehends, what one does not know – this in his view was very near to madness. He said that most people did not consider that those who blundered about things that were generally unknown were crazy, but they called crazy those who were mistaken about things that were generally known. If a man thinks that he is so tall that he stoops as he goes out through the city gates, or so strong that he tries to pick up houses or attempts any other feat which is quite obviously impossible, he is called crazy, but those who are only a little mistaken are not generally considered to be crazy. Just as it is only a strong desire that is called love, so it is only a serious eccentricity that is called madness.

Considering the nature of envy, he concluded that it was a species of grief, but not the sort that arises over the misfortunes of friends or the good fortune of enemies; he said that only those people were envious who were pained at the success of their friends. When some people expressed surprise that anyone who cared for a person should be vexed at his success, he reminded them that many people are so disposed towards certain others that they cannot ignore their troubles, but go to their help when they are unfortunate, and yet are annoyed when they are fortunate. This, he said, could not indeed happen to a sensible person, but was the regular experience of the foolish.

Considering the nature of leisure, he said that he found that most people occupied themselves in some way, because even playing draughts or making jokes was a kind of occupation; and all such people were, he said, at leisure: for it was open to them to go on to do something better. But nobody had leisure to go from better to worse; and if anyone did so, that person, he said, was acting wrongly, because he was not disengaged.

He said that it was not those who held the sceptre that were kings and rulers, nor those who were chosen by unauthorized persons, nor those who were appointed by lot, nor those who had gained their position by force or fraud, but those who knew how to rule. When anyone agreed that it was for the ruler to lay down what ought to be done and for the subject to obey, he used to point out that in a ship it is the man who knows that takes command, and that the owner and everybody else on board obeys the man who knows; and that in farming those who possess land, and in illness those who are ill, and in physical training those who are exercising their bodies, and all other persons who have anything that needs attention, if they think that they have the necessary knowledge, look after themselves; but otherwise they not only follow the advice of experts if they are on the spot, but call in their help if they are not, so that by taking their advice they may follow the right course. And he pointed out that in the case of wool-spinning women actually exercise control over men, because the former know how to do the work and the latter do not. If anyone objected that a despot can disregard good advice, he used to reply, 'How can he, when there is a penalty for disregarding it? Because in any case where a person disregards good advice he will presumably go wrong, and in going wrong he will pay the penalty.' And if anyone objected that a despot even has the power to put the wise man to death [3] he said, 'Do you suppose that the man who

3. Cf. the discussion in Plato, *Gorgias* 466B ff.

puts to death his most effective allies goes unpunished or pays only a casual penalty? Which do you think that a person who acts in this way would be more likely to do: escape the consequences or precipitate his own ruin?'

When he was asked what he thought was the best occupation for a man he replied, 'Efficient action';[4] and when he was further asked whether he considered good luck to be an occupation he replied, 'I regard luck and action as totally opposed to one another. I consider that coming upon something that you need without looking for it is good luck, but to do a thing well after learning and practising how to do it is (I think) efficient action; and it is those who make a practice of this that seem to me to be successful.'

He used to say that in every sphere of action those people were best and most favoured by the gods who did their work efficiently – whether in farming or in medicine or in politics; while the man who did nothing efficiently was neither good for anything nor favoured by the gods.

4. The Greek word is ambiguous: it can equally well mean 'success'.

CHAPTER TEN

Socrates now discusses how character and feeling are represented by the artists, and argues with an armourer about fit and proportion.

Parrhasius, the son of Evenor of Ephesus, was a celebrated painter who was working at Athens in the latter half of the fifth century. Cliton is otherwise unknown. Pistias seems to be the person referred to by Athenaeus (220E) as Piston.

It must be admitted that much of these conversations seems rather flat and obvious, but the technical description of the well-fitting corselet, and perhaps the whole conversation with Pistias, seem to be drawn from Xenophon's own experience.

AGAIN, if he was ever talking to one of those craftsmen who practise their craft professionally, he was helpful to them too. He paid a call one day on the painter Parrhasius and began to talk to him.

'Would you say, Parrhasius, that painting is copying the things that one sees? You painters represent hollows and heights, darkness and light, hard and soft, rough and smooth, young bodies and old ones by copying them with your pigments.'

'That's true,' said he.

'Also when you are painting beautiful figures, as it isn't easy to come across one single model who is beyond criticism in every detail, you combine the best features of each one of a number of models, and so convey the appearance of entirely beautiful bodies.'

'Yes, that is what we do.'

'Well, now, do you represent the personality, which is the most attractive and pleasing and friendly and desirable and lovable part of us? Or is it not a subject for representation at all?'

'How could it be, Socrates, when it has neither shape nor

colour nor any of the other qualities that you mentioned just now, and is not even visible at all?'

'Tell me, then,' said he, 'can a person look at other people in a friendly or unfriendly manner?'

'I believe so!'

'Then can this be represented in their expressions?'

'Certainly.'

'Do you think that those who care about their friends' good and bad fortune wear the same expressions on their faces as those who don't?'

'No indeed; they look glad at their friends' good fortune and dejected at their misfortune.'

'Is it possible to depict this too?'

'Certainly.'

'Then again, dignity and magnanimity, insignificance and meanness, sobriety and discretion, insolence and vulgarity show themselves both in the face and in the gestures of stationary and moving subjects.'

'True.'

'Can one represent these too?'

'Certainly.'

'Do you think it's more pleasant to see people who exhibit fine and good and admirable characters or those who exhibit base and bad and odious ones?'

'There's really no comparison, Socrates.'[1]

On another day he called on Clito the sculptor and got into conversation with him. 'I can see and appreciate, Clito,' he said, 'the variety you produce in your runners and wrestlers and boxers and all-in fighters; but the quality of seeming alive, which has the strongest visual appeal – how do you produce this in your statues?'

Clito didn't reply at once, because he didn't know what to say.

1. The implication is that painters should depict characters which are both pleasanter and more profitable to contemplate.

'Perhaps,' said Socrates, 'you make your statues more life-like by reproducing the appearance of living models.'

'Yes, indeed.'

'Do you make the various parts of the body seem more lifelike and convincing by representing them as depressed or raised, compressed or expanded, tautened or relaxed according to the pose of the model?'

'Certainly.'

'Doesn't it afford some pleasure just to see the feelings of people in action represented?'

'I suppose so,' he said.

'So you should represent the expression of warriors as threatening, and the faces of victors should be made to look joyful?'

'Definitely.'

'In that case,' said Socrates, 'the sculptor ought to make his works correspond to the type of character represented.'

He called on Pistias the armourer, and on being shown some well-made corselets, 'Upon my word,' he said, 'it's a splendid idea, Pistias, that the corselet should protect the parts of a man's body that need protection without preventing him from using his hands. But tell me, Pistias, why is it that you charge a higher price than other makers for your corselets although they are no stronger and cost no more to make?'

'Because mine are better proportioned, Socrates.'

'And is it by measurement or by weight that you display this proportion which you think enhances the value of your corselets? I presume that you don't make them all in the same or even in similar proportions, if you make them to fit.'

'Oh yes, I do,' he said. 'A corselet is no good without proportion.'

'Surely some people's bodies are well proportioned and some badly.'

'Quite so.'

'Then how do you make a corselet that fits a badly-proportioned body well-proportioned?'

'In the same way as I make it to fit. A corselet that fits *is* well-proportioned.'

'It seems to me,' said Socrates, 'that you are using the term "well-proportioned" not absolutely but in relation to the wearer, as you might say that a shield or a cloak is well-proportioned for anyone that it fits; and the same, apparently, with everything else, by your account. But perhaps fitting implies another important advantage.'

'If you've made a discovery, Socrates,' he said, 'tell me about it.'

'A corselet that fits irks you less by its weight than an equally heavy one that doesn't fit. A badly-fitting corselet either hangs entirely from the shoulders or presses severely on some other part of the body, and that makes it clumsy and uncomfortable. A well-fitting one has its weight distributed between the collar and shoulder bones, the shoulders, chest, back and abdomen; so that it seems almost more like an accessory part than something to carry.'

'That's exactly why I think my products give the best value. Some people, though, prefer to buy decorated and gilded corselets.'

'All the same,' said Socrates, 'if the consequence is that they buy misfits, it seems to me that they pay dearly for their decoration and gilding. But here's another point. The body doesn't always stay the same: sometimes it is bent and sometimes upright. How can precisely shaped corselets always fit?'

'They can't possibly.'

'When you talk of fitting you mean not what is precisely shaped but what is not uncomfortable to use.'

'You take the words out of my mouth, Socrates,' he said, 'and your grasp of the point is quite correct.'

CHAPTER ELEVEN

Socrates with some of his friends pays a call on the courtesan Theodote. This amusing conversation is in the same light-hearted vein as the Symposium. *There is nothing erotic about it: Socrates discusses with Theodote the technique of her profession and obligingly undertakes to help her; she plays up to him admirably (she is a refreshingly natural and intelligent person), and the conversation ends with an exchange of teasing civilities. The touch is remarkably delicate for Xenophon, who tends to spoil his effects by over-emphasis. Here there is just the suggestion (to anyone conversant with his views) that Socrates might introduce Theodote to a different conception of love; but there is no overt moralizing.*

At one time there was in the city a beautiful woman called Theodote who was of the sort to take up with anyone who asked her. One of the company had mentioned her, and remarked that her beauty was beyond description; and when he added that artists visited her to paint her picture, and that she let them see as much of her as was proper, 'In that case,' said Socrates, 'we ought to go and see her. We can't form a clear idea about what is beyond description from hearsay.'

'The sooner you all come with me the better,' said the informant.

Well, they went off to Theodote, found her posing for a painter, and took a good look at her. When the painter had finished, 'Gentlemen,' said Socrates, 'ought we to be more grateful to Theodote for letting us see her beauty, or she to us for looking at her? I suggest that if the display has been more to her advantage she ought to be grateful to us, and if the sight has been more to ours we ought to be grateful to her.

Somebody said, 'That's right.'

'Well, then,' he went on, 'she is already enjoying the tribute of our admiration, and when we have spread our report she will benefit still further. On the other hand we are now desirous of touching what we have seen; we shall go away with our emotions titillated; and when we have gone we shall feel an unsatisfied longing. The natural inference from this is that we are performing the service and she is receiving it.'

'I must say,' said Theodote, 'if that's how it is, I ought to be grateful to you for looking at me.'

Socrates could see that she herself was expensively got up, and that she had her mother with her, dressed and arrayed in no casual manner, and several pretty maids in attendance who similarly showed no sign of neglect; and that the house was lavishly appointed in all other respects. So he now said, 'Tell me, Theodote, have you got a farm?'

'Not I,' said she.

'Well, then, a house-property that brings in money?'

'Not a house either,' said she.

'Perhaps you have some slaves who work at a craft?'

'No, none.'

'Then how do you support yourself?'

'If anyone gets friendly with me and wants to be generous, that's how I get my living.'

'Upon my word, Theodote,' said Socrates, 'it's a splendid asset to have a lot of friends – much better than having a lot of sheep and goats and cattle. But tell me, do you leave it to chance whether a friend lights upon you, or do you devise something yourself?'

'How could I find a device to bring that about?' she asked.

'You could do it much more naturally than a spider. You know how spiders hunt to support themselves: they spin fine webs, don't they?, and feed on anything that flies into them.'

'Are you advising me,' she said, 'to weave some kind of snare too?'

'No; you mustn't expect to hunt lovers, who are the most valuable prey of all, so simply as that. Don't you see that even in hunting common game like hares people use various methods?[1] In the first place hares feed by night, so the hunters provide themselves with hounds trained for night work, and hunt them with these. Then because hares run away from their feeding-grounds when day comes, they acquire other hounds which find them by picking up the scent from the trails that they leave from the feeding-grounds to their forms. Then because they are swift-footed, so that they can escape by running even when sighted, the hunters further supply themselves with swift hounds to run them down. And because some of the hares escape even from these, people set up nets in their escape-paths, so that the hares may run into them and get entangled.'

'Well,' said Theodote, 'what method like that can I use to catch lovers?'

'Surely by providing yourself with a human hound to track down men of wealth and good taste, and after finding them to devise a means of driving them into your nets.'

'Nets!' said she; 'what nets have I got?'

'One, certainly,' said Socrates, 'which is very close-enfolding: your body. And in it is your mind, which teaches you how to look charming and talk gaily, and tells you that you must give a warm welcome to an attentive lover, but bolt the door against a fastidious one; that if a lover falls ill you must look after him devotedly; if he has a stroke of luck you must share his pleasure enthusiastically; and if he cares for you deeply you must gratify him wholeheartedly. As for loving, I am sure that you know how to love not only passively but with real affection; and you convince your lovers that you are fond of them, I know, not by words but by deeds.'

1. Here speaks Xenophon the country gentleman; cf. his *Cynegeticus* 6, 6 (but it may not be his at all).

'Honestly,' said Theodote, 'I don't use any of these methods.'

'Then again,' said Socrates, 'it's much better to keep one's human relationships natural and right. You can't capture or keep a friend by force; but by showing the creature kindness and giving it pleasure you can both catch it and keep it by you.'

'That's true,' she said.

'So in the first place,' said Socrates, 'when people care for you you should make only such demands of them as they can satisfy with a minimum of trouble. Then you should repay them by granting your favours in the same manner. In this way they are likely to become most attached to you, to go on loving you for the longest time, and to be most generous to you. And you are likely to give them most pleasure if you bestow your favours when they ask for them. You can see that even the most delightful dishes seem disagreeable if they are served before the appetite is ready, and if one has just had a full meal they actually cause disgust; whereas even inferior food served after hunger has been aroused seems quite attractive.'

'Very well,' said she, 'how am I to arouse hunger for what I have to give?'

'Why, surely,' said Socrates, 'if, when your admirers are indifferent, you neither offer nor make any reference to your favour until the satisfaction has passed and they feel the want again; and next, when they feel the want, if you encourage them by the most modest demeanour, and by dissembling your readiness to gratify them, and trying to avoid it until their eagerness reaches its climax; because the same favours are much more effective then than before the desire for them is aroused.'

Theodote said, 'Really, it's high time that you helped me in my hunt for lovers, Socrates.'

'And I will, believe me, if you persuade me.'

'How can I persuade you?'

'You'll look to that yourself,' he said, 'and you'll find a way, if you need any help from me.'

'Then come and see me often,' she said.

'Well, Theodote,' replied Socrates – poking fun at his own avoidance of public life – 'it's not very easy for me to find the time for it. I have a great deal of private and public business that keeps me occupied; and I have some girl friends[2] too who will never let me leave them by day or night, because they are learning from me about love-charms and spells.'

'Do you really know about them too, Socrates?' she asked.

'Why do you suppose that Apollodorus[3] here and Antisthenes never leave me? and that Cebes and Simmias come to visit me from Thebes? You may be sure that these effects aren't produced without a lot of love-charms and spells and magic wheels.'[4]

'Lend me your magic wheel, then, so that I may spin it first for you.'

'Certainly not,' said he. 'I don't want to be drawn to you; I want you to come to me.'

'Very well, I will,' said she. 'Only mind you let me in.'

'Yes, I'll let you in,' said Socrates, 'unless I have someone with me that I like better.'

2. He is of course using an ironical metaphor: he means the friends whom he is trying to instruct.

3. For these names see the Glossary.

4. According to Pindar, *Pythians* iv, 214, the magic wheel was invented by Aphrodite to win Jason's love for Medea: a bird called the wryneck (*iynx* in Greek) was spreadeagled on the four spokes of a wheel, which was then rotated. But in practice the bird seems to have been dispensed with. Cf. Theocritus, *Idyll* 2.

CHAPTER TWELVE

A discourse on the importance of physical fitness. If Socrates stated the theme, its zestful development may reasonably be attributed to Xenophon. Epigenes is probably the son of Antiphon of Cephisus; he was a friend of Socrates and was present at his trial and death (Plato, Apology 33E, Phaedo 59B).

SEEING that Epigenes, one of his regular companions, was in poor physical condition for a young man, he said, 'You're out of training, Epigenes.'

'I don't do physical training, Socrates,' he replied.

'But you ought to, just as much as a prospective competitor at Olympia.[1] Or do you think that the mortal struggle against her enemies in which Athens will sooner or later involve you doesn't matter? And yet in the hazards of war it's not uncommon for people to lose their lives through lack of fitness, or escape only ignominiously. For the same reason many are captured alive, and once captured either spend the rest of their lives, if fortune so wills, in the bitterest servitude, or after being subjected to the most cruel duress and paying in some cases a ransom greater than the sum of their possessions, live out their lives in want and misery. Many too win a bad reputation because their physical debility makes them appear to shirk danger. Perhaps you don't take these penalties of unfitness seriously, and assume that you can easily put up with that sort of thing? In my view, at any rate, the prospects that await a man who cares about his physical fitness are much easier and more pleasant. Or perhaps you think that unfitness is both healthier and in general more good for you than fitness, or are scornful of the results that fitness brings? In point

1. The great sanctuary of Zeus in Elis where the Olympic Games were held.

of fact the consequences of keeping oneself fit are entirely contrary to those of failing to do so.

'In the first place those who keep themselves fit are healthy and strong; and this means that many of them come through the conflicts of war with honour, and escape from all its dangers; many help their friends and do service to their country, and so earn gratitude and win great glory and achieve the most splendid honours, and consequently live out their lives with greater pleasure and distinction, and leave behind them a better start in life for their children. The fact that our country does not conduct military training at the public expense is no reason for individuals to neglect it; they should regard it no less seriously. You can take it from me that there is no feat of endurance, in fact no activity of any kind, in which you will be at a disadvantage from having your body better prepared for it. The body is involved in all human activities, and in all its uses it is very important that it should be as fit as possible. Even in the act of thinking, which is supposed to require least assistance from the body, everyone knows that serious mistakes often happen through physical ill health. Many people's minds are often so invaded, because of their poor physical condition, by forgetfulness, despondency, irritability and insanity that their knowledge is actually driven out of them. On the other hand those who are in good physical condition have ample cause for confidence and run no risk of any such misfortune on the score of debility. Their physical fitness is likely to conduce to results that are contrary to those of unfitness; results which a sane man would surely endure any hardships to secure. Besides, it is a shame to let oneself grow old through neglect before seeing how one can develop the maximum beauty and strength of body; and you can't have this experience if you are negligent, because these things don't normally happen by themselves.'

CHAPTER THIRTEEN

A selection of Socratic remonstrances and witticisms. Some of them seem distinctly heavy. No doubt a great many fabricated stories and sayings were attached to Socrates even in his lifetime, much more after his death: this is the common fate of eminent minds.

ONCE when somebody was angry because another person did not return his greeting Socrates said, 'It's funny that although you wouldn't have been angry if you had met a person in a rather poor physical state it upsets you to come across one in a rather rude state of mind.'

Somebody else said that he took no pleasure in eating.

'Acumenus[1] can tell you a good cure for that,' said Socrates.

'What sort of cure?' asked the other.

'To give up eating,' he replied. 'Once you've done that you'll find life not only more pleasant but cheaper and healthier.'

On another occasion somebody else said that the drinking-water at his house was warm.[2]

'Then whenever you want a warm bath it'll be ready for you.'

'But it's too cold to wash in.'

'Do your slaves object to drinking it and washing in it too?'

'Not at all,' said the man; 'in fact I've been surprised to see how contentedly they use it for both purposes.'

'Which is warmer to drink: the water in your house or the water in the temple of Asclepius?'[3]

1. A doctor-friend of Socrates: cf. Plato, *Phaedrus* 227A, 268A.

2. An abomination to Greek taste.

3. Better known by his Latinized name Aesculapius; he was a son of Apollo and a marvellous physician who became deified as the god of healing. The centre of his worship was at Epidaurus, but he had a shrine at Athens with a warm spring.

'The water in the temple of Asclepius.'

'And which is the colder for bathing: yours or the water at the shrine of Amphiaraus?'[4]

'The water at the shrine of Amphiaraus.'

'You should reflect, then,' said Socrates, 'that you look unpleasantly like being more fussy than a slave or an invalid.'

A man had punished a retainer severely, and Socrates asked why he was angry with his servant.

'Because he's as lazy as he is greedy, and as shy of work as he is fond of money.'

'Have you ever considered which of you needs the bigger thrashing – you or your servant?'

Somebody was afraid of travelling to Olympia.

'Why are you afraid of the journey?' asked Socrates. 'Don't you spend nearly the whole day walking when you're at home?[5] On your way to Olympia you will walk for a while and then have lunch; then walk for another while, have dinner and go to bed. Don't you realize that if you joined together, end to end, the walks that you take in five or six days, you would easily cover the distance from Athens to Olympia?[6] Besides, it is pleasanter to start a day too soon than to arrive too late. It's awkward to be forced to lengthen the stages of your journey too much, but to cover several stages in one day gives a great sense of relief. So it's better to hurry at the start than on the journey.'

When someone else said that he was exhausted after making a long journey Socrates asked him whether he was carrying baggage too. 'Good heavens, no,' he said; 'only my coat.'

4. A hero and seer who perished in the operation described by Aeschylus in his play *Seven against Thebes*. He had a shrine at Oropus near the east end of the Attic-Boeotian frontier.

5. This probably means 'at Athens' as distinct from 'abroad'.

6. Even by the shortest route (which involves some stiff climbing) this is about 150 miles.

'Were you travelling alone,' asked Socrates, 'or had you a servant with you?'

'Yes, I had.'

'Empty-handed or carrying something?'

'Carrying my bedding, naturally, and my other belongings.'

'And how did he get through the journey?'

'Better than I did, I should say.'

'Well, now,' said Socrates, 'if you had had to carry his luggage, what sort of state do you think you would have been in?'

'Very poor; or rather, I couldn't have brought it at all.'

'Do you really think it's natural for an athletic man to be so much less capable of effort than a boy servant?'

CHAPTER FOURTEEN

A chapter of anecdotes showing how Socrates helped people to improve their manners in relation to food and eating.

The situation described in the first example is familiar to us in the case of picnics and requires no comment, but the other anecdotes need a little explanation. Greek diet consisted (broadly speaking) of two elements: (a) bread, (b) something to give it a taste – rarely meat, usually fish, cheese, pickle or vegetables; the latter was called collectively opson, *translated here by 'relish' for want of a better word. Good manners demanded that you should take a little relish with or between each bit of bread, but to eat relish without any bread at all was a mark of sheer greed (so within living memory in this country it was considered decidedly odd not to take bread or potato in some form with meat, fish and egg).*

The final paragraph, which is intended to sum up the chapter, misfires because it turns on a piece of etymology that is not very obvious. The Greek verb in question does indeed mean to eat, but in the fuller sense of 'feast' or 'enjoy oneself', and with the accessory notions of health and comfort. Hence Socrates' contention that 'good living' consists in eating food which is wholesome and easily procured.

WHEN there was a communal dinner and some of the party brought more food than others, Socrates used to tell his servant either to pool the smaller contributions or to distribute them in equal shares. The result was that those who brought a large quantity felt ashamed to refuse a share of the pooled food and also felt ashamed to keep their food to themselves; so they put their food into the pool too. And since they got no more than those who brought a small quantity, they gave up spending large sums on food.

On one occasion Socrates noticed that one of the company

at dinner had stopped eating bread and was eating relish by itself. As the conversation was about the proper application of names to occupations, 'Can we say, gentlemen,' said Socrates, 'what sort of conduct gets a man called a relish-eater? Of course everybody eats relish with his bread if he's got any; but I presume that this is not enough to earn the name of relish-eater.'

'No, indeed,' said one of the company.

'Well, now,' he went on, 'if somebody eats relish by itself without bread, not with a view to training but for pleasure, do you think he is a relish-eater or not?'

'There could hardly be a better claim for the title.'

Another member of the company said, 'What about a man who eats a lot of relish with a little bread?'

'In my view,' said Socrates, 'it would be fair to call him a relish-eater too. And when everyone else is praying to the gods for a good harvest, I suppose he would pray for a good supply of relish.'

When Socrates said this the young man realized that the discussion had been aimed at him, and although he did not stop eating relish he took bread with it. Observing this, Socrates said, 'I want you who are sitting near to him to watch and see whether he will treat the bread as relish or the relish as bread.'

He once saw another of his dinner-companions sampling several kinds of relish with one piece of bread.[1] 'Could there be,' he asked, 'a form of epicurism more extravagant or more ruinous of good food than is practised by a person who eats several dishes at once and puts all kinds of flavourings into his mouth at the same time? By combining more ingredients than his cooks use he is acting more extravagantly; and since he combines what they refuse to combine, as being incompatible, if they are right, he is wrong, and is desecrating their

1. I.e., dipping it into several dishes.

art. And yet it is surely absurd for a man to engage the most expert cooks and then interfere with their menus when he doesn't even profess the art in question. Besides, there's another thing that happens to a man who has made a habit of eating several kinds of food at once. If he hasn't got several kinds he is likely to feel discontented through missing what he is accustomed to. On the other hand a man who has made a habit of helping down one piece of bread with one kind of relish could be content with one kind if more were not available.'

He also used to say that in Attic 'good living' was synonymous with 'eating', and that the qualification 'good' referred to eating foods which were innocuous to both mind and body, and not difficult to procure. Thus he regarded even good living as the privilege of those whose lives are well-ordered.

BOOK FOUR

CHAPTER ONE

The reader is again assured of the beneficial effect that Socrates had upon all his friends. It was their mental and moral qualities that attracted him, and he inferred these from their conduct. He was at pains to disillusion those who prided themselves on their natural ability or education.

As this chapter contains nothing new, it has been denounced as the work of an 'editor' of Xenophon's memoirs who wanted an introduction for the chapters which follow; but Xenophon was perfectly capable of writing it himself, and since it is quite in his manner he may be credited with the authorship.

SOCRATES was so helpful in every activity and in every way that anyone who considers the subject and estimates it fairly must see that nothing was more profitable than associating with Socrates and spending one's time with him in any place or circumstances. Indeed, even to recall him now that he is gone is no small help to those who have been used to live in his company and who accept his views.

His influence on his companions was just as salutary in his lighter moments as when he was serious. He would often say that he loved somebody; but anyone could see that what attracted him was the state of being gifted not with physical beauty but with excellence of mind and character. He inferred that his friends had natural talent from their learning quickly anything to which they applied their minds, and remembering what they had learned, and from their eagerness for any kind of instruction that enables one to manage a household or a community efficiently, and in general to be successful in one's dealings with people and in one's management of human affairs. He thought that anyone who had received this sort of training would not only be happy himself and manage his household well, but would be able to make other persons and communities happy too.

He did not approach everyone in the same way. If people thought that they were naturally talented and were scornful of instruction, he explained to them that the natures which are regarded as the best have the greatest need of training. He pointed out that the best-bred horses are spirited and lively, and that if they are broken in when they are quite young they become most manageable and better than any others; but if they grow up unbroken they are very difficult to control and worse than any others. Again, puppies of the best breeds which are tireless and eager to attack their prey,[1] if they are properly trained become very good hounds and most serviceable for hunting; but if they grow up untrained they become wild and erratic and very difficult to control. In the same way the best types of men, people with exceptional strength of mind and ability to carry through whatever they undertake, if they are educated and learn to do their duty, become excellent and most useful citizens, because they perform a great many important services; but if they grow up uneducated and ignorant they turn out worse and cause more harm than anybody. Not knowing how to decide where their duty lies, they often set their hands to wicked deeds; and since they are proud and overbearing they are difficult to restrain or divert from their course; and consequently they commit a great many serious crimes.

As for those who were proud of their wealth and thought that they had no need of education as well, but assumed that their riches would be quite enough to secure for them any result that they wanted and to win the esteem of their fellowmen, he tried to put sense into them by saying that a man was a fool if he expected to be able to distinguish beneficial and harmful activities without learning how to do so; and a fool

1. Cf. *Cynegeticus* 3, 11.

if, unable to draw this distinction but using his wealth to procure whatever he wanted, he nevertheless thought that he
would be able to act to his own advantage; and if he could not
act to his own advantage it was stupid to think that he was
fortunate and well or adequately provided for life; and also
stupid to think that he would be considered good for anything
because of his wealth if he had no knowledge, or that he
would enjoy popularity if he was considered good for
nothing.

CHAPTER TWO

*This long chapter describes how Socrates succeeded in convincing
Euthydemus that he was ignorant and needed instruction.*

*The account is impressive, especially as regards Socrates' cautious
approach, the details of which are convincingly vivid. When
Euthydemus has had his interest aroused and has disclosed that he
wants to enter politics, Socrates proceeds methodically to show him
that questions of right and wrong, and indeed value-judgements in
general, are much less straightforward than they seem. Forced into
contradictions, Euthydemus loses faith in himself but clings to
Socrates, who, satisfied that the elenchus is now complete, begins to
help his friend towards a more philosophical outlook.*

*The method of argument is authentic: it might be paralleled in
most of Plato's 'Socratic' dialogues. What is doubtful is whether
Euthydemus is a real person (see Glossary); the problem is probably
insoluble.*

I SHALL next describe what his attitude was towards those who
thought that they had received the best education and prided
themselves on their wisdom.

He discovered that the handsome Euthydemus had collected
a great many writings of the best-known poets and sophists,
and that consequently he now considered himself to be more
enlightened than anyone of his age, and entertained high hopes
of becoming unrivalled in eloquence and administrative
ability. So first of all, realizing that because of his youth
Euthydemus did not yet go into the market-place if he wanted
to conduct any business but took up his position in a saddler's
shop close by, Socrates went to the shop himself with some
of his friends. Someone opened the conversation by inquiring
whether it was through association with one of the sophists
or by natural talent that Themistocles rose so far above his

fellow-citizens that the state looked to him whenever it needed a man of action. Socrates wanted to stir up Euthydemus, and observed that it was silly to imagine that, although the lesser arts were not practised seriously without the help of competent teachers, the art of public administration, which was the greatest accomplishment of all, came to people of its own accord.

On another occasion when Euthydemus was present Socrates noticed that he was withdrawing from the group and taking care not to seem impressed by Socrates' wisdom. 'Gentlemen,' he said, 'it is easy to see from the way in which our friend Euthydemus spends his time that when he is old enough he won't refrain from advising the state on any political issue that comes up. And it seems to me that by carefully avoiding the appearance of learning anything from anybody he has provided himself with a splendid preface to his public speeches. Evidently when he begins to speak he will introduce what he has to say like this: "Gentlemen, I have never learned anything from anybody, nor have I sought the company of any persons whose abilities in speech and action I had heard of, nor have I troubled to acquire a teacher from among those who understand these matters. On the contrary I have consistently avoided not only learning anything from anybody but even giving the impression of doing so. However, I shall offer you whatever advice occurs to me of its own accord." Such an introduction would be appropriate for candidates applying for a public medical post. They could suitably begin their application in this way: "Gentlemen, I have never learned medicine from anyone, nor have I tried to secure any doctor as a teacher. I have consistently avoided not only learning anything from medical men, but even giving the impression of having learned this art. However, I ask you to give me this medical post. I shall try to learn by experimenting on you."'

This introduction made everybody present laugh.

It was now obvious that Euthydemus was paying attention to what Socrates was saying, although he was still careful not to say anything himself, thinking by his silence to invest himself with an air of discretion. Socrates wanted to stop him behaving like this, and said:

'I can't understand how it is that people who want to be competent performers on a stringed or wind instrument, or on horseback, or in any other similar skill, try to practise the desired accomplishment as continuously as possible, not only by themselves but under the supervision of acknowledged experts, going to all lengths in their anxiety to do nothing without these experts' advice, because they feel that they cannot otherwise earn recognition; whereas some of those who wish to become proficient in public speaking and administration expect to be able to do this of their own accord off-hand, without preparation or application. Yet political proficiency seems to be harder to achieve than the other kinds, inasmuch as more people pursue political ends and fewer achieve them. So obviously political ambition calls for more and closer application than other kinds.'

Socrates began by making observations of this sort in the hearing of Euthydemus. When he noticed that Euthydemus was enduring his comments more readily and listening with greater interest, he went alone to the saddler's shop, and when Euthydemus sat down near him he said, 'Tell me, Euthydemus, is it true what I hear, that you have collected a large number of books by reputed experts?'

'Indeed it is, Socrates,' replied Euthydemus, 'and I'm going on collecting them still, until I have got as many as I can.'

'Upon my word,' said Socrates, 'I do admire you for not preferring hoards of silver and gold to the possession of wisdom. Evidently you think that silver and gold make people no better, whereas the maxims of the wise enrich their possessors with moral goodness.'

Euthydemus cheered up as he heard this, thinking that Socrates approved of his method of pursuing wisdom; but when Socrates noted that he was pleased at this commendation, he said,

'What exactly is it that you want to become good at, Euthydemus, by collecting these books?'

When Euthydemus remained silent, wondering what he should reply, Socrates went on: 'Can it be medicine? There are a great many treatises written by doctors.'

'That's not my idea at all,' said Euthydemus.

'Perhaps you want to become an architect? That's another profession that calls for a skilled mind.'

'Not for my taste,' he said.

'Perhaps you are keen to become a good geometrician, like Theodorus?'[1]

'Not that either,' he said.

'Perhaps you want to be an astronomer?'

When he denied this too, 'Perhaps a reciter?[2] They say that you have got all the poems of Homer.'

'Certainly not,' he said. 'I know that professional reciters are word-perfect, but they have very little intelligence themselves.'[3]

At this Socrates said, 'You don't mean to tell me, Euthydemus, that you are aiming at that kind of proficiency that makes people politicians and administrators and capable of governing, and helpful both to others and to themselves?'

'I am very anxious to acquire this kind of proficiency,' replied Euthydemus.

1. Of Cyrene, a famous mathematician who taught Plato and is one of the characters in Plato's *Theaetetus* and *Sophist*.

2. A 'rhapsodist' or professional reciter of epic poetry; cf. Plato's *Ion*.

3. Cf. *Symposium* 3, 6.

'Dear me!' said Socrates, 'it's a most splendid and important art that you have set your heart on. It's the province of kings, and is called the art of kingship. But have you satisfied yourself whether it is possible to become good at these things without being morally good?'

'Certainly I have,' said he, 'and it's impossible to become even a good citizen without moral goodness.'

'Well,' said Socrates, 'have you achieved this?'

'I think, Socrates, that I should prove to be as moral a man as anyone.'

'Well, then: do moral men have "works" in the same way that carpenters do?'

'Yes, they have.'

'Carpenters can display their works; can moral men give an account of theirs too?'

'Are you suggesting,' said Euthydemus, 'that I can't give an account of the works of morality? I assure you that I can do it for the works of immorality too! There are plenty of them to be seen and heard every day.'

'Look here,' said Socrates, 'shall we write an R here and a W there, and then put down whatever we think is a right thing to do under R and whatever we think is wrong under W?'

'If you think there's any point in it, do that.'

Socrates wrote the letters as he had suggested.

'Is there such a thing in human life as telling lies?'

'Yes, there is.'

'On which side shall we put that?'

'Obviously under Wrong.'

'Is there such a thing as deception?'

'Certainly.'

'On which side shall we put that?'

'Obviously that too under Wrong.'

'What about doing injury?'

'That too.'

'And depriving of liberty?'

'That too.'

'And we shall list none of these under Right, Euthydemus?'

'No, that would be shocking.'

'Well, now, suppose that a man who has been appointed to a military command reduces a wicked and hostile city to slavery, shall we say that he is acting wrongly?'

'Of course not.'

'Shall we not say that he is acting rightly?'

'Certainly.'

'And supposing that he deceives them in fighting against them?'

'That is right too.'

'And if he steals and plunders their possessions will he not be acting rightly?'

'Certainly,' said he. 'I thought at first that you were asking about these actions only in relation to one's friends.'

'So perhaps all the things that we have put under Wrong ought to be put under Right too.'

'It looks like it.'

'Now that we have settled that, shall we revise our definition and say that it is right to do this sort of thing to enemies but wrong to do it to friends, and that to the latter one should be as sincere as possible; is that what you wish?'

'Very much so,' said Euthydemus.

'Well, then,' said Socrates, 'supposing that a general sees that his force is downhearted, and issues a false statement that help is approaching, and by this falsehood restores the morale of his men: on which side shall we put this deceit?'

'I think under Right.'

'And supposing that someone has a son who needs medical treatment and refuses to take his medicine: if the father surreptitiously gives him the medicine in his food and by this artifice restores him to health, where should we put this example of deceit?'

'I think in the same category.'

'Well, now, supposing that someone has a friend who is in a state of depression, and is afraid that he will make away with himself; and supposing that he covertly or openly removes a weapon from him – in which column should we put this?'

'Surely this ought to go under Right too.'

'Do you mean that we ought not *always* to deal straight-forwardly even with our friends?'

'Of course not,' said he. 'I am revising my earlier statement; that is, if I'm allowed to.'

'At any rate that's much better than making wrong as-sumptions,' said Socrates. 'But take the case of those who de-ceive their friends for their harm (so as not to leave even this aspect unconsidered); which is the worse morally, to do it voluntarily or involuntarily?'[4]

'Well, Socrates, I've lost confidence in my answers. Every-thing that I said before seems to be different now from what I thought then. However, take it that I say that voluntary is morally worse than involuntary deception.'

'Do you think that one can learn and understand morality as one can grammar?'

'Yes, I do.'

'Which do you consider to be more grammatical, the man who deliberately reads or writes wrongly or the man who does it involuntarily?'

'The former, I think, because he could do the same thing correctly if he wanted to.'

'So the man who deliberately writes incorrectly would be grammatical, and the one who does it involuntarily would be ungrammatical?'

4. Cf. the discussion of voluntary and involuntary error in Plato, *Hippias Minor* 373C ff.

'Of course.'

'Which knows what is right – the man who lies and deceives voluntarily or the one who does so involuntarily?'

'The latter, obviously.'

'You hold that the man who knows his grammar is more grammatical than the one who doesn't.'

'Yes.'

'And that the man who knows what is right is morally better than the one who doesn't?'

'Obviously. I think that is, in a sense, implied in what I said.'

'Well, now, take the man who wants to tell the truth, but never says the same about the same things: who in describing the same route calls it sometimes eastward and sometimes westward, and in totalling up an account makes the same total now bigger and now smaller – what do you think about him?'

'He's a clear case of not knowing what he thought he knew.'

'You know that there are people whom we call uneducated?'[5]

'Yes.'

'Because of their wisdom or because of their ignorance?'

'Obviously because of their ignorance.'

'Is it because they are ignorant of metal-working that they get their description?'

'Of course not.'

'Ignorant of carpentry, then?'

'Not that either.'

'Well, of cobbling?'

'None of those reasons; just the opposite. Most of the people who understand these crafts are uneducated.'

5. Literally 'slavish' or 'servile'; but the point is that most Greek slaves were non-Greek and therefore (from the Greek point of view) uneducated.

'Then does this name apply to those who don't know what is honourable and good and right?'

'So I believe.'

'In that case we ought to use every effort to avoid being uneducated.'

'By Heaven, Socrates,' said Euthydemus, 'I quite thought that I was following a philosophy of life which I believed would give me the right sort of education for one whose object is all-round perfection. But now you can't think how depressed I feel when I see that my past efforts have left me unable to answer questions even about the most important subjects, and with no other course available by which I can make myself better.'

Socrates said, 'Tell me, Euthydemus, have you ever been to Delphi?'

'Yes, indeed, twice.'

'Did you notice the inscription somewhere near the shrine, "Know thyself"?'[6]

'Yes, I did.'

'Did you ignore the inscription, or did you pay attention to it and try to examine what sort of person you were?'

'Dear me, no!' he said. 'You see, that was one thing I thought I did know. I could hardly have known anything else if I hadn't even been acquainted with myself.'

'Which do you think "knows himself" – the man who merely knows his own name, or the one who behaves like people buying a horse? They don't consider that they know a horse in which they are interested until they have satisfied themselves whether it's obedient or disobedient, strong or weak, swift or slow, and how it stands with respect to all the other qualities, desirable and undesirable in a horse with a view to its usefulness; and the man I am thinking of has in the

---

6. Cf. Plato, *Phaedrus* 230A.

same way ascertained his own ability by examining his own qualifications in respect of human relationships.'

'To my mind,' he said, 'the man who doesn't know his own ability is ignorant of himself.'

'And isn't this obvious,' said Socrates, 'that people derive most of their benefits from knowing themselves, and most of their misfortunes from being self-deceived? Those who know themselves know what is appropriate for them and can distinguish what they can and cannot do; and by doing what they understand they both supply their needs and enjoy success, while by refraining from doing things that they don't understand they avoid making mistakes and escape misfortune. Self-knowledge also enables them to judge the quality of others; and it is through their relations with others that they provide themselves with what is good and guard against what is bad for them. Those who do *not* know themselves and are totally deceived about their own ability are in just the same position with regard to other people and the rest of human affairs. They don't know what they want or what they are doing or what means they are using; and through making gross mistakes about all these they miss the good things and get into trouble. People who know what they are doing succeed in their activities and become famous and respected. Those who are like them gladly associate with them, while those who are unsuccessful in their affairs are anxious for these men to make decisions for them and to represent their interests, and pin to them their hopes of prosperity, and for all these reasons regard them with special affection. But those who don't know what they are doing make bad choices and fail in their attempts, and so not only suffer loss and punishment in respect of the actions themselves but damage their reputations in consequence, and get themselves laughed at, and live despised and unhonoured. You can see, too, that any states which have gone to war with stronger ones through not knowing their own capability either lose their territory or exchange freedom for slavery.'

Euthydemus said, 'You can take it from me, Socrates, that I quite recognize the importance of knowing oneself. But I am looking to you in the hope that you may be willing to explain to me at what point one should begin self-examination.'

'You are quite clear in your mind, I suppose,' said Socrates, 'what things are good and what are bad?'

'Certainly,' he said, 'if I don't even know that I should be worse than illiterate.'

'Come on, then, and expound them to me.'

'Well, that's not difficult. In the first place I think that health is a good thing in itself, and sickness an evil. Then the things conducive to each of these: drinks and foods and occupations that promote health are good, and those that cause illness are bad.'

'Surely even health and illness may be good things when they have a good result and bad when they have a bad one.'

'When could health have a bad result and disease a good one?'

'Why, to be sure,' said Socrates, 'in the case of a shameful expedition or a disastrous voyage or many other such events, when those who have taken part because they were able-bodied have perished, while those who have been excluded by infirmity have escaped.'

'True. But you see that in the case of beneficial activities too some people participate through fitness and others are excluded by infirmity.'

'Then if these things are sometimes beneficial and sometimes harmful, are they any more good than bad?'

'Not a bit, it seems, according to your argument. But surely wisdom, Socrates, is beyond all question a good thing. What action is there that a person would not perform better if he is wise than if he were ignorant?'

'Why, haven't you heard of Daedalus,' said Socrates, 'how he was captured by Minos because of his skill and compelled to serve him, and was deprived at the same time of his country and of his liberty, and how when he tried to escape with his son he both lost the boy and didn't even reach safety himself, but was carried away into a hostile country and there became a slave again?'

'That is certainly the story.'[7]

'And haven't you heard of the fate of Palamedes?[8] All the poets sing of how he fell a victim to Odysseus' jealousy because of his cleverness.'

'That again is the story.'

'And how many[9] other people do you think owe it to their cleverness that they have been carried off to the king of Persia, and served there as slaves?'

'It looks as if the most unquestionable good was happiness, Socrates.'

'Provided that it isn't composed of questionable goods, Euthydemus.'

'Why, what constituent of happiness could be questionable?'

'None; unless we include in it beauty or strength or wealth or fame or something else of that kind.'

'But we certainly shall include them. How could anyone be happy without them?'

'Then I assure you that we shall be including constituents

---

7. Some of the details are unusual: see Glossary.

8. One of the Greeks who attacked Troy. He was credited with the invention of letters and numbers. He exposed Odysseus' attempt to evade military service, and in revenge Odysseus, by forged evidence, got him executed for treason (Plato, *Apology* 41B; *Republic* 522D; Virgil, *Aeneid* ii, 81 ff.).

9. Probably plenty, but the often-quoted example of Democedes is not a good one, because his appointment as chief physician to Darius could be regarded as highly enviable (Herodotus iii, 129 ff.).

from which many unpleasant consequences follow for mankind. Beauty often brings disaster through the excitement
aroused by physical attraction; wealth often causes ruin
through self-indulgence or the covetousness of others; fame
and political power often lead to great calamities.'

'Really,' said Euthydemus, 'if I'm not even right in praising
happiness, I must admit that I don't even know what to pray
to the gods for.'

'Well,' said Socrates, 'probably you haven't so much as
considered the question, because you were so confident in
your knowledge. But since you are proposing to be a leader
in a city with a popular government, obviously you know
what popular government is.'

'Perfectly, of course.'

'Do you think it's possible to know popular government
without knowing the people?'

'No, indeed I don't.'

'So you know what the people is?'

'I believe so.'

'And what do you think the people is?'

'The poor among the citizens.'

'So you know the poor also?'

'Of course.'

'Then do you know the rich too?'

'No less well than the poor.'

'What sort of persons do you call "poor" and "rich"?'

'I suppose I call those who have not got enough to pay for
what they need, poor; and those who have more than enough,
rich.'

'Have you noticed that some of those who have very little
not only find it enough but actually save out of it, and that for
some a great many possessions are not enough?'

'Yes, indeed,' said Euthydemus, 'you are quite right to re-
mind me; I know even some despots who are driven to do

wrong because they haven't enough, just like the neediest classes.'

'Well, then,' said Socrates, 'granted that this is so, we shall class the despots among the people, and those who have few possessions among the rich, if they are good managers.'

Euthydemus said, 'I'm forced to admit that too. Evidently the fault lies with my own incompetence; and I am considering whether it may be best to keep my mouth shut. It looks as if I knew absolutely nothing.'

He went away very much dejected, because he had come to despise himself, and felt that he really was a blockhead.

Many of those who were treated in this way by Socrates stopped going to see him; these he considered to lack resolution. But Euthydemus decided that he would never become a person of any importance unless he associated with Socrates as much as possible; and from that time onwards he never left him unless he was obliged to, and he even copied some of Socrates' practices. When Socrates realized that Euthydemus was in this frame of mind he stopped teasing him and explained as simply and precisely as he could what he thought it was necessary for Euthydemus to know, and what lines of action were best for him to follow.

CHAPTER THREE

The next three chapters, or parts of them, have incurred much sus-
picion because (a) they contain repetitions or amplifications of what
has been said already, (b) they express or presuppose views (such
as the discussion of Providence in ch. 3) which seem more appro-
priate for a post-Aristotelian philosopher. But neither reason is de-
cisive. The effective arrangement of subject-matter was always
difficult for ancient writers, who not only lacked card-indexes but had
no means even of giving accurate references; division into chapters
and sections was quite a late invention, and writing on rolls (as
Greeks did at least until Hellenistic times) they had not even pages
to help them – only their memories, some notes on waxed tablets,
and perhaps something in the nature of a rough draft written on the
back of an old roll. Few modern authors would care to write a
serious work under such conditions. The wonder is how (say) a sub-
stantial Platonic dialogue with a coherent train of thought running
through it was composed at all. Xenophon, for all his military effi-
ciency, was not very good at this sort of thing; and what strike us as
flaws may be due to his imperfect (and perhaps incomplete) editing.
As for the doctrines, we don't know how much reached Stoicism
through Cynicism and its founder Antisthenes from Socrates him-
self. It may be objected that Socrates is unlikely to have delivered
such a detailed discourse involving so much observation and reflec-
tion; but he was certainly capable of doing so, and if we are to attach
any weight to Plato's evidence in Phaedo 97D–99C, *he took a very*
poor view of attempts to explain the universe on a mechanistic basis.
It seems best, therefore, to regard the doctrines as possibly Socratic.

The chapter is written with liveliness and conviction. It is still
worth reading, especially by those who are so credulous as to suppose
that the irrational can – even by the aid of an infinity of failures –
generate reason.

For a possible change in Euthydemus' status see the Glossary.

HE was in no hurry for his associates to become eloquent or capable or inventive; he thought that they ought first to acquire self-control, because he considered that without this the possession of those other faculties made them more unscrupulous and more capable of mischief.

In the first place, then, he tried to make his associates think rightly about religion. Different people were present at different discourses of his on this subject, and recorded them; I was present when he was having the following discussion with Euthydemus.

'Tell me, Euthydemus,' he said, 'has it ever occurred to you to reflect how carefully the gods have supplied all human needs?'

'No, as a matter of fact it hasn't,' said he.

'Well, you know that in the first place we need light, with which the gods supply us.'

'Certainly; without it we should be no better than blind for all the good our eyes could do us.'

'Then we also need rest; and they provide us with night as the best possible time for it.'

'We ought to be very grateful for that too.'

'And since the sun is bright and enables us to distinguish the times of the day, as well as everything else, while the night because of its darkness is more obscure, they have made stars shine in the night which inform us how the time is passing, and so enable us to do many of the things that we need to do. Isn't that so?'

'Yes, it is.'

'Then the moon marks us the divisions not only of the night but of the month.'

'Quite so.'

'There is also the fact that we need food, and the gods produce this from the earth, providing for the purpose appropriate seasons, which supply us with all kinds not only of necessaries but also of enjoyments.'

'That is very kind of them too.'

'And the fact that they give us water, which is so precious that it helps the earth and the seasons to make germinate and grow everything that is useful to us, and helps also to feed us ourselves, and by combining with all the things that feed us makes them more digestible and beneficial and agreeable; and because we need a great deal of it, they supply it in the greatest possible abundance.'

'This too shows their forethought.'

'And their providing us with fire as an ally against cold and darkness and as a partner in every art and in supplying all the things that people prepare for their own convenience. To put it briefly, of all the aids for living with which people equip themselves, not one of any importance is independent of fire.'

'That is another outstanding example of kindness.'

'And the fact that after the winter solstice the sun comes nearer, ripening some things and drying up others which have passed their prime; and that after finishing this task it comes no closer, but turns back for fear of injuring us by too much heat. And then when as it recedes again it reaches the point where even we can see that if it recedes any further we shall be frozen stiff by the cold, it turns again and approaches, so that it traverses just that part of the heavens in which it can do us most good.'

'Yes, indeed,' he said, 'that too gives a very strong impression of happening for the benefit of mankind.'

'And then, since it is also plain that we could not endure either the heat or the cold if it came on suddenly, the fact that the sun approaches and recedes so gradually that we don't notice that we are passing into either extreme of temperature.'

'I have been wondering already,' said Euthydemus, 'whether the gods have any function other than looking after men. My only difficulty is that the animals share these benefits as well.'

'Naturally,' said Socrates, 'because it's obvious, isn't it, that animals too are born and reared for the benefit of mankind? What other creature enjoys so many benefits as man does from goats and sheep and cattle and horses and donkeys? More, it seems to me, than from plants. At any rate people obtain food and profit from the former no less than from the latter; and there are many tribes which don't use the produce of the earth for food, but support themselves on the milk and cheese and flesh of their herds; and all nations tame and domesticate useful animals and employ their help for war and for many other purposes.'

'I agree with you about that too,' he said. 'I observe that even those animals which are much stronger than ourselves are brought so far under human control that people use them just as they like.'

'And what of the fact that they have equipped us with senses corresponding to the different kinds of beautiful and beneficial objects that surround us, so that by their help we can enjoy all good things? And the fact that they have implanted in us reason, which enables us to reckon up and remember our sensations, and so discover the effects of each class of objects, and devise various means for enjoying what is good and avoiding what is bad for us? Then there is their gift of communication, which enables us through instruction to share reciprocally with others everything that is good, and to enact laws and live in organized communities.'

'There is every reason to suppose, Socrates, that the gods show great concern for human beings.'

'Then there is their direct assistance in a sphere in which we are incompetent, that is in foreseeing our future interests; by means of prophecy they reveal to those who consult them what is going to happen, and explain how it can be turned to the best advantage.'

'And they seem to be on even friendlier terms with you

than with the rest, Socrates, if it is true that they forewarn[1] you
what to do and what not to do, without even being asked.'

'You will discover for yourself that what I say is true if
instead of waiting until you see the gods with your own eyes
you are content to worship and honour them on the evidence
of their works. You should reflect that the gods intimate as
much themselves. They give us good gifts, but never reveal
themselves in any act of giving; and in particular he who[2]
controls and regulates the whole universe, with all its good
and beautiful contents, which he ceaselessly supplies for our
use, fresh and healthy and unmarred by age, obeying his
commands unfailingly and faster than thought; he can be
seen to be carrying out the greatest works, but in the detailed
administration he is invisible to our eyes.[3] Reflect that the sun,
which is supposed to be manifest to all, does not permit
human beings to regard him directly: anyone who attempts
to observe him without due reverence is deprived of sight.
Even the agents of the gods, you will find, are invisible. The
thunderbolt is obviously discharged from above and over-
comes everything that it meets; but neither in its approach
nor at the moment of impact nor in its withdrawal can it be
seen. Winds are themselves invisible, but their effects are plain
to us and we can perceive their approach. Moreover, there is
the human soul, which partakes of divinity if anything else
human does; that it is the ruling part[4] of us is evident, but even
it cannot be seen. You should lay this to heart, and not despise
things that are unseen, but appreciate their power from the
effects of it, and honour the Deity.'

1. Cf. i, 1, 4; 4, 15.

2. This supreme deity might suggest the Stoic Zeus; but such a concept was certainly achieved by Plato (e.g. *Sophist* 265B–E, *Politicus*
269C–E), *Timaeus* 30), and why not by Socrates?

3. The effects of his activity are seen, but not his actions.

4. This recalls the Stoic *hegemonicon*; but the primacy of soul is a
doctrine at least as old as Plato (*Phaedo* 94).

'Speaking for myself, Socrates,' said Euthydemus, 'I am quite sure that I shall not disregard the Deity even in a small degree. What does depress me is that it seems to me that no human being could ever repay the goodness of the gods towards us by adequate gratitude.'

'Don't feel depressed about that, Euthydemus,' said Socrates. 'You can see that the god at Delphi, when he is asked how one can show gratitude to the gods, replies "By the law of the state." And I presume that it is the law everywhere to please the gods to the best of one's power by sacrificial offerings.⁵ Well, then, how can we honour them better and more devoutly than by doing as they themselves direct? But one must not fall short of one's capacity; when a man does this it is surely obvious that he is not honouring the gods. So if one consistently honours the gods to the best of his power he may feel confident and expect the greatest blessings. It wouldn't be sensible to expect greater ones from any other source than from those who can grant the greatest benefits, or on any other ground than that of pleasing them. And how can one please them better than by the greatest possible obedience?'

By enunciating such principles as these and by putting them into practice himself he made his associates more devout and self-disciplined.

5. Cf. i, 3, 3.

CHAPTER FOUR

The chapter consists of four introductory sections and a discussion with Hippias about morality and law. The former have been thought to be spurious, partly because they contain repetitions or amplifications of what has been said already, partly on the more solid ground that emotional appeals to the jury seem to have been perfectly legitimate in Xenophon's day, although they were later prohibited. But it is hard to believe that at any period an actually illegal procedure was generally accepted in the courts; so either Xenophon (or his 'editor') has written carelessly or the illegality was felt only by Socrates himself. The dialogue with Hippias also has difficulties. In the main it reads like a normal Socratic dialogue, apart from the encomium on obedience to the laws (sections 15–18), which is perhaps just an ill-timed display of Xenophon's popular rhetoric. But it is strange to find an argument with Hippias interrupting a sort of course of instruction for Euthydemus; and the argument to prove that incest brings its own punishment is distinctly feeble. See also the footnotes. Certainly if the chapter is by Xenophon it is not one of his happiest efforts.

As for his views about what is right, so far from concealing them he demonstrated them by his actions. In all his personal relationships he was law-abiding and helpful; in public life he obeyed the authorities in respect of their lawful requirements, both in civil affairs and on military service, so punctiliously that he was conspicuous for exceptional loyalty. When he was appointed president in the Assembly[1] he did not permit the people to pass an illegal motion, but in support of the law he resisted a popular outburst which no other man, I suppose, could have withstood. He disobeyed the illegal orders of the Thirty: when they not only forbade him to con-

1. Cf. i, 1, 18.

verse with the young[2] but instructed him, with some others, to arrest a citizen[3] for execution, he alone disobeyed the instruction on the ground that it was illegal. When he was facing prosecution by Meletus he rejected as illegal the usual practice in courts of law. All other accused persons used to address the jury ingratiatingly and flatter them and appeal to them illegally, and many of them by this sort of behaviour often secured an acquittal. But although Socrates might easily have been acquitted if he had made even a moderate concession to common practice, he chose to abide by the law and die rather than break it and live.[4]

He actually expressed these convictions on many occasions to others; and in particular I know that one day he had the following discussion about right conduct with Hippias[5] of Elis. Hippias had arrived at Athens after a long absence and joined Socrates just as he was saying to some of his friends how remarkable it was that if one wanted to have somebody taught cobbling or joinery or metal-work or horsemanship there was no difficulty about knowing where to send him for this purpose, but if one wanted to learn oneself what is right, or to have a son or a slave taught this knowledge, one did not know where to go in order to get it. When Hippias heard this he said playfully, 'Dear me, Socrates, are you still saying the same things that I heard you say all that time ago?'

Socrates replied, 'Yes, and what is stranger still, Hippias, I'm not only saying the same things but about the same subjects. You, no doubt, because of your wide learning, never say the same thing about the same subject.'

'To be sure,' he said, 'I always try to say something new.'

'Even about facts that you know? I mean, if somebody asks

2. Cf. i, 2, 32 ff.
3. Leon of Salamis; cf. *Hellenica* ii, 3, 39; Plato, *Apology* 32C–D.
4. Cf. Plato, *Apology* 38D–E.
5. See Glossary.

you how many letters there are in "Socrates", and what they are; do you try to say something different now from what you said before? or if you are asked about numbers, whether twice five is ten, don't you give the same answer now as before?'

'About things like these, Socrates, I always make the same statements, just as you do; but about what is right I am quite confident that I have something to say that neither you nor anyone else could contradict.'

'Dear me!' said Socrates, 'you certainly claim to have made a valuable discovery if it will stop jurymen from disagreeing over their verdicts, and ordinary citizens from arguing and litigating and rioting about their rights, and stop states from disputing and going to war about theirs. For my part I don't know how I can tear myself away from you before hearing about this priceless discovery from the man who made it.'

'No, no,' said Hippias, 'you shan't hear about it until you have told us your view about what is right. You content yourself with making fun of other people by questioning them all and arguing them down, while you won't state your own case or disclose your own opinions to anyone about anything.'

'Why, Hippias,' he said, 'aren't you aware that I never stop expounding what I think is right?'

'I should like to know what this account of yours is.'

'If I don't expound my views in a formal account I do so by my conduct. Don't you think that actions are more reliable evidence than words?'

'Much more, of course. People often say what is right and do what is wrong; but nobody can be in the wrong if he is doing what is right.'

'Well, then: have you ever known me give false evidence or lay malicious information or stir up trouble between friends or in the state, or do anything else that is wrong?'

'No, I haven't,' said he.

'And refraining from what is wrong is right, don't you think?'

'I can see, Socrates, that you are still trying to avoid explaining about what you think "right" means. You are describing not what right-minded people do but what they don't do.'

'Well,' said Socrates, 'I should have thought that to refuse to do wrong was a sufficient demonstration of moral rectitude. But if you don't agree, see whether you like this better. I say that what is lawful is right.'

'Do you mean that "lawful" and "right" are the same, Socrates?'

'Yes, I do,' said he.

'I really don't feel clear what you mean by "lawful" and "right".'

'You know what is meant by a country's laws?'

'Yes.'

'And what do you think they are?'

'What the citizens have had recorded after agreement about what they ought to do and what they ought to refrain from.'

'So a law-abiding[6] person would be one who orders his life in the community in accordance with these, and a lawless person one who transgresses them?'

'Certainly,' said he.

'So a person who obeyed them would be doing what is right, and one who disobeyed them what is wrong?'

'Certainly.'

'So the person who did what was right would be right, and the one who did wrong would be wrong?'

'Of course.'

6. Greek uses the same adjective *nomimos* to mean 'lawful' of things and 'law-abiding' of people.

'Then a law-abiding person is right, and a lawless one wrong.'

Hippias objected, 'How can one regard laws or obedience to them as a serious thing when the very same people who enacted them often repudiate and alter them?'[7]

'As a matter of fact,' said Socrates, 'states often undertake a war and then make peace.'

'Very true.'

'Do you think there is any difference,' he said, 'between belittling obedience to the laws on the ground that the laws may be repealed, and criticizing good discipline in time of war because peace may be made? Or do you actually find fault with those who help their country whole-heartedly in time of war?'

'No, I certainly don't,' he said.

'Are you aware,' said Socrates, 'that Lycurgus[8] the Lacedaemonian would have made Sparta no better than any other city if he had not inculcated in it the greatest obedience to the laws? Don't you know that the best ministers of state are those who are most efficient in making the people obey the laws? and that a city in which the people are most obedient to the laws has the best life in time of peace and is irresistible in war? And then concord is accepted to be the greatest blessing in a state, and very commonly in a state the senate[9] and aristocracy call upon the citizens to agree; and everywhere in

7. A good example of the critical attitude adopted by many sophists towards accepted beliefs; cf. Thrasymachus in Plato, *Republic* 338. Xenophon's Socrates makes an inept reply. He should have pointed out at once (instead of drawing later, in §19, a rather artificial distinction between written and unwritten laws) that some laws, e.g. those designed to protect people and property, are indispensable for a civilized society, while others have only a temporary purpose or validity and can be repealed when this has ceased.

8. Traditional founder of the Spartan constitution and possibly a real person of the seventh century B.C.

9. The Greek word is the official name for the senate at Sparta.

Greece there is a law laid down that the citizens take an oath to agree, and everywhere this oath is taken. I presume that the purpose of this is not that the citizens may come to the same decision about plays, or praise the same musicians, or choose the same poets, or take pleasure in the same things, but that they may obey the laws; because it is when the inhabitants abide by these that countries become strongest and happiest, but without agreement a state cannot be well organized nor a household well managed.

'And in private life how can anyone incur less punishment or more honour from the state than by obeying the laws? How could he be less likely to lose or more likely to win in the courts? To whom would one more confidently entrust one's money or one's sons and daughters? Whom would the state as a whole consider more dependable than the law-abiding man? and from whom would parents or relations or servants or friends or fellow-countrymen or foreigners be more likely to obtain their rights? To whom would an enemy more readily entrust the making of truces or treaties or terms of peace? To whom would people be more willing to ally themselves than to the law-abiding man? and to whom would allies more readily entrust supreme command or the defence of a fortress or the protection of cities? From whom would a benefactor expect to receive more gratitude than from a law-abiding man? and whom would one be more inclined to benefit than a person from whom one anticipates a return of gratitude? Whom would one wish more to have for a friend, or less to have for an enemy? Whom would one be less likely to fight than the man whom one would wish most to be one's friend and least to be one's enemy, and to whom the largest number wished to be friends and allies, and the smallest number enemies and foes? Personally, Hippias, I express the view that lawful and right are the same. If you hold the opposite view, explain it to me.'

'No, really, Socrates,' said Hippias, 'I don't think I do hold the opposite view to yours about what is right.'

'Do you know any unwritten laws,[10] Hippias?' he asked.

'Yes; those which are observed in every country with respect to the same circumstances.'

'Can you assert that it was men that laid them down?'

'How could it be, considering that they couldn't all meet together and don't speak the same language?'

'Then who do you think are the authors of these laws?'

'I suppose that these laws were ordained for men by gods. At any rate among all peoples the first established custom is to worship gods.'

'Isn't it a custom everywhere also to honour parents?'

'Yes, that too.'

'And that parents should not copulate with their children or children with their parents?'

'I don't think that this is a god-given law like the others, Socrates.'

'Why? tell me.'

'Because I observe that some people break it.'

'In point of fact,' he said, 'they break a good many other laws. But those who transgress the laws laid down by the gods pay a penalty which is quite inescapable in the way that some transgressors of man-made laws escape paying the penalty, some by escaping detection and others by the use of force.'

'Why, Socrates, what penalty cannot be escaped by parents who copulate with their children or children with their parents?'

'The greatest of all, I can tell you. What greater misfortune could happen to human beings in the procreation of children than to procreate them badly?'

10. The concept was not uncommon; cf. Sophocles, *Antigone* 454 (and *Oedipus Tyrannus* 865 ff.); Plato, *Laws* 838; Demosthenes, *De Corona* 275.

'Why should they procreate them badly,' said Hippias, 'seeing that there is no reason why the fathers should not be good themselves and beget them on good mothers?'

'Because surely the partners in procreation ought not only to be good but at their physical prime.[11] Or do you suppose that the seed of those who are in their prime is no different from that of those who have not yet reached it or who have already passed it?'

'No, indeed,' he said, 'it isn't likely that there is no difference.'

'Which is the better, then?'

'Obviously the seed of those who are in their prime.'

'So that of the others is not of high quality.'

'It is certainly not likely to be.'

'Then one ought not to procreate under these conditions.'

'No, indeed.'

'So those who do so are procreating under unsatisfactory conditions.'

'So it seems to me.'

'Who else could procreate badly if not these?'

'I accept your view about this too.'

'Well, now: isn't it customary everywhere to repay benefits?'

'Yes, it is,' he said; 'but this is transgressed too.'

'Don't those who transgress it pay the penalty as well, by being deprived of good friends and being compelled to pursue the company of people who dislike them? Isn't it a fact that people who do good to those who have contact with them are good friends, and that those who don't repay their benefactors are disliked by them for their ingratitude, and at

11. He seems to assume a very short period. Plato's eugenic theory (*Republic* 460E) reckons 25–55 as the prime for males and 20–40 as the prime for females, which allows ample margin. But the argument is obviously invalid and unworthy of Socrates.

the same time pursue them especially because of the special benefit to be had from their company?'

'Certainly, Socrates,' he said, 'all this looks like the work of the gods. That the laws themselves should entail the appropriate penalties for their transgressors seems to me to imply a law-giver of more than human excellence.'

'Well, then, Hippias, do you think that the gods' legislation is right or other than right?'

'Certainly not other than right. It's hard to see how anyone else could lay down what is right if a god couldn't.'

'So it follows, Hippias, that the gods are satisfied that "right" and "lawful" mean the same.'

By this sort of conversation and conduct he made those who came into contact with him better men.

CHAPTER FIVE

Socrates promoted his friends' physical and mental fitness partly by example and partly by convincing them of the importance of self-discipline, as in the following conversation with Euthydemus.

I SHALL now tell how he made his associates more efficient. Believing that self-discipline was a good thing for anyone to have who intended to achieve a creditable result, in the first place he let his companions see clearly that he himself kept the strictest training that anyone could; and in the second, in his conversation he was always urging his companions on to self-discipline. He was always constantly mindful himself, and reminding all his companions, of the things that are conducive to moral goodness; and I know that he once had a discussion about self-discipline with Euthydemus to the following effect:

'Tell me, Euthydemus,' he said, 'do you think that liberty is a fine and splendid possession both for an individual and for a state?'

'Yes, in the highest possible degree.'

'If a man is governed by the pleasures of the body and because of them cannot act as is best, do you think that he is a free man?'

'Far from it.'

'Presumably you say that because you think it is the mark of a free man to act in the best way; and consequently that to have impulses to prevent you from so acting is unworthy of a free man.'

'Absolutely,' he said.

'So it seems to you that those who have no self-control are absolutely unworthy of the name of free men?'

'It does indeed, naturally.'

'Do you think that these people are merely prevented from acting in the best way, or that they are actually forced to do the most disgraceful things?'

'In my opinion,' he said, 'they are just as much compelled to do the one as they are prevented from doing the other.'

'And what sort of masters do you think those are who prevent the best actions and compel the worst?'

'Surely the worst possible,' he said.

'And what do you consider to be the worst form of servitude?'

'I think it is servitude under the worst masters.'

'So self-indulgent people endure the worst form of servitude.'

'That's my opinion,' he said.

'Don't you think that self-indulgence debars people from wisdom, which is the greatest good, and drives them into the opposite state? Don't you think that, by dragging them off in pursuit of pleasure, it prevents them from studying and apprehending their real interests; and that it often confuses their perception of good and bad alternatives and makes them choose the worse instead of the better?'

'That does happen,' said he.

'And who, Euthydemus, can we say has less concern with self-discipline than the self-indulgent man? because surely the effects of self-discipline and of self-indulgence are directly opposed.'

'I admit that too,' he said.

'Do you think that anything is more likely to hinder one from devoting oneself to the proper objects than self-indulgence?'

'No, I don't.'

'Do you think there is anything worse for a man than that which makes him choose what is bad for him instead of what is good, and persuades him to cultivate the former and disregard the latter, and compels him to behave in the opposite way to that which is adopted by sensible people?'

'No, nothing,' said he.

'Isn't it likely that self-discipline brings results, for those who practise it, which are opposite to those of self-indulgence?'

'Certainly.'

'Isn't it also likely that the cause of these opposite results is supremely good?'

'Yes, it is,' he said.

'So it looks as if self-discipline were the best thing for a man.'

'Very likely, Socrates,' he said.

'Have you ever reflected on this, Euthydemus?'

'On what?' he asked.

'The fact that although self-indulgence is supposed to be the sole guide to pleasure it cannot take us there itself; it is self-discipline, above all things, that causes pleasure.'

'How so?' he asked.

'Self-indulgence doesn't allow us to endure hunger or thirst or sexual desire or sleeplessness, which are the only things that make eating and drinking and sexual intercourse pleasurable, and likewise rest and sleep; it doesn't permit us to hold out and wait for the moment of maximum enjoyment; and consequently it prevents us from getting any appreciable pleasure from the most necessary and regularly recurrent acts.[1] On the other hand, self-discipline, which is the only thing that gives us endurance in the cases I have described, is also the only thing that in these cases gives us any pleasure worth mentioning.'

'What you say is absolutely true,' said he.

'Then again there is the process of learning something really good, and taking an interest in one of those activities by means of which a man can maintain his physical fitness and manage

1. Cf. ii, 1, 30.

his household efficiently and make himself useful to his friends and to the state, and get the better of his enemies – activities which offer not only the greatest benefits but also the greatest pleasures – the self-disciplined practise these activities and enjoy them, but the self-indulgent have no part in any of them. Whom could we call worse qualified for such activities than the man who is least capable of performing them, obsessed as he is by his eagerness for the pleasures that are nearest to hand?'

Euthydemus replied, 'It seems to me, Socrates, that you are saying that a man who can't resist physical pleasure is quite incapable of any goodness at all.'

'Yes, Euthydemus, because how can a man without self-discipline be any better than the most ignorant beast? If a person doesn't consider what is best, but tries by every means to do what is most pleasant, how can he be any better than the most senseless animals? Only the self-disciplined have the capacity to consider what are the best objects of action, and, by dividing them into classes, both in theory and in practice, to choose the good and abstain from the bad.'

This was the way, he said, in which people became best and happiest and most capable of logical discussion.[2] He also said that discourse was so called from the fact that when people join together for a discussion they divide their subject-matter into classes.[3] Hence one should try to prepare oneself as fully as possible for this activity, and devote the fullest attention to it; because it was through it that people developed the highest qualities of character and leadership and reasoning ability.

2. Not an anticlimax, because discussion is the method of discovering and disseminating truth. Besides, this is a preparation (whether Xenophon's or not) for the theme of the next chapter.

3. The point (difficult to convey in translation) is that there is an etymological connexion between the Greek verbs meaning respectively 'discuss' and 'divide into groups'.

CHAPTER SIX

Socrates attached great importance to definition as an aid to clear thinking, and his method of reaching a definition is illustrated by a number of examples. (The general approach, and the underlying assumptions, are much as one would expect from reading Plato's dialogues; the arguments here seem rather childish and the logic is often faulty, but Xenophon was no logician, and although Socrates was one of the founders of logic he died before the syllogism was invented.) Finally Socrates' opinions on certain forms of government are quoted, and an illustration is given to show how he referred difficult questions back to first principles.

I SHALL now try to describe how Socrates made his associates better at logical discussion. He believed that those who understood the nature of any given thing would be able to explain it to others as well, whereas it was no wonder (he said) if those who did not understand made mistakes themselves and misled others. Consequently he never stopped investigating, with the help of his companions, the meaning of every single term. It would be a laborious task to describe fully all the distinctions that he drew; I shall mention only those examples which I think will serve to illustrate his method of inquiry.

First of all he examined the meaning of Piety in some such way as this. 'Tell me, Euthydemus,' he said, 'what sort of thing do you think piety is?'

'A very fine thing, to be sure,' said he.

'Can you say what sort of person a pious man is?'

'I think he is a man who worships the gods.'

'Can one worship the gods in any way one likes?'

'No; there are laws which must be observed in worshipping.'

'Then a person who knows these laws would know how one ought to worship the gods.'

'That is my opinion.'

'Does a man who knows how one ought to worship the gods think that one ought not to worship them in a different way from the one that he knows?'

'Surely,' he said.

'Does anyone worship the gods in a different way from that in which he thinks he ought to worship?'

'I imagine not,' he said.

'So the man who knows what is lawful with regard to the gods is likely to worship them lawfully.'

'Certainly.'

'Does the man who worships lawfully worship as he ought?'

'Of course.'

'And the man who worships as he ought is pious?'

'Certainly.'

'So we may take it that the man who knows what is lawful with regard to the gods would be correctly defined as pious.'

'That is how it seems to me.'

'Is one allowed to treat people just as one likes?'

'No; here again there are points of law in accordance with which people have to be treated.'

'Do people who treat one another in accordance with these treat one another as they ought?'

'Certainly,' said he.

'Do those who treat people well conduct their human affairs well?'

'Presumably,' said he.

'Do those who obey the laws do what is right?'

'Certainly.'

'Do you know what is meant by "right"?'

'What the law commands,' he said.

'So those who do what the law commands do what is right and what they ought to do?'

'Of course.'

'Are those who do what is right righteous?'

'I presume so,' he said.

'Do you think that any people obey the laws without knowing what the laws command?'

'No, I don't.'

'Do you think that any people who know what they ought to do think that they ought not to do it?'

'I imagine not,' he said.

'Do you know of any people who do things other than what they think they ought?'[1]

'No, I don't.'

'So those who know what is lawful with regard to men do what is right?'

'Certainly.'

'Are those who do what is right righteous?'

'Yes; who else could be?' he said.

'So we should be correct if we defined righteous persons as those who know what is lawful with regard to men.'

'I think so,' said he.

'And how can we define wisdom? Tell me, do you think that a wise man is wise in relation to what he understands, or are some people wise in relation to what they don't understand?'

'Obviously in relation to what they do understand,' said he. 'How can anyone be wise in relation to what he doesn't understand?'

'Then are the wise wise because of their understanding?'

'What else could make one wise if not understanding?'

'And do you think that wisdom is anything other than that which makes people wise?'

'No, I don't.'

'So wisdom is understanding.'

1. See Introduction, p. 8.

'So it seems to me.'

'Does it seem to you that it is possible for a human being to understand everything that there is?'

'No, indeed; not even the minutest portion of it.'

'So it isn't possible for a human being to be wise in respect of everything?'

'No, certainly not.'

'Then every man is wise only in respect of that which he understands.'

'So it seems to me.'

'Should we, then, look for the good in this way too, Euthydemus?'

'How?' he asked.

'Do you think that the same thing is beneficial to everyone?'

'No, I don't.'

'Put it in this way: don't you think that what is beneficial to one person is sometimes harmful to another?'

'I do indeed,' he said.

'Would you say that "good" is anything else than "beneficial"?'

'I should not,' he said.

'So what is beneficial is good for anyone to whom it is beneficial?'

'I think so.'

'Can we give any different account of beauty? Can you name a beautiful body or article or anything else which you know to be beautiful for all purposes?'

'No, indeed I can't,' said he.

'Is it proper to use everything for the purpose for which it is useful?'

'Certainly.'

'Is a thing beautiful for any purpose other than that for which it is proper to use it?'

'No, in relation to nothing else.'

'So what is useful is beautiful for the purpose for which it is useful?'

'So it seems to me.'

'Next, courage, Euthydemus; do you think that it is a fine thing?'

'I should say that it is a very fine thing.'

'You don't consider that courage is useful in relation to the most trivial things?'

'On the contrary,' he said, 'in relation to the biggest things.'

'Does it seem to you that it is useful in relation to dangers and perils to be unaware of them?'

'Not at all,' he said.

'So those who are not afraid of such things because they don't know what they are are not brave?'

'No, indeed,' he said; 'on that basis a great many lunatics and cowards would be brave.'

'What about those who fear even what is not dangerous?'

'Surely they are even less brave,' said he.

'Then do you consider that those who are good in relation to perils and dangers are brave, and those who are bad in relation to them are cowardly?'

'Certainly.'

'Do you think that anyone is good at these things apart from those who can deal with them well?'

'No; only those.'

'And the bad are those who are of the kind to deal with them badly?'

'Yes; who else?'

'Do both types deal with them as they think they should?'

'Yes; how else?'

'Do those who can't deal with them well know how they ought to deal with them?'

'Of course not,' said he.

'So those who know how they ought to deal with them also have the ability to deal with them?'

'Yes, and they are the only ones who have.'

'Well, now: do those who don't fail in their object deal with these situations badly?'

'I think not,' said he.

'So it is those who deal with them badly that fail in their object?'

'Presumably.'

'So those who know how to deal well with dreadful and dangerous situations are brave, and those who fail in this attempt are cowardly?'

'So it seems to me,' he said.

Socrates considered that monarchy and despotism were both forms of government, but differed from one another. He thought that government with the consent of the people and in accordance with the laws of the state was monarchy, whereas government without consent and in accordance not with the laws but with the whim of the ruler was despotism. Where offices were filled by men who acted in accordance with custom he considered the constitution to be an aristocracy; where they were filled in accordance with a property qualification, a plutocracy; where they were filled by anybody, a democracy.

If anyone was arguing with him about some appointment and had nothing definite to say, but claimed (without proof) that his own nominee was the wiser or more statesmanlike or more courageous or superior in some other such quality, Socrates used to refer the whole argument back to first principles in this sort of way:

'Do you maintain that your candidate is a better citizen than mine?'

'Yes, I do.'

'Then hadn't we better first consider what is the function of a good citizen?'

'Let us do that.'

'If it were a matter of financial administration wouldn't the better man be the one who increased the public revenue?'

'Certainly.'

'And in war he would be the one who gave his country the upper hand over its opponents?'

'Of course.'

'And in diplomacy the man who makes friends instead of enemies?'

'Naturally.'

'Then in politics he is the one who stops party strife and creates a spirit of unity?'

'So it seems to me.'

When the argument was referred back to first principles in this way the truth became apparent to his opponents too. And when he himself was setting out a detailed argument he used to proceed by such stages as were generally agreed, because he thought that this was the infallible method of argument. Consequently when he was talking he used to win the agreement of his audience more than anyone else that I have known. He used to say that Homer himself attributed to Odysseus the quality of being an infallible speaker,[2] because he could base his arguments on the accepted beliefs of his hearers.

2. The reference seems to be to *Odyssey* viii, 171.

CHAPTER SEVEN

Socrates was deeply interested in his friends' education, and even advised them how far to carry their studies, i.e. no further than could be shown to be practically useful. He strongly deprecated the study of natural science (especially astronomy) for its own sake, and criticized Anaxagoras for his physical doctrines.

IT is obvious, I think, from the foregoing account that Socrates used to reveal his opinions candidly to those who sought his company. I shall now show that he also tried to ensure that they should be self-sufficient in their appropriate activities.

Of all the people that I have known he was the most concerned to know the extent of any of his associates' special knowledge, and the most enthusiastic to teach, so far as he was competent, the subjects which a really good man should know; and where he himself was not well qualified he put them in touch with experts. He also instructed them how far a properly educated person should be informed about each subject. For example, he thought that geometry should be learnt so far as to enable one to receive or to convey or to apportion land accurately in point of measurement, or to carry out a task. This, he said, was so easy to learn that a man who applied his mind to the act of measuring could at one and the same moment know the extent of the ground and carry away the knowledge of how it was measured. But he deprecated the learning of geometry so far as figures difficult of comprehension. He said that he didn't see the use of them – although he was not unacquainted with them – and he said that these studies were capable of wasting a man's life and debarring him from learning many other useful things. He told them to become acquainted also with astronomy, but here

again only so far as to be able to recognize the time of night
and the day of the month and the day of the year, with a view
to a journey or a voyage or keeping a watch, and to be able to
use the evidence in relation to all other activities of the night
or month or year by distinguishing the proper times within
these periods. This too, he said, was easy to learn from night-
hunters and pilots and many others whose business it was to
know such things. But to learn astronomy to the extent of
even acquiring a knowledge of bodies moving in different
orbits, such as the planets and other irregularly moving bodies,
and to wear oneself out with trying to discover their distances
from the earth and their paths and the cause of them – from
this he vigorously tried to dissuade them. He said that in these
studies too he saw no utility (although he was not unin-
structed in them either); and they too, he said, could waste a
man's life and debar him from much that was profitable. In
general he dissuaded them from concerning themselves with
the way in which God regulates the various heavenly bodies;[1]
he thought that these facts were not discoverable by human
beings, and he did not consider that a man would please the
gods if he pried into things that they had not chosen to reveal.
He said that a person who bothered about these things would
run the risk of going just as crazy as Anaxagoras,[2] who prided
himself enormously on his exposition of the workings of the
gods. When Anaxagoras said that fire and sun were identical he
did not realize that men can easily look at the fire, but cannot
fix their gaze upon the sun; and that exposure to the sun makes
their skins darker, but exposure to fire does not. He failed also
to realize that no plant can grow properly without sunlight,
whereas all plants die when they are heated by fire. And when
he said that the sun was a red-hot stone he also failed to realize
the fact that if a stone is placed in a fire it neither shines nor

1. Cf. i, 1, 11–15.
2. See the Glossary.

persists for any length of time, whereas the sun remains all the time the brightest of all things.

Socrates recommended the study of arithmetic; but here too, just as in the case of the other subjects, he told his companions to guard against purposeless research; and he himself helped them in their investigations and explanations only so far as was useful. He also strongly encouraged his companions to be careful about their health, not only learning all that they could about it from those who knew, but also each one studying his own constitution all through life to see what food or drink or what kind of exercise was good for him, and by what use of these he could live the healthiest life. He said that anyone who watched himself in this way would find it hard to discover a doctor who could prescribe what was good for his health better than he could himself.

If anyone wanted help beyond the resources of human wisdom he advised him to take up divination.[3] A man who knew the means by which the gods made revelations to men about events, he said, was never in lack of divine counsel.

3. Cf. i, 1, 6–10.

CHAPTER EIGHT

A justification of Socrates' conduct at the time of his trial. A reported conversation with Hermogenes shows why he faced the prospect of death with equanimity. The author closes with his own personal tribute to Socrates' memory.

IF anyone thinks that Socrates was convicted of making a false claim to his 'divine sign',[1] on the ground that he was condemned to death by the jury although he claimed that the divine sign warned him in advance what he ought and ought not to do, let him reflect that Socrates was already so far advanced in age that he would soon have reached the end of his life, even if he had not done so then:[2] and that he escaped the most disagreeable part of life, in which everybody's intellect deteriorates; and instead of this not only displayed his strength of mind but also won distinction by pleading his cause with unparalleled veracity, dignity and integrity, and facing the death-sentence with the utmost serenity and fortitude.[3] It is generally agreed that no one in the memory of man has ever met his death more nobly. He had to live on for thirty days after his trial, because the festival of Delos[4] fell in that month, and the law does not permit any public execution until the mission has returned from Delos.[5] It was evident to his intimate friends that during this time he did not deviate at all from his former way of life – although he had previously been remarkable above all men for the cheerfulness and equanimity of his life.

1. Cf. i, 1, 2 ff.
2. Cf. Plato, *Apology* 38C.
3. Cf. ibid. 40A–C.
4. See Glossary.
5. Cf. Plato, *Crito* 43C–D; *Phaedo* 58A–C.

How could anyone die more nobly? or what death could be nobler than the noblest that one could die? and what death could be more happy than the noblest? or what could be more blessed than the happiest?[6]

I shall relate also what I heard about him from Hermogenes the son of Hipponicus. He said that after Meletus had already laid his indictment, hearing Socrates discoursing about anything rather than the trial, he told him that he ought to be considering his defence. At first Socrates said, 'Don't you see that I have been preparing it all through my life?' and when Hermogenes asked him how, he replied that he had spent all his time in nothing else than studying questions of right and wrong, doing what was right and refraining from what was wrong; and he considered that this was the finest preparation for a defence. Then Hermogenes said again, 'Don't you see, Socrates, that the jurors at Athens have often before now been prevailed upon by argument to put innocent men to death and to acquit guilty ones?'

'Well, as a matter of fact, Hermogenes,' he said, 'I have already set about considering my defence before the jury, and my divine sign opposed it.'[7]

'That's an extraordinary statement,' said Hermogenes.

Socrates answered, 'Do you think it's extraordinary that God should decide that it is better for me to end my life now? Don't you know that up to the present I should have conceded to nobody that he had lived a better or more pleasant life than I? because I believe that the best life is lived by those who take the best care to make themselves as good as possible, and the pleasantest life by those who are most conscious that they are becoming better. Up to the present time I have felt that this was happening to me, and in my contacts with other

6. A distressingly artificial piece of rhetoric, perhaps not to be debited to Xenophon, but cf. *Cyropaedia* viii, 2, 8 f.

7. Xenophon says the same in his *Apology* 4.

people and in comparing myself with others I have invariably come to this conclusion about myself. And not only I, but my friends have always come to this conclusion; not because they love me (because if that were all, everyone who is fond of somebody else would come to the same conclusion about his friends) but simply because they believe that they too are likely to become best by associating with me. But if I go on living, I suppose I shall have to pay the penalty of old age: to see and hear less, and think less well, and become in consequence denser and more forgetful; and become inferior to those to whom I used to be superior. Now even if one were unconscious of this, life would not be worth living; and when one is conscious of it, surely it must make one's life worse and more disagreeable. Then again, if I am wrongly executed, this may be discreditable to those who wrongly put me to death, because if it is shameful to do wrong, it is surely shameful to do anything wrongly; but what disgrace is it to me if other people fail to decide or act rightly with regard to me? And I see also that the reputation left behind them among later generations by men of earlier times is not the same for the doers as for the sufferers of wrong. And I know that even if I die now people will regard me and those who put me to death in different lights; because I know that I shall always have testimony that I never wronged anybody or made anybody a worse person, but always tried to make my associates better men.'

This was what he said in conversation with Hermogenes and the rest.

Of those who knew what Socrates was like, all whose hearts are set upon goodness continue still to miss him more than anything, because they feel that he was their greatest help in the cultivation of goodness.

Socrates was, as I have described him, so devout that he never did anything without the sanction of the gods; so upright that he never did the smallest harm to anybody, but conferred the greatest benefits upon those who associated with him; so self-disciplined that he never chose the more pleasant course instead of the better; so judicious that he never made a mistake in deciding between better and worse, and needed no advice, but was self-sufficient for such decisions, capable of stating and distinguishing such alternatives, and capable both of otherwise appraising and of exposing errors and encouraging towards goodness and excellence of body and mind. In view of these qualities he seemed to me to be the perfect example of goodness and happiness.

If anyone disapproves of this assessment, let him compare other people's characters with these qualities, and then make his own decision.

SYMPOSIUM

THE DINNER-PARTY

CHAPTER ONE

*Callias invites Socrates and others to dine at his house in Piraeus.
The beauty of the young Autolycus has an almost paralysing effect
on the company, to the alarm of the comedian Philippus when he
arrives uninvited and at first fails to raise a laugh.*

IT seems to me that in writing about great men it is proper to
record not only their serious activities but their diversions too.
I should like to describe an experience which led me to this
conclusion.

There was a horse-race at the Great Panathenaic festival.[1]
Callias the son of Hipponicus happened to be strongly attracted
by a boy called Autolycus and had brought him along to
watch, fresh from his victory in the pancratium.[2] When the
race had finished Callias set off to his house in Piraeus,[3] taking
Autolycus and his father with him. He was accompanied
also by Niceratus. Seeing a group consisting of Socrates,
Critobulus, Hermogenes, Antisthenes and Charmides, Callias
arranged for somebody to show the way to Autolycus and
his party while he himself went up to Socrates and the others
and said, 'I've met you just in the nick of time. I'm having
Autolycus and his father to dinner. I'm sure that my establish-
ment would seem much more stately if my dining-room
were graced by persons of pure aspiration, like yourselves,
than if my guests were generals or cavalry-officers or ambitious politicians.'

'You're always teasing us,' said Socrates; 'you turn up your

1. The Panathenaea was an annual festival in honour of Athena.
Every fourth year it was held on a grander scale and was called the
Great Panathenaea; cf. Introduction p. 22.

2. A kind of all-in wrestling in which almost anything was allowed
except biting and gouging out the eyes.

3. See *Mem.* ii, 7, 2. He had a town house in Athens.

nose at us because you've paid a lot of money to Protagoras
and Gorgias and Prodicus[4] and a lot of others for expert
instruction, and you can see that we are, so to speak, amateur
philosophers.'

'Up to the present,' said Callias, 'I've kept you in the dark
about my powers of fluent and witty conversation; but now
if you'll visit me I'll show you that I deserve your very serious
attention.'

Well, naturally Socrates and his friends began by thanking
Callias for his invitation but excusing themselves from dining
with him; but when it became clear that he really would be
annoyed if they didn't come too, they joined the party. In
due course they presented themselves, some rubbed down
with oil after their exercise and others freshly bathed as well.
Autolycus sat down[5] beside his father, and the others, as you
would expect, reclined. An observer of the scene would at
once have reflected that beauty has something naturally regal
about it, especially if it is combined with modesty and self-
control in the possessor, as it was then in Autolycus. In the
first place his beauty drew everyone's attention to him, as
surely as a light draws all eyes towards it in the dark; and
secondly there was not a man there whose feelings were not
moved at the sight of him. Some became more silent, and
others underwent a sort of transformation. Possession by a
god always seems to have a remarkable effect. Those who are
influenced by other gods tend to become more intimidating
in their appearance, more truculent in their speech, and more
aggressive in their conduct; but those who are inspired by a
pure love wear a kindlier expression and speak in a gentler
tone and behave in a more civil manner. Such was the effect
that Callias' love had upon him on this occasion, as was duly
noted by those who were initiates of this god. So they pro-

4. Well-known sophists: see Glossary.
5. Not being an adult. His father was Lycon (2, 4).

ceeded to dine in silence, as if they were under orders to do so.

At this point Philippus the 'funny man' knocked at the front door, and told the man who answered it to announce who he was and why he wanted to be let in. He said that he came fully equipped with everything he needed for dining at another person's house, and added that his servant was quite exhausted because he had nothing to carry and had had no breakfast.

When Callias heard this he said, 'Well, gentlemen, it would be a shame to grudge him shelter, at any rate. Let him come in.' As he spoke he glanced at Autolycus, evidently looking to see how the comedy appealed to him.

Philippus paused in the doorway of the dining-room and said, 'You all know that I'm a funny man. I've come here on purpose, because I thought it was funnier to come to dinner without an invitation than with one.'

'Sit down, then,' said Callias. 'The company are full of seriousness, as you see, but perhaps a little short of humour.'

They went on with the meal, and Philippus at once tried to make a joke, to fulfil the usual purpose for which he was invited to dinner-parties. When he didn't get a laugh he was obviously hurt. A little later he ventured another joke; and when they still failed to laugh at him he suddenly stopped in the middle of eating, covered his head[6] and lay down.

'What's the matter, Philippus?' asked Callias. 'Have you got a pain?'

Philippus uttered a loud groan. 'I certainly have, Callias,' he said, 'a violent one. If laughter has gone from the world, my occupation's ruined. Up till now I have been invited to dinner-parties to entertain the company by making them laugh, but now what reason will anyone have for inviting me? I can no more be serious than I could make myself im-

6. With his cloak; a conventional sign of distress.

233

mortal; and nobody will invite me in the hope of being invited back, because everyone knows that it's quite without precedent for a dinner to be held at my house.'

As he spoke he blew his nose, and his voice showed unmistakably that he was crying. So everybody assured him that they would laugh again, and told him to eat his dinner; and Critobulus actually guffawed at his pitiful complaint. When Philippus heard him laugh he uncovered his head and telling his heart to take courage,[7] because there would still be engagements,[8] he went on with his dinner.

7. In the epic manner. So Odysseus addresses his heart, *Odyssey* xx, 17 f.

8. There is a pun here: the word can mean either 'conflicts' or 'parties'.

CHAPTER TWO

A Syracusan impresario provides a kind of cabaret show. Callias offers to supply his guests with perfume, but Socrates demurs. After a general exchange of badinage Philippus burlesques the dancers' acts, and his consequent thirst raises the subject of drinking. Socrates recommends the principle of 'little and often'.

WHEN the table had been cleared and they had poured libations and sung a grace,[1] a Syracusan came in to provide entertainment. He had with him a girl who was an expert flautist,[2] another who was an acrobatic dancer, and a very attractive boy who both played the lyre and danced extremely well. The man made a living by exhibiting these turns as a novelty. When the girl had played her flute for them and the boy his lyre, and both performances seemed to give a very satisfactory amount of pleasure, Socrates said, 'Upon my word, Callias, this is perfect entertainment. You have not only served us an irreproachable dinner; you are providing us with most delightful sights and sounds.'

Callias said, 'What about having some perfume[3] brought in, so that we can enjoy its fragrance?'

'No, please don't,' said Socrates. 'You know that one kind of clothing looks well on a woman and another on a man: in the same way the smells that suit men and women are different. No man, surely, daubs himself with scent for the benefit of another man. At the same time women, especially if they're newly married, like the wives of Niceratus here and

1. More accurately 'a hymn of thanksgiving'.

2. The Greek *aulos* was not really a flute: it had its blow-hole at the end, like a recorder.

3. Perfume and scented oil were very popular with the Greeks, especially at parties, although some people (like Socrates) thought they were effeminate.

Critobulus, don't need the help of perfume: they smell of it themselves. And the smell of oil in the training-rooms gives women more pleasure by its presence and excites more longing by its absence. A daub of scent automatically makes everyone, slave or free, smell alike; but the smells that come from strenuous effort in sport call first for strict training over a long period if they are to be pleasing and worthy of a cultured person.'

'That may be so for the young,' said Lycon, 'but what about us who are too old for violent exercise – what ought we to smell of?'

'Decency and goodness, of course,' said Socrates.

'And where can one get this lotion?'

'Not at a perfumery, certainly.'

'Well, where, then?'

'Where Theognis told us:[4]

> Good company will edify you: bad
> Will rob you even of the wits you had.'

'Hear that, son?' said Lycon.

'Of course he does,' said Socrates, 'and he acts upon it. At any rate when he wanted to win the pancratium he looked about, with your help, for the best trainer, and now he will attach himself to the person who seems best qualified to give him this other kind of training.'

Here several people spoke at once: one said 'Where will he find a teacher of this subject?' and another said that goodness wasn't a thing that could be taught at all; and someone else that if anything was to be learnt, that was. But Socrates said, 'As this is a debatable subject,[5] let's defer it to another occasion. Let us proceed now with our programme. I see that this

4. Theognis 35 f.; cf. *Memorabilia*. i, 2, 20.
5. Cf. *Mem*. iii, 9. It is extensively debated in Plato's *Meno* and *Protagoras*.

dancer here has taken up her position, and somebody is bringing her some hoops.'

At this moment the other girl began to play for her on the flute, and a man standing by the dancer handed her out hoops to the number of twelve. She took them and threw them spinning up into the air as she danced, judging how high to throw them so as to catch them in time with the music.

Socrates said, 'It's evident from this girl's display, gentlemen, as well as on many other grounds, that women have no less natural ability than men; only they lack judgement and physical strength. So any one of you who has a wife can teach her with confidence any skill that he would like her to acquire and practise.'

'If that's your view, Socrates,' said Antisthenes, 'why don't you train Xanthippe[6] instead of having a wife who is of all living women – and I believe of all that ever have been or will be – the most difficult to get on with?'

'Because I notice that people who want to become good horsemen keep not the most docile horses but ones that are high-spirited, because they think that if they can control these they will easily manage any other horses. In the same way, since I wish to deal and associate with people, I have provided myself with this wife, because I'm quite sure that if I can put up with her I shall find it easy to get on with any other human being.' This explanation was felt to be not far off the mark.

Next a circular frame was brought in, closely set all round with upright sword-blades; and the dancer turned somersaults into this and out again over the blades,[7] so that the spectators were afraid that she would hurt herself; but she went through her performance confidently and safely. Socrates hailed Antisthenes and said, 'I don't imagine that the witnesses of this act will continue to deny that courage is a

6. Cf. *Mem*. ii, 2.   7. Cf. *Mem*. i, 3, 9.

thing that can be taught,[8] when this girl in spite of her sex throws herself so daringly on to the swords.'

Antisthenes replied, 'Don't you think that this Syracusan had better exhibit his dancing-girls to the state, and say that if it will pay him a fee he will make all Athenians dare to charge on to the spear-points?'

'Yes, indeed,' said Philippus; 'speaking for myself, I should love to see that tub-thumper Pisander[9] learning how to tumble on to the swords; as it is, he won't serve in the army at all, because he can't look a spear in the face.'

After this the boy performed a dance, and Socrates said, 'Did you see how, beautiful as the boy is, he nevertheless looks even more beautiful with the help of the dance-figures than when he is keeping still?'

'You seem to be commending his dancing-master,' said Charmides.

'I certainly am,' said Socrates. 'I've noticed something else too, that in the dance no part of his body was idle: neck, legs and arms were exercised together; it was just the sort of dancing to develop bodily grace and agility. Personally,' he said, 'I should very much like you, my Syracusan friend, to teach me the figures.'

'What use will they be to you?' asked the man.

'I shall dance them, of course.'

This raised a general laugh. Socrates went on, with a perfectly straight face, 'Are you laughing at me? Is it at the idea of my wanting to take exercise to improve my health, or to enjoy my food and sleep better? or is it because I'm bent on a particular kind of exercise, not wanting to develop my legs at the expense of my arms like a long-distance runner, nor my arms at the expense of my legs like a boxer, but by work-

8. Cf. *Mem.* iii, 9, 1.

9. An oligarch prominent in the revolution of 411; ridiculed for cowardice by Aristophanes, *Birds* 1556 ff.

ing hard with my whole body to make it evenly proportioned all over? Or are you laughing because I shan't have to find myself a training-partner, or undress in public at my advanced age, because a moderate-sized [10] dining-room will serve for me to work up a sweat in, just as this room served for our young friend here; and in cold weather I shall exercise under cover, and in a heat-wave beneath the shade? Or is *this* why you're laughing, because my stomach is larger than it should be and I want to reduce it to a more normal size? Don't you know that the other day Charmides here caught me dancing at daybreak?'

'Yes, begad!' said Charmides, 'and at first I was astonished and afraid that you were out of your mind, but when I heard you explain in the way that you are doing now, I went home myself and – well, I didn't dance, because I've never learnt how, but I waved my arms about, because I knew how to do that.'

'Quite so,' said Philippus; 'and as a result you seem to have your legs so evenly matched with your arms that I believe if the market-inspectors made you weigh the lower items against the upper ones, like the loaves on a stall, [11] they wouldn't be able to fine you.'

Callias added, 'Call me in, Socrates, when you start to take dancing-lessons, so that I can act as your partner and learn along with you.'

'Come on, now,' said Philippus, 'let the girl play for me so that I may dance too.' He stood up and went through a parody of the two dances, the boy's and the girl's. First, because they had praised the boy for looking even more beautiful as he danced the figures, Philippus on the contrary made every part of the body that he moved look funnier than normal;

10. Literally 'with seven couches'. Cf. *Oeconomicus* 8, 13.

11. The loaves would not be quite the same size or weight; and the practice of putting the biggest on the top of the display (not unknown to some modern greengrocers) was punishable by a fine. Philippus means that Charmides' legs and arms are equally puny.

and because the girl had formed the shape of a hoop by bending over backwards, he tried to produce the same effect by bending the same parts of himself forward.[12] Finally, because they had praised the boy for exercising the whole of his body in the dance, Philippus told the flautist to speed up the tempo, and let fly legs, arms and head all together.

When he was exhausted he said, as he lay down again, 'Here's proof, gentlemen, that my dances provide good exercise: I, at any rate, am thirsty; and I should like the waiter to pour me a bumper.'

'Yes, indeed,' said Callias, 'and the same for us, because we're thirsty too with laughing at you.'

But Socrates said, 'Well, gentlemen, I'm entirely in favour of drinking, because it's a fact that wine refreshes the heart, and both allays worry like a sedative and like oil feeds the flame of gaiety. But it seems to me that the human body is affected in just the same way as plants are. When God gives plants too much to drink at a time, they can't stand up or breathe in fresh air; but when they drink only as much as is pleasant they grow up quite straight and flourish and reach the fruiting stage. In the same way if we pour out all the drink at once both our bodies and our minds will quickly let us down; we shan't be able to breathe, much less speak; but if the waiters drop for us frequent dew in goblets small, to borrow a phrase of Gorgias,[13] then instead of being forced into intoxication by the wine we shall reach a more playful mood through gentle persuasion.'

This proposal was immediately adopted, Philippus adding a rider to the effect that the waiters should follow the example of racing drivers and send the cups round with increasing speed; and the waiters did so.

12. This seems a rather feeble form of parody.
13. Gorgias, the Sicilian rhetorician (see Plato's dialogue), was famous for his metaphors and poetic diction.

CHAPTER THREE

After another song Socrates proposes that his friends prove their ability to entertain one another. Callias undertakes to display his skill if each guest will inform the party what he considers to be his greatest asset or accomplishment. Some of the resulting disclosures are highly paradoxical.

THE boy now tuned his lyre to the flute and sang to his own accompaniment.[1] At this everybody applauded, and Charmides further remarked, 'It seems to me, gentlemen, just as Socrates said about the wine, that this combination of youthful beauty and music allays one's cares and awakens thoughts of love.'

Socrates now interposed again. 'These people, gentlemen, show that they are capable of entertaining us. I'm sure that we believe ourselves to be much better than they are. Won't it be a disgrace if, while we are together here, we don't even try to improve or amuse one another?'[2]

At this several people said, 'Well, you tell us how we are most likely to succeed; what sort of subject should we discuss?'

'What I should like best,' he replied, 'is to take up Callias' offer. He said, I believe, that if we would dine with him he would give us a display of his skill.'

'And so I will,' said Callias, 'if each one of you will inform the company what his special gift is.'

'Well, nobody objects to the proposal that each of us should state what he *thinks* is his most valuable asset.'

'Very well, then, let me tell you what I am most proud of. I believe that I can make people better.'

1. Evidently the flautist accompanied him too.
2. Cf. Plato, *Protagoras* 347C–E.

Antisthenes said, 'By teaching them what? – some mere skill, or all-round excellence?'[3]

'The latter – if all-round excellence means moral goodness.'

'Of course it does,' said Antisthenes, 'most unquestionably. Courage and wisdom are admitted to be sometimes injurious both to one's friends and to one's country;[4] but moral goodness has no connexion at all with wickedness.'

'Well, when each of you has told us what his special gift is, I won't object to tell you the art by which I produce this effect. It's your turn, Niceratus; tell us what accomplishment you're proud of.'

Niceratus said, 'My father, in his anxiety to make me a good man, made me learn the whole works of Homer; and I could now repeat by heart the entire *Iliad* and *Odyssey*.'

'Has it escaped you,' asked Antisthenes, 'that the professional reciters[5] all know these poems?'

'How could it,' he replied, 'when I listen to them almost every day?'

'Well, do you know any class of people sillier than they are?'

'No indeed,' said Niceratus, 'I don't think I do.'

'No,' said Socrates, 'because they obviously don't understand the underlying ideas.[6] But you have paid a lot of money to Stesimbrotus[7] and Anaximander[8] and many others, and so none of the important points has escaped you. What about you, Critobulus? what do you pride yourself on most?'

3. 'Beauty and goodness'; Introduction p. 9.

4. Courage obviously can have awkward results; for the dangers of 'wisdom' see *Mem.* iv, 2, 33 (but the example is unfair, because Daedalus was more inventive than wise).

5. Rhapsodists: bards who went round reciting epic poetry.

6. Cf. *Mem.* iv, 2, 10, and Plato, *Ion*, especially 536E–end.

7. A biographer from Thasos who also wrote on Homer (Plato, *Ion* 530D).

8. Not the philosopher but the author of a book on Greek heroes (Athenaeus 498B).

'On my appearance.'

'Will you really be able to claim that you can make us better by your good looks?'

'If I can't I obviously shan't look very good.'

'What about you, Antisthenes?' said Socrates; 'what are you proud of?'

'My wealth,' said he.

Hermogenes asked him if he had a great deal of money, and he swore that he hadn't so much as a shilling.[9]

'Well, do you own a lot of land?'

'It might be just enough to serve as a dust-bath[10] for Autolycus here.'

'We shall have to hear from you too. What about you, Charmides? what are you proud of?'

'For my part,' he said, 'I'm proud of my poverty.'

'Certainly a gratifying asset,' said Socrates. 'Nothing could provoke less jealousy or rivalry; it remains safe without protection, and neglect improves it.'

'You, now,' said Callias, 'what are you proud of, Socrates?'

He lengthened his face into a very serious expression, and said, 'My skill as a procurer.' They laughed at him. 'You can laugh,' he said, 'but I know that I could make a great deal of money if I chose to follow the profession.'

'In your case, anyhow,' said Lycon to Philippus, 'it's obvious that you pride yourself on raising laughs.'

'And with better reason, I fancy,' he replied, 'than the actor Callipides,[11] who gives himself extraordinary airs because he can set vast audiences weeping.'

9. In Greek 'an obol'.

10. Wrestlers powdered themselves with fine sand to afford a better grip. Apparently it also had a cooling effect, like talc.

11. A famous tragic actor who won the prize at the Lenaea in 418; criticized by Mynniscus (Aristotle, *Poetics* 1461b 34 f.) for his lack of restraint.

'Won't you tell us, Lycon,' said Antisthenes, 'what you are proud of?'

He answered, 'Why, surely you all know that it's this son of mine.'

'And he,' said somebody, 'is obviously proud of being a champion.'

'Certainly not!' said Autolycus, blushing.

Everyone looked towards him in pleasure at hearing his voice, and someone asked him, 'Well, what *are* you proud of?'

'My father,' he said, leaning up against him as he spoke.

When Callias saw this he said, 'Do you know, Lycon, that you're the richest man alive?'

'No, that I certainly don't.'

'Don't you realize that you wouldn't accept all the wealth of the Great King[12] in exchange for your son?'

'It seems to be a clear case against me,' he said; 'I'm the richest man in the world.'

'You, Hermogenes,' said Niceratus, 'what do you delight in most?'

'The goodness and influence of my friends,' he said, 'and the fact that, having these qualities, they care for me.'

This turned all eyes towards him, and several people at the same time asked if they too might be introduced to his friends. He said that he wouldn't object.

12. The king of Persia, to a Greek the personification of wealth and prosperity.

CHAPTER FOUR

The next stage is for each guest to justify his assertion. Callias begins by explaining that he makes people better by giving them money. Niceratus argues that his knowledge of Homer enables him to advise on all subjects. Critobulus maintains that his beauty gives his friends the same enjoyment and benefit that he receives from his favourite Clinias. Socrates challenges him to a beauty contest of which the dancers shall be the judges. This leads to a lot of banter.

SOCRATES now said, 'I suppose it remains for each of us to demonstrate the value of what he claimed to possess.'

'You can hear my statement first,' said Callias. 'While I have been listening to all of you puzzling about what moral goodness is, I have been making people morally better.'[1]

'How, my good friend?' asked Socrates.

'By giving them money, to be sure.'

Antisthenes got up and stood over him and questioned him very critically. 'Callias, do you think that people keep their morality in their souls or in their pockets?'

'In their souls.'

'Then do you make their souls morally better by putting money into their pockets?'

'Certainly.'

'How?'

'Because when they know they've got something with which to buy what they need they don't want to risk committing crimes.'

'Do they repay all that they get from you?'

'Dear me, no!' he said, 'indeed they don't.'

1. Not at this party, but in the past generally.

'Well, then, do they do you favours in return for your money?'

'Oh no,' he said, 'they don't do that either; some of them are even more hostile than they were before.'

'It's a curious thing,' said Antisthenes, fixing him with an accusing stare, 'if you can make them act fairly towards everyone else, but not towards you.'

'What is there curious about that?' asked Callias. 'Don't you realize that there are plenty of carpenters and builders who make houses for large numbers of other people, but can't do it for themselves, and live in rented homes? You must really accept that you're confuted, professor!'

'He must, indeed,' said Socrates. 'Prophets, too, I believe, are supposed not to foresee what is coming to themselves, although they foretell the future for others.'

That was the end of that topic. Next Niceratus said, 'You can now hear from me how you will be improved if you associate with me. You know, I presume, that the inspired Homer has sung about practically every aspect of human affairs; so if any one of you wants to become a good manager or politician or general, or to become like Achilles or Ajax or Nestor or Odysseus,[2] let him give his attention to me; because I have all this knowledge.'

'Do you know how to be a king too?' said Antisthenes, 'just because you are aware that Homer praised Agamemnon as "both, a good king and a stout warrior"?'[3]

'Indeed I do,' he said, 'and that when one is driving a chariot one must turn close to the post

> and smoothly lean out of the polished car
> to the left of them, but goad the off-side horse,
> cheering him on, and slacken off his reins.[4]

2. See Glossary.
3. *Iliad* iii, 179; cf. *Mem*. iii, 2, 2.
4. *Iliad* xxiii, 335-7, quoted also by Plato, *Ion* 537A-B.

And besides this I know something else, which you can try this very moment. Homer said somewhere

> and onion as a relish for their drink.[5]

So if someone provides an onion, you can have this benefit immediately: you will enjoy your drinking more.'

'Gentlemen,' said Charmides, 'Niceratus is set on going home smelling of onions, so as to convince his wife that nobody would even have thought of kissing him.'

'No doubt,' said Socrates, 'but I think there's a risk of our creating another ridiculous impression besides. Onion does really seem to be a kind of relish, because it adds pleasure not only to food but to drink too. So if we munch it after dinner as well, we must be careful that someone doesn't say that we went to Callias' house and wallowed in luxury.'

'That would never do,' said Callias.[6] 'It's all right for a soldier going into action to munch an onion first, just as some people feed their cocks on garlic before they set them on to fight;[7] but we are presumably planning to give somebody a kiss, not to start a battle.'

That was more or less how this topic came to an end.

'Now I'll tell you,' said Critobulus, 'why I'm proud of my appearance.'

'Go on,' they said.

'Well, then, if I am not beautiful, as I think I am, you could properly be sued for fraud, because you're always voluntarily stating under oath that I am beautiful. What's more, I believe you: because I regard you as men of the highest character. But if I am really beautiful, and if you feel just the same towards me as I feel towards the person who

---

5. *Iliad* xi, 630, quoted also (in the wrong context) by Plato, *Ion* 538C.

6. It is not clear who is the speaker.

7. Cf. Aristophanes, *Knights* 494 f.

seems beautiful to me, I swear by all the gods that I wouldn't choose the throne of Persia[8] in preference to being beautiful. As things are, I get more pleasure from looking at Clinias[9] than from all the beauty in the world; and I would rather be blind to everything else than to the one person Clinias. Night and sleep exasperate me because then I can't see him; but I overflow with gratitude to the day and the sun, because they show me Clinias.

'There is another ground on which we who are good-looking are entitled to be proud: a strong man has to exert himself to gain his ends, and a brave man to run risks, and a wise man to utter his thoughts; but a handsome man can achieve all his effects without moving a muscle. For my part, although I know that it's a pleasant thing to have money, it would please me better to give all that I have to Clinias than to receive as much from somebody else; and it would please me better to be a slave than to be free, if Clinias would be my master. Working for him would be easier than resting, and to face danger for him would be more pleasant than a life of security.

'So if you, Callias, pride yourself on the ability to make people more upright, I have a better claim than you to lead them on to goodness of every kind. The inspiration that we beautiful people give to our admirers makes them more generous with their money, and in danger gives them a greater zeal for effort and a greater thirst for glory; it also makes them more modest and self-controlled, because they feel reverence for what they most desire.

'It is madness, too, not to choose beautiful people as military leaders. Personally I would go through fire in Clinias' company, and I know that you would do the same in mine.

8. Cf. 3, 13 above.
9. Son of Axiochus and grandson of Alcibiades; he appears as a handsome youth in Plato's *Euthydemus*.

So you needn't wonder any more, Socrates, whether my beauty will do people any good.

'There is no reason, either, for disparaging beauty on the ground that it quickly passes its prime; as we find a beauty of childhood, so we do of adolescence, of maturity and of age. Here is the evidence: they choose beautiful old men to carry the olive-shoots in honour of Athena,[10] which shows that beauty is the accompaniment of every age. And if it is a pleasant thing to have one's wishes granted willingly, I am sure that at this very minute I could persuade this boy and girl here to kiss me more quickly without saying a word than you could, Socrates, even if you spouted wisdom.'

'What's this?' said Socrates. 'You're bragging as if you were more beautiful than I am.'

'Of course,' said Critobulus; 'otherwise I should be uglier than any Silenus[11] in the satyr-plays.'

'All right, then,' said Socrates, 'mind that you remember to settle the question of our beauty when the topics that we have tabled have gone all round. Our judge shall be not Alexander[12] the son of Priam but these very persons who you think are eager to kiss you.'

'Couldn't you leave it to Clinias, Socrates?' he said.

'No; I wish you'd stop thinking of Clinias!'

'Do you suppose I think of him any the less if I don't mention his name? Don't you know that I have such a clear picture of him in my mind that if I were a sculptor or a

10. In the Panathenaic procession; cf. above, 1, 1, and see Aristophanes, *Wasps* 544.

11. A gross and clownish person, 'tutor' to Dionysus, and a regular character in Satyric drama (cf. Euripides, *Cyclops*); for Socrates' resemblance to him cf. Alcibiades' remarks about Silenus and satyrs in Plato, *Symposium* 215A–216E.

12. Better known as Paris, judge of the famous beauty contest between three goddesses; cf. Homer, *Iliad* xxiv, 25–30 and Euripides, *Helen* 23–30.

painter I could have executed a portrait of him just as well from that picture at by looking at him?'

Socrates retorted, 'Well, then, if you've got such an accurate picture of him, why do you plague me by dragging me about to where you can see him?'

'Because, Socrates, the sight of Clinias himself has the effect of making me happy, but the picture in my mind gives me no pleasure – it only fills me with longing.'

Hermogenes said, 'Look here, Socrates, I don't think it's at all like you to let Critobulus get so infatuated.'

'Do you imagine,' said Socrates, 'that he got into this state after he came under my influence?'

'Well, when *did* it happen?'

'Don't you see that the down on his face is just creeping down by the ears, whereas on Clinias it's already climbing up towards the back?[13] Well, Critobulus was fired with a violent passion for him while they were going to the same school; so when his father noticed it he handed him over to me in case I could do anything to help him. And he is really much better already. Before, he used to gaze at Clinias with a fixed stare, as though he was looking at a Gorgon,[14] and never left his side; but now I've seen him actually blink already. All the same, I do assure you, gentlemen, it seems to me,' he said, 'between ourselves, that he has even kissed Clinias; and nothing is a fiercer incitement to love than that. It's an insatiable thing, and it produces a kind of delicious anticipation. That's why I say that anyone who wants to be able to behave decently ought to refrain from kissing the young and attractive.'[15]

'Come, come, Socrates,' said Charmides, 'what do you mean by trying like this to scare us, your friends, away from

13. A puzzling description because Critobulus is obviously the elder.
14. And had consequently been turned into stone.
15. Cf. *Mem.* i, 3, 8 ff.

beautiful people, although I've seen you yourself, I swear,' he said, 'with my own eyes, when you were both in the school-room searching for something in the same book, with your head touching Critobulus' head and your bare arm against his.'

'Dear me!' said Socrates, 'so that's why I had a sore arm for more than five days, as if some wild beast had bitten me, and felt a sort of ache in my heart. Well, I now give you warning, Critobulus, before all these witnesses, not to touch me until your chin is as hairy as your scalp.'

In this way they combined joking with seriousness.

Charmides now explains that his poverty has freed him from his former anxieties, Antisthenes that his wealth is due to the simplicity of his life, and Hermogenes that the friends whom he values so much are the gods.

Critias now said, 'It's your turn, Charmides, to tell us why you are proud of your poverty.'

'It's an admitted fact,' said he, 'that it's better to be confident than to be frightened, and to be free than to be a slave, and to be courted than to court others, and to be trusted by one's country than to be distrusted. Well, in the days when I was a rich man in this city, in the first place I used to be afraid that somebody would break into my house and take my goods and do me myself some injury. Then I used to make myself agreeable to the informers,[16] knowing that I was more vulnerable than they were. Besides this, the state was always ordering me to finance[17] something, and I was never able to leave the country. But now that I'm deprived of my properties abroad, and get nothing out of these that I have here, and the

16. Cf. *Mem.* ii, 9.

17. I.e., to undertake a 'liturgy' or public duty (like the training of a chorus, *Mem.* iii, 4, 3) involving heavy expense.

contents of my house are sold, I sleep happily and fully relaxed; I have won the confidence of my country; I am no longer threatened, I now threaten others; and I am free to go abroad or stay in the country. Rich men now give up their seats to me and make way for me in the street.[18] Now I am like a dictator, but then I was clearly a slave; then I used to hand over money regularly to the people, but now the state imposes a tax and supports me.[19] They even denounced me for associating with Socrates when I was rich; but now that I've become poor it doesn't matter any more to anybody. Besides, when I had many possessions I was always losing something, thanks to the state or to fortune; but now I lose nothing (because I haven't got anything), but I'm always hoping to get something.'

'So you actually pray,' said Callias, 'never to be rich; and if you dream of any stroke of luck, you sacrifice to the gods who protect us from harm?'[20]

'Good heavens, no!' he said, 'I don't do that; I stand my ground very gallantly if I expect to get anything from anywhere.'

'Well, come along now, Antisthenes,' said Socrates, 'you tell us how it is that you pride yourself on your wealth although you have such limited means.'

'Because, gentlemen, I believe that it's not in their houses that people have wealth or poverty, but in their minds. I see many private persons who, although they have very great wealth, consider themselves so poor that they submit to any hardship and any hazard with a view to increasing their possessions; and I know cases too of brothers who have in-

18. Presumably because he is a potential informer.

19. He means that instead of always paying out money he now gets remuneration from public funds for minor services like attendance in the Assembly or the courts.

20. Especially Apollo: cf. Aristophanes, Birds 61.

herited equal shares, and although one of them has more than enough to cover his expenditure, the other is in need of everything. And I observe some despots too who are so hungry for wealth that they commit far more dreadful crimes than the desperately poor. It is need, no doubt, that makes these steal and break into houses and kidnap; but there are some despots who destroy whole houses, and commit mass-murders, and often sell whole populations away into slavery for the sake of money. Personally I feel very sorry for these people in their most distressing disease: it seems to me that they are in much the same state as a man with ample provisions who eats heavily and is never satisfied. I have so few possessions that I myself can hardly discover them; but still I have quite enough to satisfy my hunger when I eat, and to quench my thirst when I drink, and to clothe myself so that out of doors I am no colder than Callias here for all his great wealth. And when I get home the walls of my house seem to me like a really warm tunic, and the roof like a really thick cloak; and my bedclothes are so adequate that it's hard work even to wake me up. If my body ever feels the need for sexual inter-course I am so content with what is available that any women I approach welcome me with open arms, because nobody else will go near them. And, mark you, I find such pleasure in all these things that my prayer would be to enjoy doing each one of them not more, but less; I have such a feeling that some of them give me more pleasure than is good for me.

'But I reckon that the most precious possession in my for-tune is this: that if I were robbed even of what I now possess, I can imagine no kind of work so mean that it couldn't pro-vide me with enough to live on. For instance, when I want to have a good time I don't buy luxuries in the market – it costs too much – I supply myself from my own mind. And it gives me far greater pleasure when I wait until I feel the need before I refresh myself than when I enjoy some luxury;

as at this present moment I am drinking this Thasian[21] wine not because I am thirsty but because the opportunity presented itself.

'Besides, those who are more concerned with economy than with extravagance are likely to be far more moral in their conduct, because those who are most content with what they have are least attracted by other people's property. And it is worth reflecting that this sort of wealth makes people generous. Socrates here, from whom I obtained it, didn't supply me by quantity or weight, but handed over to me as much as I could carry away, and I now grudge nobody; I exhibit my generosity to all my friends, and I give a share of my mental wealth to anyone who wants it. What is more, you can see that I have always at hand that supreme luxury, leisure; so that I can see what is worth seeing and hear what is worth hearing and – what I value most – spend my days at leisure with Socrates. And he on his part doesn't look up to those who pay the most money, but persists in keeping company with anyone that he likes.'

When Antisthenes had finished this speech Callias said, 'Upon my word, I do envy you your wealth, for two reasons especially: first that the state doesn't treat you like a slave by imposing tasks upon you,[22] and secondly that people aren't angry if you don't lend them anything.'

'No, no,' said Niceratus, 'don't envy him. Before I leave him I shall have borrowed his faculty for needing nothing. Homer has taught me to reckon by weight and number:[23]

> Seven new cauldrons, talents ten of gold,
> Twenty bright cooking-pots, and horses twelve[24]

21. Thasian was, next to Chian, the best Greek wine.
22. Cf. note on 4, 30 above.
23. Unlike Socrates: cf. 43 above.
24. *Iliad* ix, 122 f., repeated 264 f. The talent was properly a unit of weight, i.e. about 37 kilos of silver.

so I never stop craving for the utmost wealth. Consequently some people probably think I'm rather fond of money.' At this all shouted with laughter, thinking that he had said no more than the truth.

Next somebody said, 'It's up to you now, Hermogenes, to tell us who your friends are, and to demonstrate that they have great influence and take care of you, so that your pride in them may be shown to be justified.'

'Well, it's quite plain that both Greeks and non-Greeks believe that the gods know everything that is and will be; at any rate all states and all peoples inquire of the gods by means of divination what they ought and ought not to do. Next, it's also clear that we believe they can do us both good and harm; at least everyone asks the gods to avert what is evil and grant what is good. Well, now, these omniscient and omnipotent gods are such good friends to me that because of their concern for me I am never beyond their notice night or day, wherever I am bound and whatever I intend to do. And because of their foreknowledge they indicate to me the result of every action, sending me messages by utterances and visions and omens[25] telling me what I ought to do and what I must not; and when I obey these I am never sorry for it, but when I have sometimes disobeyed in the past I have been punished for it.'

'Well,' said Socrates, 'there is nothing incredible in this. But one thing I should like to know: what sort of service you render them to keep them so friendly to you.'

'Certainly,' said Hermogenes; 'a very economical kind. I praise them, which costs me nothing; I always make them a return out of what they give me; I do my best not to offend in my speech; and when I call them to witness I never voluntarily tell a lie.'

'Upon my word,' said Socrates, 'if that's how you keep

25. Cf. *Mem.* i, 1, 3.

their friendship, it seems that the gods do take pleasure in perfection of character.'[26]

The foregoing topic was treated seriously in the manner I have described.

Philippus briefly defends his talent for making jokes, and the Syracusan protests that his greatest asset is not the boy dancer but the gullibility of the public. Finally Socrates explains that his art of procuring consists in introducing people for their mutual benefit, and observes that Antisthenes is very good at it too.

When they came to Philippus they asked him what he saw in making jokes that led him to pride himself upon it.

'Why, isn't it right that I should?' he said. 'Everybody knows that I make jokes, and when they have a bit of good luck they're glad to call in my professional help, but when they've had a piece of bad luck they scurry away without looking behind them, they're so terrified of laughing against their will.'

'Well, you certainly have a right to be proud,' said Niceratus. 'I find, with my friends, that it's the lucky ones that take themselves well out of one's way, but any who have had a piece of bad luck draw up a pedigree to prove our relationship, and never leave my side.'

'All right,' said Charmides. 'Now for you, my Syracusan friend: what are you proud of? I suppose it's obviously your boy?'

'My God, no,' he said, 'not at all; I am violently alarmed for him; I find that some people are plotting his destruction.'

When Socrates heard this he said, 'Good heavens! what fearful wrong do they think your boy has done them that they want to kill him?'

26. Once again the untranslatable quality.

'No, of course they do not want to kill him,' said he, 'but to persuade him to sleep with them.'

'And apparently you think that if that happened it would be the ruin of him.'

'Yes, indeed, absolutely.'

'Don't you sleep with him yourself, then?'

'Certainly; all night and every night.'

'Upon my word,' said Socrates, 'it's great luck for you to have been born with such a unique body that you alone have no bad effect on those who sleep with you; so you're entitled to take a pride in your body, if in nothing else.'

'No, really,' he protested, 'I don't take any pride in that.'

'Well, in what then?'

'Why, in my simple-minded public, to be sure. They provide me with a living by gazing at my puppets.'

'Ah,' said Philippus, 'that's why I heard you the other day praying to the gods to grant, wherever you were, a glut of fruit and a dearth of wits.'

'Very good,' said Callias. 'Now then, Socrates, how do you justify your claim to pride yourself on the disreputable calling that you mentioned?'

He replied, 'Let's decide first what the duties of a procurer are. Don't hesitate to answer all the questions I ask, so that we may know how far we agree. Do you approve?'

'Quite,' they said; and having once said 'quite' they all kept to this same answer for the rest of the discussion.[27]

'Do you think that it's the duty of a good procurer to represent his client to everyone he meets as a pleasing person?'

'Quite,' they said.

'Doesn't one aid towards pleasing consist in having a suitable arrangement of hair and clothing?'

'Quite,' they said.

27. Perhaps this is a skit on the monotony of affirmative replies in dialogue.

'Are we aware that it's possible for the same person to give friendly and hostile looks with the same eyes?'

'Quite.'

'Next, is it possible to speak modestly and insolently with the same voice?'

'Quite.'

'Next, aren't there some ways of talking that are offensive and others that are agreeable?'

'Quite.'

'Well, wouldn't a good procurer inculcate such of these qualities as are conducive to pleasing?'

'Quite.'

'Which would be the better – the man who can make his clients agreeable to one person or the one who can make them agreeable to many?'

Here the company was divided, some saying 'The man who can do it to most', and others saying 'Quite.'

Socrates remarked that this too was agreed, and went on, 'Supposing that somebody could represent them as pleasing to the whole city, wouldn't that in itself make him a supremely good procurer?'

'Yes, undoubtedly,' they all said.

'So if somebody could produce this effect on his clients, he would be justified in feeling proud of his skill, and justified in taking large fees?' When they all agreed upon this too, he said, 'I think Antisthenes here is just the type.'

'Are you conceding your art to *me*, Socrates?' asked Antisthenes.

'Certainly,' he replied. 'I can see that you have carried to perfection the art that follows from it.'

'What is that?'

'Pandering,' said he.

Antisthenes was very indignant. 'And what, Socrates, are you aware of that I have done in this line?'

'I know,' he said, 'that you introduced Callias here to the sophist Prodicus[28] when you saw that the one had a passion for philosophy and the other needed money. And I know that you introduced him to Hippias[29] of Elis, from whom he learned the art of memorizing – which has made him more amorous than he was before, because he never forgets anything beautiful that he's seen. And of course there was our visitor from Heraclea[30] the other day; you first excited my interest in him by praising him and then brought him to see me. And indeed I'm grateful to you; I think he's a very fine character. And Aeschylus of Phlius[31] – didn't you praise us to each other so effectively that your descriptions made us fall in love and set us hunting for each other? It's because I see that you can do these things that I think you're a good pander. It seems to me that a man who is able to recognize people who are likely to benefit each other, and who can make them desire each other's company, could develop friendship between states and arrange suitable marriages,[32] and would be a very valuable ally for both states and individuals to possess. But you thought you were insulted because I said you were a good pander, and got angry.'

'Well, I assure you I'm not now,' he said. 'If I have those qualities, my mind will soon be absolutely crammed with wealth.'

So this round of conversation was completed.

28. Cf. 1, 5 above.

29. See Glossary.

30. Perhaps Zeuxippus (Plato, *Protagoras* 318B).

31. An unknown character; Phlius was about fourteen miles west of Corinth.

32. Probably a metaphor for political alliance, but possibly intended in a literal sense; the text of the sentence that follows is uncertain.

CHAPTER FIVE

Socrates asserts his claim to be more beautiful than Critobulus. When the ballot is taken he expresses great indignation at the judges' decision.

'I say, Critobulus,' said Callias, 'are you holding back from the beauty contest with Socrates?'

'To be sure he is,' said Socrates. 'I expect he can see that the procurer is in favour with the judges.'

'In spite of that,' said Critobulus, 'I'm not backing out. If you've got some subtle argument, explain to me how you are more beautiful than I am. Only,' he added, 'I want the lamp brought up.'

'Well, now,' said Socrates, 'I summon you first to a preliminary investigation of the case.[1] Answer my questions.'

'Ask away.'

'Do you think that beauty is found only in man, or in other things as well?'

'I certainly believe that it's found in horses and cattle and in many inanimate objects. At any rate I know that a shield is beautiful, and a sword, and a spear.'

'Why, how can all these things be beautiful when they are nothing like one another?'[2]

'Surely,' said Critobulus, 'anything that's well constructed for the particular function for which we possess it, or well adapted by nature to meet one's needs, is also beautiful.'

'Well, then, do you know what we need eyes for?'

'Obviously to see with.'

1. The word means a formal inquiry before a magistrate to decide whether there is ground for an action.
2. Cf. *Mem.* iii, 8, 5.

'Then in that case it would follow directly that my eyes are more beautiful than yours.'

'How, pray?'

'Because yours only see straight in front, but mine see sideways too, because they project.'

'Do you mean that a crab has better eyes than any other creature?'

'In every way, surely; because its eyes are also better provided by nature in respect of strength.'[3]

'All right,' said Critobulus, 'which of our noses is more beautiful – yours or mine?'

'I think that mine is,' said Socrates, 'that is, if the gods have created our noses for the purpose of smelling. Your nostrils look down at the ground, but mine are opened right up so as to admit smells from every direction.'

'Come, though; how can snubness in a nose be more beautiful than straightness?'

'Because it doesn't set up a barrier, but lets the eyes have a direct view of whatever they like. A high-bridged nose looks haughty and forms a dividing wall between them.'

'As for the mouth,' said Critobulus, 'I give you that; if it's made for biting, you can take a much bigger bite than I can. But as your lips are thick, don't you think I've got a softer kiss than you have?'

'By your description I seem to have an uglier mouth than a donkey's. But don't you think this is evidence that I'm more beautiful than you are: the fact that the Naiads, who are goddesses, are mothers of the Sileni,[4] who resemble me more than you?'

3. If this means what it appears to mean it is untrue. Crabs' eyes, with the stalks on which they are set, can be retracted for protection into sockets in the carapace.

4. The Naiads were water-nymphs and so belonged to the same class of nature-spirits as satyrs and Sileni, but the relationship seems unlikely. For Socrates and Silenus see above, 4, 19.

'I can't argue against you any more,' said Critobulus. 'Let them record their votes, so that I may know as quickly as possible what penalty or fine I've got to pay. Only,' he added, 'let it be a secret ballot. I'm afraid that your and Antisthenes' wealth will be too much for me.'

So the girl and the boy recorded their votes in secret. Meanwhile Socrates made two arrangements: to have the lamp brought up in front of Critobulus, so that the judges might not be misled, and to fix as the token of victory given by the judges to the winner not garlands but kisses. When the votes were turned out and were all[5] for Critobulus, 'Tut, tut!' said Socrates, 'Critobulus, your money doesn't seem to be like Callias's. His makes people better,[6] but yours, like most other money, is capable of corrupting both judges and juries.'

5. Humorous exaggeration; there were only two voters.
6. Cf. above, 4, 1–5.

CHAPTER SIX

Hermogenes is rallied for being unsociable, and the Syracusan tries to provoke Socrates. An argument develops about Philippus' talent for satirical comparison.

HERE some urged Critobulus to receive the kisses that he had earned by his victory, and others to prevail upon the dancers' master, and others uttered other pleasantries; but Hermogenes remained obstinately silent. Socrates addressed him and said, 'Hermogenes, could you tell us what drunkenness is?'

'If you're asking for its definition,' he said, 'I don't know; but I could tell you what I think.'

'Well, what you think will do.'

'All right: I consider that drunkenness consists in annoying one's companions over the wine.'

'Do you realize, then,' said Socrates, 'that you're now annoying us by your silence?'

'Even while you're talking?' he asked.

'No, but when we leave a pause.'

'Has it escaped you that when you people are talking there's no gap to poke even a thread in, let alone a remark?'

'Callias,' said Socrates, 'could you lend a hand to a debater in distress?'

'Yes, I can,' he replied. 'Whenever the flute sounds we keep absolutely silent.'

Hermogenes said, 'You know how the actor Nicostratus[1] used to recite poetry to a flute accompaniment; do you want me to converse with you to the sound of the flute in the same way?'

'Do that, for Heaven's sake, Hermogenes,' said Socrates.

1. Not otherwise known.

'A flute accompaniment makes a song more agreeable, and I presume that in the same way your remarks will be improved by the tune, especially if you gesticulate to suit the words, like the flute-player.'

'What shall the music be,' asked Callias, 'when Antisthenes here argues somebody down in the course of the party?'

'I think the right music for the loser in the argument,' said Antisthenes, 'would be a hiss.'[2]

As this conversation went on the Syracusan saw that they were paying no attention to his displays, but entertaining one another; so he felt aggrieved with Socrates and said, 'Socrates, are you the person that they call the Thinker?'[3]

'That's nicer than if they called me the Thoughtless,' he replied.

'Yes, if you weren't regarded as a thinker about things that are too high for us.'

'Do you know anything higher than the gods?'

'No, no,' said the man, 'it's not in them that you're said to be interested, but in things far above our heads.'

'Even so,' said Socrates, 'I might be showing interest in the gods. It's from above that they help us by sending rain, and from above that they give us light. If that's a flat answer,' he added, 'it's your fault for bothering me.'[4]

'Never mind that,' said the man. 'Tell me how many feet away from me a flea is; they say you can solve these problems in geometry.'[5]

Antisthenes broke in, 'You're clever at expressing like-

2. The Greek word means both a tune on a shepherd's pipe and a derisive hiss or cat-call.

3. Cf. Aristophanes, *Clouds* 266; the Syracusan evidently knows the play.

4. The answer contains some frigid puns, almost impossible to reproduce in English.

5. Cf. *Clouds* 144 ff.

nesses,[6] Philippus; don't you think this man is like someone who wants to be abusive?'

'Yes, indeed,' he said, 'and a good many other things too.'

'But still,' said Socrates, 'you'd better not describe what he's like, for fear that *you* may be like an abusive person.'

'But if I liken him to all the beauties and best characters I should be more fairly likened to an effusive person than to an abusive one.'

'You're like an abusive one as it is if you say that everything is better than he is.'

'Well, do you want me to liken him to worse people?'

'No, not to worse ones either.'

'Well, then, to nobody?'

'No, don't liken him to any of them.'

'But I don't know how I shall earn my dinner if I say nothing.'

'Quite easily, if you say nothing about what is better left unsaid.'

In this way the alcoholic heat of this discussion was cooled down.[7]

6. I.e., taking off a character by means of a witty comparison; cf. Alcibiades on Socrates in Plato, *Symposium* 215 ff.

7. And no wonder, considering how frigid the word-play is.

CHAPTER SEVEN

Preparations are made for a 'novelty' dance, but Socrates asks for something quieter and more graceful, and the Syracusan agrees.

THE others now joined in, some urging Philippus to 'do a likeness' and others objecting. There was an uproar, and Socrates interposed again. 'As we're all eager to speak, perhaps this would be the right moment to sing together'; and with these words he started a song. When it was over they began to bring in a revolving platform[1] for the dancer, who was going to show off a novelty dance on it. At this Socrates said, 'My Syracusan friend, it looks as if I really am a thinker, as you say; at any rate I am now considering how this boy and girl of yours can have the easiest time, and how we can get the greatest pleasure from watching them – which, I am sure, is what you want too. Well, it seems to me that to turn somersaults on to sword-blades is an exhibition of danger, which is quite out of place at a drinking-party. Then again, to write or read as one spins round on the wheel is no doubt a remarkable feat; but I can't make out what pleasure this could afford either. Nor, again, is it more pleasant to watch attractive young people twisting their bodies round into hoops than to see them in repose. In fact it isn't at all uncommon to find things to wonder at, if that's what one wants: for example we can wonder why on earth it is that the lamp gives light because it has a bright flame, whereas the bronze reflector, although it's bright, doesn't *make* light, but gives off the light that is reflected in it from other sources; and how it is that oil, which is liquid, feeds the flame, but water, because it's liquid, puts the fire out. However, even these topics don't promote the same end as the wine does. If your young people

1. Literally 'a potter's wheel', but this suggests something too small.

266

danced, with a flute accompaniment, figures representing Graces and Seasons and Nymphs,[2] I believe that they would have an easier time and the party would be artistically more attractive.'

The Syracusan said, 'Yes, indeed, you are right, Socrates, and I will put on turns which you will enjoy.'

2. The Graces (*Charites*) were goddesses of grace and beauty, often associated with Aphrodite; the Seasons (*Horae*) were nature-spirits who presided over the several stages of the year and the gifts of the earth; Nymphs haunted natural objects such as woods, springs and mountains; all were represented in art as beautiful young women.

CHAPTER EIGHT

Socrates declares that honour should be shown to Love, who is a
great god and is worshipped by them all in their various ways.
There are two kinds of Love, Celestial and Common: the latter,
being physical, is often defective and short-lived, whereas the former,
being concerned with the personality, is complete and enduring.

HE went out amid applause; Socrates once more introduced
a new subject.

'Gentlemen, we are in the presence of a great deity, as old
in time as the eternal gods, and yet most youthful in appearance; pervading all things in his greatness, and yet enshrined
in the heart of man: I mean Love. Isn't it natural that we
should make some mention of him, especially when we are
all his worshippers? I can't name a time when I haven't been
continuously in love[1] with someone; I know that Charmides
has acquired a number of lovers, and has lost his own heart to
more than one; and Critobulus, who still has his admirers, is
already setting his heart on others. Then Niceratus too, as I
hear, is in love with his wife and is loved by her in return.
And Hermogenes – don't we all know that, whatever nobility
of character is, he is wasting away with love of it? Don't you
see how serious are his brows, how calm his countenance,
how measured his speech, how gentle his voice, how cheerful
his disposition? and how, although he enjoys the friendship of
the most holy gods, he shows no disdain for us mortals? Have
you alone, Antisthenes, no love at all?'

'Yes, by Heaven! I have,' he replied; 'a violent love for you.'

Socrates replied banteringly, with mock coyness, 'Don't
bother me now at the moment; you can see that I'm otherwise
engaged.'

1. Cf. *Mem.* iv, 1, 2.

268

'No mistake about it,' said Antisthenes, 'you're always the same, playing the coquette. At one time you refuse to talk to me on the pretext of your "divine sign",[2] and at another because you're attracted by somebody else.'

'For Heaven's sake, Antisthenes,' said Socrates, 'only don't shatter me completely! The rest of your unkindness I bear, and will continue to bear, in a friendly spirit. But let's draw a veil over your love for me, because it's inspired not by my character but by my elegance. That you, Callias, are in love with Autolycus is known to the whole of our city and, I expect, to a good many foreigners too, the reason being that you are both sons of famous fathers,[3] and distinguished men yourselves. I have always admired your nature, but now I admire it much more, because I see that the person you love is not pampered by luxury or enervated by effeminacy but displays to the eyes of all his strength, endurance, courage and self-discipline. To be attracted by these qualities is evidence of the lover's own character.

'Whether there is one Aphrodite or two, Celestial and Common,[4] I don't know; Zeus has many titles although he is regarded as the same deity. But I do know that there are different altars and shrines and offerings for each of them: more casual for the Common and of a devouter kind for the Celestial goddess. One might guess that the former inspires physical love, while the latter inspires love of the personality, of friendship, and of noble deeds. That, I believe, is the sort of love that possesses you, Callias. I base my belief on the fine character of the one whom you love, and on the fact that I see you invite his father to be present when you are together,

2. Cf. *Mem*. i, 1, 2, 4; iv, 8, 1, 5.
3. Hipponicus belonged to a famous and wealthy family, but Lycon seems to have had little claim to distinction.
4. The interpretation of these cult-titles is probably due to Plato (or Socrates); cf. Plato, *Symposium* 180D–185C, and Introduction, p. 21.

because there is nothing in these associations that need be concealed from the father by an honourable lover.'

'Upon my word, Socrates,' said Hermogenes, 'the thing I admire most in you (and there are many others) is this way of yours: at the same time paying Callias a compliment and instructing him just how he ought to behave.'

'Quite so,' he replied, 'and to give him even greater encouragement I want to show him evidence that love of the personality is much better than physical love. We all know that without affection there can be no companionship worthy of the name. Now the affection of those who admire the character is recognized as a pleasant and acceptable compulsion; but many of those whose desires are sensual criticize and dislike the characters of those whom they love; and even if they are fond of them in both ways, the bloom of youth (as we know) quickly passes its prime, and when this fails the affection must fade together with it; but so long as the soul is progressing towards greater wisdom the more lovable it becomes. Then again, the enjoyment of physical beauty involves a sort of satiety, so that one is bound to lose interest in a boy-favourite in just the same way as repletion makes one lose interest in food. But affection for the personality, being pure, is less liable to satiety; yet this does not imply (as might be supposed) that it is lacking in attraction: on the contrary the prayer in which we ask the goddess to grant us charm of speech and action is manifestly fulfilled. That a nature which is endowed with the elegance of good breeding and with a modest and noble character, which even among its contemporaries combines authority with friendliness – that such a nature admires and loves its lover needs no explanation; but I shall prove to you that it is natural also for such a lover to enjoy the affection of his beloved.'

Celestial Love is reciprocated, but Common Love is often selfish;

*the former ennobles, the latter degrades. It is Celestial, not Common
Love that incites soldiers to acts of gallantry, and it is also Celestial
Love that inspires confidence.*

'In the first place, who could hate a person by whom he
knows that he is idealized, who he can see is more concerned
about what is good for the boy than what is pleasant to himself, whose affection, too, he believes could not be diminished
even by calamity or a disfiguring disease? Then those whose
affection is mutual must look at each other with pleasure and
converse in amity; they must trust and be trusted, be considerate to each other, share pleasure in their successes and
sorrow if anything goes wrong; continue in happiness so long
as they are together in good health, and, if either falls ill, keep
him company much more constantly, and care for each other
even more in their absence than in their presence. Aren't all
these characteristics attractive? It's this sort of conduct that
maintains people's mutual devotion to their friendship and
their enjoyment of it even into old age.

'As for the lover whose attachment is physical; why should
the boy return his affection? Because he assigns to himself the
gratification of his passion, leaving to the boy the extremity
of shame? Or because the favour that he is eager to exact cuts
the favourite off completely from his family and friends? Then
again the very fact that he uses not force but persuasion makes
him more detestable, because a lover who uses force proves
himself a villain, but one who uses persuasion ruins the character of the one who consents. Again, is one who sells his
youth for money any more likely to love the purchaser than
one who trades in the market? Certainly the fact that he is
young and his partner is not, or that he is beautiful and his
partner is so no longer, or that he is not in love and his
partner is – this will not stir his affection. A boy does not share
the man's enjoyment of sexual intercourse as a woman does:

he is a sober person watching one drunk with sexual excitement. In view of all this it is no wonder if he develops an actual contempt for his lover. Investigation would also show that no serious result has ever been caused by those who are loved for the sake of their characters, whereas the shameless form of intercourse has led before now to many atrocious deeds.

'I shall now show that the association is more degrading for the lover of the body than for the lover of the personality. The person who teaches you to say and do what you ought may fairly be held in honour as Chiron and Phoenix were by Achilles,[5] but the one who has a physical craving may reasonably be treated like a mendicant, because he always follows his favourite round begging and soliciting either a kiss or some other caress.

'Don't be surprised if I am rather outspoken. It's partly because the wine helps to carry me away, and partly because the love which is my constant companion spurs me on to speak out against its adversary. It seems to me that a person who is obsessed with outward appearance is like one who has rented a plot of land: his object is not to increase the value of the land but to secure for himself the maximum enjoyment of its mature produce. But the man who desires friendship is more like the owner of his own holding; at any rate he gathers together from every quarter whatever he can get to increase the worth of what he loves. Besides, in the case of the favourite, one who knows that enough outward beauty will enable him to dominate his lover is likely to take little trouble over any other quality; but if he knows that unless he maintains the highest standards[6] he will not retain the friendship,

---

5. Chiron was a centaur who ran a sort of preparatory school for the sons of heroes; Phoenix was chosen as an emissary to Achilles because he had been tutor to him (Homer, *Iliad* ix, 438–43).

6. One more attempt to convey the meaning of that difficult phrase (Introduction, p. 9).

then it is natural that he should care more about goodness.

'But the supreme advantage enjoyed by one who is eager to convert his favourite into a good friend is that he is compelled to cultivate goodness himself, because if he behaves wickedly it is impossible for him to make his companion good; and if he shows himself shameless and dissolute it is impossible for him to make the one he loves self-controlled and modest.

'I feel moved also to invoke myth[7] to show you, Callias, that not only men but gods and demigods set affection based on character above physical gratification. All the mortal women whom Zeus loved for their beauty he allowed after their union to remain mortal, but all those persons who won his regard by their nobility of soul he made immortal. Examples of these are Heracles[8] and the Dioscuri;[9] and we are told of others as well. I myself maintain that Ganymede[10] too was carried off by Zeus to Olympus on account of not his body but his mind. His very name supplies the evidence. Homer, I believe, has the phrase

and hearing he is gay,[11]

which means "and hearing he is pleased". And somewhere else there is this phrase

in his heart knowing shrewd conceits.[12]

This again means "in his heart knowing wise counsels".

7. Xenophon does this much more clumsily than Plato, and the example here will impress nobody.

8. Cf. *Mem*. ii, 1, 21 ff.

9. Castor and Pollux, sons of Tyndarus and Zeus respectively by Leda. Their immortality was alternate; see Homer, *Odyssey* xi, 300 f.; Pindar, *Nemean* 10, 55 ff.

10. Son of Tros or some other Trojan prince; carried off to become cupbearer to the gods (Homer, *Iliad* v, 265 f.; xx, 231–5).

11. Not in our text, but the word which Socrates regards as the first member of the name Ganymede occurs at *Iliad* xiii, 493 and xx, 405.

12. A conflation of *Iliad* vii, 278 and xxiv, 674.

Putting these two together we find that Ganymede is held in honour among the gods by a name which means not "pleasing in body" but "pleasing in mind".[13] Besides, Niceratus, Homer has made Achilles exact his world-famous vengeance for Patroclus not as his favourite but as a dead comrade.[14] Also Orestes and Pylades[15] and Theseus and Pirithous[16] and many other leading heroes are celebrated in song for having jointly performed the greatest and noblest exploits not because they slept together but out of mutual admiration.

'Take the case of gallant acts in our own day: wouldn't you find that they are all done to win praise by men who are willing to endure hardship and danger rather than by those who are accustomed to choose pleasure before glory? And yet Pausanias the lover of Agathon the poet,[17] in his defence of those who wallow in debauchery,[18] has said that an army composed of boys and their lovers would be braver than any other, because he said he thought that they would be most ashamed to desert one another – a remarkable statement, that those who make a habit of flouting censure and acting shamelessly towards each other should be most ashamed of doing

13. As the name is probably not Greek at all, the etymological quirk is doubly pointless.

14. Cf. Plato, *Symp.* 179E. These arguments, weak as they are, illustrate the almost Biblical authority of the Homeric poems.

15. For their unselfish affection see Euripides, *Iph. in T.* 578 ff.

16. Pirithous helped Theseus in many exploits, but finally involved him in a disastrous attempt to abduct Persephone (Virgil, *Aen.* vi, 601, 617 f.; Horace, *od.* iv, 7, 27; Ovid, *Tristia* i, 5, 19 f.

17. For Pausanias and Agathon see Plato, *Protagoras* 315E-D, *Symposium* 193B.

18. Pausanias does make a speech in Plato's *Symposium* (180C-185C), in which, incidentally, he draws the distinction between Celestial and Common Love made by Socrates in §9 above; but although the superficial idealism of the speech barely serves to gild over its shabby morality, Socrates' description seems a little harsh. Probably Xenophon's memory is at fault. See Introduction, p. 21, and cf. the next note.

something shameful! And he adduced as evidence the fact that this was the policy of both Thebes and Elis,[19] at any rate he said that although they slept with their favourites they nevertheless had them posted by their sides for battle – quoting this as an illustration, although the cases are not at all parallel, because paederasty is an accepted custom with those peoples, but with us it is a matter for reproach. Also it seems to me that those who arrange for this formation are probably not sure that their favourites will acquit themselves like brave men if they are separated. The Spartans, who believe that if a man so much as entertains a carnal desire he can no longer attain any good and noble object,[20] train up their favourites to such a perfect pitch of bravery that even among strangers, even if they are not stationed in the same country as their lovers, they are just as much ashamed to desert the comrades at their side. This is because the goddess that they believe in is not Immodesty but Modesty.

'It seems to me that we should all come to an agreement on the subject that I am discussing if we looked at it from this point of view: which kind of love would inspire one with greater confidence to entrust a boy with money or one's children or favours? I imagine that even the man who enjoys the external beauty of his beloved would be more ready to commit all these things to the one with the lovable personality.'

Callias should be thankful that the object of his love is a young man of such fine character. He should earn Autolycus' respect by entering public life and using his talents and resources for the benefit of his country.

19. He refers to 'Elis and Boeotia' (Plato, *Symposium* 182B), but only as countries where paederasty is taken for granted. The notion of an army composed of 'lovers and beloved' is introduced by Phaedrus (ibid. 178E); see Introduction, p. 19 and the article there cited.

20. This astonishing statement seems to have no foundation; see Introduction, p. 13.

'As for you, Callias, I think you should be grateful to the gods for implanting in you a love of Autolycus. It's easy to see that he is eager for honour, because he endures a great many hardships and discomforts for the sake of being proclaimed victor in the pancratium.[21] Now if he thought that he would not only distinguish himself and his father, but be enabled by his manly prowess both to help his friends and to raise the prestige of his country by winning victories over its enemies, and that he would consequently be a marvel and celebrity among both Greeks and foreigners: don't you think he would treat with the deepest respect the person who he thought would be his most effective helper to this end? So if you want to find favour in his eyes you should consider what sort of knowledge enabled Themistocles to liberate Greece, and what sort of wisdom it can have been that earned Pericles the reputation of being his country's best adviser; you must consider what sort of profound reflection preceded Solon's provision for our city of a matchless legal code; and you must also inquire what sort of qualities the Spartans cultivate that make them regarded as the best leaders. You are their representative[22] at Athens, and the most important of them are always given hospitality at your house. You may be sure that your country would readily put itself in your charge, if that is your wish, because you have the essential qualifications. You are of noble birth, a priest of the gods descended from Erechtheus,[23] who marched with Iacchus against the barbarians;[24] and now at the festival you are thought to be a more distinguished holder of that sacred office than any of

21. Cf. above, 1, 2.

22. Diplomatic representative (*proxenus*); though an Athenian citizen he looked after Spartan interests at Athens.

23. See Glossary.

24. Iacchus was properly a minor deity associated with the mysteries of Demeter at Eleusis, but he was sometimes identified with Bacchus = Dionysus. The precise reference is unknown.

your predecessors, and you have a body which is the come-
liest in the city to look at, and capable of enduring hardships.
If you think that I have spoken more seriously than is appropriate over the wine, don't be surprised at that. I have always
shared my country's love for those who are naturally good
and make virtue their keen ambition.'

The others began discussing what had been said, but
Autolycus kept his eyes fastened on Callias. Callias, with a
glance at him, said, 'Then are you going to seduce me into
public life, Socrates, so that I may engage in politics and always
be in favour with my country?'

'Yes, indeed,' he replied, 'if they see that your interest in
goodness is not superficial but genuine. A false reputation is
soon exposed when it comes to the test, but true manliness,
unless a god interferes,[25] by its actions always helps to make
renown more glorious.'

25. A characteristic touch of Greek pessimism: cf. Herodotus' concept of the 'jealous deity' (ii, 40).

CHAPTER NINE

Lycon and Autolycus leave to go home. A short ballet scene between the two dancers represents the love of Dionysus and Ariadne so charmingly and realistically that the guests are deeply moved, and breaking up the party go their several ways.

THAT was the end of this discussion. Autolycus got up to walk home, because it was time for him to go. As his father Lycon was going out with him he turned back and said, 'By Heaven, Socrates, it does seem to me that you are a good and honourable man.'[1]

At this point first a sort of raised couch was set up in the room, and then the Syracusan came in and said, 'Gentlemen, Ariadne will enter the bedchamber which she shares with Dionysus; and after that Dionysus will arrive, after having a few drinks with the gods, and will go in to her; and then they will make fun with each other.'[2]

Hereupon first Ariadne[3] came in dressed up as a bride and sat down on the couch, and as there was still no sign of Dionysus the Bacchic rhythm[4] was played on the flute. At this point the choreographer won admiration, because as soon as Ariadne heard it she acted in a way that showed unmistakably that she was delighted at it; she did not go to meet her bridegroom or even stand up, but she obviously could hardly keep still. When Dionysus caught sight of her he came

1. As always, the supreme compliment.
2. This fault of idiom is intended to represent the man's lapse into Doric dialect.
3. Ariadne helped Theseus to escape from the labyrinth and fled with him from Crete, but he left her on the island of Naxos, where Dionysus found and married her.
4. Or perhaps 'melody'; but what exactly is meant cannot be determined.

dancing across and sat down on her lap in the most affectionate way imaginable, flung his arms round her and kissed her. She conveyed the impression of shyness, but nevertheless returned his embraces lovingly.

When the guests saw this they clapped and shouted 'Encore!' Dionysus got up and helped Ariadne to stand up too; and then there was an opportunity to watch the figures that they danced as they kissed and embraced each other. When the guests saw that Dionysus was really handsome, and Ariadne young and pretty, and that they were not pretending but actually kissing with their lips, they were all carried away with excitement as they watched. They heard Dionysus asking her if she loved him, and the girl reassuring him in such a way that not only Dionysus but the whole company would have sworn with one voice that the two young people really did love each other. They did not seem to have rehearsed their movements; it seemed as if they were free at last to do what they had long desired.

When at last the guests saw them in each other's arms as if they were going off to bed, the bachelors swore that they would get married, and the married men got into their carriages and drove away to their own wives, with the same end in view. Socrates and those who were still left set out to walk with Callias to the home of Lycon and his son. That is the way in which this party came to an end.

GLOSSARY OF PROPER NAMES

ACHILLES. Son of Peleus, and the best Greek warrior at Troy; affronted by Agamemnon, he withdrew from the fighting, but when Patroclus was killed by Hector he took the field again, killed Hector, and dragged his body round the walls of Troy.

AGAMEMNON. King of Mycenae (or Argos); commanded the Greek force that attacked Troy.

AJAX. Son of Telamon and second only to Achilles as a warrior; for his tragic end see Sophocles, *Ajax*.

ALCIBIADES. Son of Clinias, ward of Pericles, pupil and friend of Socrates; but he seems not to have profited much from Socrates' mora lteaching (the picture of him in Plato's *Symposium* is probably not unfair). Brilliant and selfish, admired and distrusted, he helped his country and her enemies by turns, and was finally (404 B.C.) murdered in exile at the instigation of the Thirty (q.v.). The Alcibiades mentioned at *Mem.* i, 3, 8 was probably another person.

ANAXAGORAS. Of Clazomenae (*c.* 500–428 B.C.), a notable thinker whose astronomical (and other) views were a good deal nearer the truth than Xenophon realized. He was prosecuted for impiety and had to leave Athens in 450. According to Plato (*Apology* 26D–E, *Phaedo* 97B) Socrates did not think much of him.

ANTISTHENES. Lived about 455–360 B.C.; friend and follower of Socrates (cf. Plato, *Phaedo* 59B); regarded as founder of the Cynic sect. He wrote dialogues, some fragments of which are preserved. The person mentioned at *Mem.* iii, 4, 1 is clearly quite different.

APOLLODORUS. The narrator in Plato's Symposium; he was with Socrates when he died (*Phaedo* 59A, 117D).

ARISTIPPUS. Of Cyrene, born perhaps about 430 B.C., a friend of Socrates and an entertaining person according to Diogenes Laertius (ii, 65 ff.), and perhaps the founder of the Cyrenaic school of hedonism; but there is some confusion between him and his grandson of the same name.

CALLIAS. Son of Hipponicus (about 450–370). Very rich and a great patron of sophists; his house in Athens, 'the finest in the city', was the scene of Plato's dialogue *Protagoras*.

CARTHAGE. Founded about 800 B.C. in the Gulf of Tunis by Phoenicians from Tyre; it became the chief maritime power of the West Mediterranean and acquired a large empire in North Africa.

CEBES. Of Thebes, a young friend of Socrates who plays an important part in Plato's *Phaedo*.

CHAERECRATES. Younger brother of Chaerephon.

CHAEREPHON. One of Socrates' closest friends; cf. Plato, *Apology* 21A, *Charmides* 153B, *Gorgias* 447A; ridiculed by Aristophanes, *Clouds* 102 ff., 503 f.

CHARMIDES. Son of Plato's uncle Glaucon; appears as a very handsome youth in Plato's dialogue to which he gives his name. In spite of Socrates' high hopes for him (*Symp.* 8, 39 f.) he threw in his lot with Critias and shared his fate.

CLINIAS. (1) Father of Alcibiades; (2) son of Axiochus and grandson of (1), figuring in Plato's *Euthydemus* as a very handsome youth.

CRITIAS. Son of Callaeschrus and first cousin of Plato's mother Perictione; wrote poetry and seems like Charmides to have been at one time a close friend of Socrates (he appears in several of Plato's dialogues besides the unfinished one that bears his name). He took part in the oligarchic revolution of 411 and was exiled when it failed; returning in 404 after the fall of Athens he became the leader (and apparently the worst) of the Thirty (q.v.). He was killed in battle against the resurgent democrats in 403.

CRITO. Close friend of Socrates. Plato shows him (in the *Crito*) trying to persuade Socrates to escape from prison. See also *Apology* 33E, 38B; *Phaedo* 59B, 115B; and *Euthydemus* (beginning and end).

CRITOBULUS. Son of Crito, an amiable and amorous young man who seems to have had a real affection for Socrates: he was present at his trial and death (Plato, *Apology* 33E, *Phaedo* 59B).

DAEDALUS. Craftsman and inventor; fled from Athens to Crete, where *inter alia* he built the labyrinth to house the Minotaur; forcible detained, he made wings for himself and his son Icarus; the latter crashed in the sea, but D. flew safely to Sicily.

DELOS. One of the Cyclades islands, venerated as the birthplace of

Apollo and Artemis; it was the centre of the famous maritime confederacy organized by Athens after the Persian Wars. A quinquennial festival was held there (*Mem*. iii, 3, 12), not to be confused (as X. seems to confuse it) with the annual mission from Athens which delayed Socrates' execution (ibid. iv, 8, 2).

DELPHI. A town in Phocis containing the ancient shrine of Apollo generally regarded as the centre of Greek religion. The oracle was freely consulted by individuals as well as by states. For the inscriptions, especially 'Know thyself', cf. Plato, *Charmides* 164D, *Phaedrus* 230A, *Philebus* 48C, *Protagoras* 343B.

ERECHTHEUS. A legendary king of Athens whose name is still recalled by the well-known temple on the Acropolis. In a quarrel between Athens and the neighbouring city Eleusis the latter was aided by Eumolpus, king of Thrace; Erechtheus was victorious at the price of sacrificing one of his daughters.

EUTHYDEMUS. Not, of course, the sophist from Chios in Plato's dialogue of that name, but a young Athenian, probably the one mentioned by Plato in *Symposium* 222B (or possibly the son of Cephalus, *Republic* 328B). At his first conversation with Socrates (*Mem*. iv, 2) he reveals a recognizable character, but later the name seems to be used without personal significance.

GLAUCON. (1) Brother of Plato and one of the principal characters in the *Republic*, where he talks very sensibly; (2) grandfather of the above and father of Charmides.

HERMOGENES. No doubt the son of Hipponicus and brother of Callias (q.v.); he was a keen Socratic who takes a leading part in the discussion in Plato's *Cratylus* and is mentioned at *Phaedo* 59B.

HESIOD. Of Ascra in Boeotia; a didactic poet regarded by the Greeks as second only to Homer in antiquity and poetic authority.

HIPPIAS. A celebrated sophist and polymath from Elis. He appears in Plato's *Protagoras* and in two other dialogues (one of which may be spurious) which bear his name.

HOMER. Traditionally the oldest and greatest Greek poet; but whether he was one person or several, and when the poems ascribed to him were composed, are still disputed questions. He is quoted (directly or indirectly) at *Mem.* i, 2, 58; ii, 6, 11; iii, 1, 4; 2, 1 f.: *Symp.* 4, 6; 8, 30.

LACEDAEMONIANS. Inhabitants of Laconia in the S.E. Peloponnese; a Dorian state, from the seventh to the fourth century the strongest land-power in Greece. Its capital (and the state as a whole) is commonly called Sparta, but the official name was Lacedaemon, of which the adjective Lacon(ian) was a convenient abbreviation.

LIBYANS. A term for Africans in general.

LYDIA. A large territory in the west of Asia Minor, once a rich and independent kingdom under Croesus, but in Xenophon's time a satrapy of the Persian empire.

MAEOTIANS. A tribe living to the N.E. of the Sea of Azov, on the River Don.

MELETUS. Socrates' chief accuser (Plato, *Apology* 19C, 23E–28A; cf. *Euthyphro* 2B, 5A–C, etc.).

MYSIANS. A people of N.W. Asia Minor.

NESTOR. Oldest and most sagacious of the Greeks at Troy.

NICERATUS. Son of Nicias, mentioned by Plato (*Laches* 200D, *Republic* 327C).

NICIAS. Son of the elder and father of the younger Niceratus; born about 470; moderate politician and general whose excessive caution was largely responsible for the Athenian disaster in Sicily; he was put to death by the Syracusans in 413. Thucydides' tribute to him (vii, 86, 5) is well known. He appears in Plato's *Laches*, discussing courage with Socrates.

ODYSSEUS. Latinized as Ulixes, whence Ulysses; hero of the *Odyssey*, in which he displays not only amazing fortitude and resource but other admirable qualities; in the *Iliad* he is formidable and unscrupulous, and in tragedy generally (apart from Sophocles' *Ajax*) a ruthless opportunist.

ORESTES. Son of Agamemnon, whose death he avenged with the help of his friend Pylades.

PERICLES. The Athenian statesman who virtually ruled Athens for thirty years and made her the most important city in Greece and its cultural centre; he died of the plague in 429. The Pericles of *Mem.* iii, 5 was his son by Aspasia, his second wife or mistress.

PERSIA. In the early fourth century the Persian empire included, besides modern Iran, all Asia Minor, Syria, Lebanon, Jordan, Israel, Egypt, Iraq, Afghanistan and Baluchistan; it was highly cultured and well organized, and had no serious rival in military power until the rise of Alexander. The king of Persia was naturally regarded as the richest and most powerful man in the world.

PHAEDONDAS. Present at Socrates' death (Plato, *Phaedo* 59C).

PHILIPPUS. Appears in the *Symposium* as a maker of jokes which are not always very funny.

PHRYGIANS. Inhabited the south-central part of Asia Minor; once a powerful people, they were now not only subject but largely servile.

PRODICUS. Of Ceos; a distinguished sophist, interested in the correct use of words and distinction of apparent synonyms. He takes part in Plato's *Protagoras* and is mentioned with rather ironical respect in several other dialogues. His 'Choice of Heracles' seems to be mentioned in Plato's *Symposium* 177B.

PROTAGORAS. Of Abdera in Thrace; one of the earliest (he lived about 485–415 B.C.) and ablest of the sophists; practised mainly at Athens; famous for his dictum 'Man is the measure of all things', usually thought to imply the denial of any objective reality, but probably much more moderately intended. Plato portrays him as a match for Socrates in the dialogue called after him; criticizes his views in *Theatetus* 152–83; and often refers to him elsewhere, usually with respect.

SCYLLA. A monster opposite the whirlpool Charybdis in the Straits of Messina (*Odyssey* xii, 85 ff., 235 ff.); she had six heads and twelve 'waving' feet – presumably tentacles.

SCYTHIANS. Nomadic tribes occupying the area between the Carpathians and the Don. Their mounted archers were formidable.

SIMMIAS. Of Thebes, friend of Cebes (q.v.).

SOLON. Statesman and poet (about 640–560 B.C.); by abolishing bondage for debt, introducing various economic and legal reforms, and establishing a fairly representative system of government he removed the most active causes of civil strife and laid the foundations of Athenian democracy.

SYRIA. In Xenophon's time this included the whole district occupied by the modern states of Syria, Lebanon, Israel and Jordan, together with the peninsula of Sinai.

THEBES. The principal city in Boeotia, and generally hostile to Athens. Under Epaminondas it was for a few years (372–362) the most powerful state in Greece.

THEMISTOCLES. The ablest Athenian statesman (about 528–462). By getting Piraeus fortified and increasing the fleet he made Athens the chief sea-power in Greece; he was largely responsible for the repulse of the Persian invasion in 480; and after the war he enabled Athens to rebuild her walls and urged her to challenge Sparta's supremacy. Made unpopular by his vanity, he was charged with treason and fled the country; reached Persia, where he was honoured by the king, and died there a few years later.

THEOGNIS. Of Megara; sixth-century aristocrat who wrote elegiac poetry on themes partly moralizing, partly erotic – but some think that the poems were composed at Athens a century later.

THESEUS. Son of Aegeus (or Poseidon), Athenian hero of numerous exploits, notably the killing of the Minotaur; see also *Mem.* ii, 1, 14; iii, 5, 10: *Symp.* 8, 31; 9. 3.

THIRTY (TYRANTS). See *Mem.* i, 2, 31 n.

THRACE. In classical times this name was applied to most of the south-eastern corner of Europe below the Taurus range.

SELECT BIBLIOGRAPHY

FOR further information about the life and writings of Xenophon the following sources are suggested:

Delebecque, É., *Essai sur la vie de Xénophon*, Paris (Klincksieck), 1957.
Usher, S., 'Xenophon', *History Today*, July 1962.
Usher, S., *The Historians of Greece and Rome*, Hamish Hamilton, 1969.

Any of the standard Histories of Greek Literature may be consulted with profit.

The case of Socrates is more difficult. Many books have been written about him, but (a) few are free from distortion, (b) Socrates really needs to be seen in perspective. The following are probably still the best:

Cornford, F. M., *Before and After Socrates*, Cambridge University Press (paperback), 1960.
Field, G. C., *Plato and his Contemporaries*, Methuen, 1930.

The standard Histories of Greek Philosophy may also be consulted; in particular the third volume of that by Professor W. K. C. Guthrie (Cambridge University Press, 1970) may be confidently predicted to give a clear and well-balanced account.

The reader is also referred to the following Penguin Classics:

Guthrie, W. K. C., *Protagoras* and *Meno* (Plato).
Hamilton, W., *Gorgias* (Plato).
Hamilton, W., *Symposium* (Plato).
Lee, H. D. P., *Republic* (Plato).
Lee, H. D. P., *Timaeus* (Plato).
Tredennick, Hugh, *The Last Days of Socrates* (Plato, *Euthyphro*, *Apology*, *Crito* and *Phaedo*).
Warner, Rex, *The Persian Expedition* (Xenophon, *Anabasis*).
Warner, Rex, *A History of My Times* (Xenophon, *Hellenica*).

A list of the most recent Penguin Classics
is described on the following page.

THE PENGUIN CLASSICS

The Most Recent Volumes